Brothers

Guy Lanoue

The creation of a huge artificial lake in western Canada led to the flooding of prime hunting and trapping territory of the Sekani Indians, thus depriving them of their traditional occupations and livelihood. This caused considerable social distress resulting in drastic increases in alcohol consumption and violence and seriously disrupting social relationships. While some Sekani have made efforts to create new ties of solidarity through the adoption of Pan-Indianism, it is an ideology which is not proving very effective, being marred by the same factionalisms which characterized their personal relationships, as the author concludes in his provocative analysis of this nativist movement.

Guy Lanoue is a lecturer at the Università di Chieti 'G.D'Annunzio' at Pescara.

Explorations in Anthropology
A University College London Series
Series Editors: Barbara Bender, John Gledhill and Bruce
Kapferer

Joan Bestard-Camps, *What's in a Relative? Household and Family in Formentera*

Henk Driessen, *On the Spanish–Moroccan Frontier: A Study in Ritual, Power and Ethnicity*

Tim Ingold, David Riches and James Woodburn (eds), *Hunters and Gatherers*
> Volume 1. *History, Evolution and Social Change*
> Volume 2. *Property, Power and Ideology*

Bruce Kapferer, *A Celebration of Demons* (2nd edn)

Jadran Mimica, *Intimations of Infinity: The Mythopoeia of the Iqwaye Counting System and Number*

Barry Morris, *Domesticating Resistance: The Dhan-Gadi Aborigines and the Australian State*

Thomas C. Patterson, *The Inca Empire: The Formation and Disintegration of a Pre-Capitalist State*

Pnina Werbner, *The Migration Process: Capital, Gifts and Offerings among Pakistanis in Britain*

Forthcoming:

Alfred Gell, *The Anthropology of Time: Cultural Constructions of Temporal Maps and Images*

Max and Eleanor Rimoldi, *Hahalis and the Labour of Love: A Social Movement on Buka Island*

Terence Turner, *A Critique of Pure Culture*

Brothers

*The Politics of Violence among the Sekani
of Northern British Columbia*

Guy Lanoue

BERG
New York/Oxford

**Distributed exclusively in the US and Canada by
St Martin's Press, New York**

First published in 1992 by
Berg Publishers Limited
Editorial offices:
165 Taber Avenue, Providence, RI 02906, USA
150 Cowley Road, Oxford OX4 1JJ, UK

Library of Congress Cataloging-in-Publication Data

Lanoue, Guy
    Brothers: the politics of violence among the Sekani of northern
British Columbia / Guy Lanoue.
        p.   cm. — (Explorations in anthropology)
    Includes bibliographical references and index.
    ISBN 0–85496–746–X : $49.50
    1. Sekani Indians—Social conditions.   2. Sekani Indians—
Economic conditions.   3. Indians, Treatment of—British
Columbia—Williston
Lake Region.   I. Title   II. Series.
E99.S26L36   1991
971.1'004972—dc20   91–18433
                                                                                              CIP

British Library Cataloguing in Publication Data

Lanoue, Guy
    Brothers: the politics of violence among the
    Sekani of Northern British Columbia.
    – (Explorations in anthropology)
    I. Title   II. Series
    305.897

    ISBN   0–85496–746–X

Printed and bound in Great Britain by
Billing and Sons Ltd, Worcester

Contents

Tables, Appendices, Figures and Maps

Tables

Appendices

Figures

Maps

Preface

The research upon which this book is based was the product of luck, both good and bad. In 1977 and 1978 I had originally hoped to undertake research in Fort Good Hope, Northwest Territories, studying the political implications of Hare social organization. After a two-month preliminary visit during the spring of 1977 I returned to Toronto and wrote a research proposal for my doctoral dissertation based on information gathered and impressions formed on this trip. Tensions were running high in the middle of the Mackenzie Valley Pipeline inquiry on establishing the feasibility of pipeline construction and the economic development of the Northwest Territories, and for perhaps the first time many northern Athabaskan people were in the political spotlight. In December I learned that permission to conduct the proposed research had not been granted by the Settlement Council. Since there was only one other community that was primarily composed of Hare Indian residents and it had been the subject of a major study by Savishinsky,[1] I was unsure of what to do.

Roger McDonnell, then at the University of Toronto, suggested that I study the Sekani of Fort Ware in northern British Columbia (see Map 1). Little was known about these northern Athabaskan speakers. They had last been studied by Diamond Jenness in 1924.[2] The National Museum, which had provided me with funds for the proposed Fort Good Hope study, agreed to the change in location. In early 1978 I left Toronto for Fort Ware. Once I arrived in Vancouver I learned that another Sekani band, at McLeod Lake, wanted a researcher to undertake some of the initial background work so that a land claims proposal could be initiated by the band. I contacted the Chief and council, explained my circumstances and established myself in the community.

I had planned on spending six months in McLeod Lake in

order to acquaint myself with the Sekani language and learn
some of the basic issues which were important to them and which,
I thought, formed the basis of their system of social categories. I
would then proceed for a longer stay in Fort Ware, which, because of its greater isolation from White influence, would be
more traditional in its cultural expression. At least, this is what
I had planned.

Once I was settled in McLeod Lake Reserve I discovered that
learning the language would entail more work than I had anticipated. Although older people could still speak and understand
some Sekani, they could not always agree on the English meanings. This was not so much due to their imperfect knowledge of
English as to their increasing loss of Sekani. English was the
lingua franca of the community; there was only one old mono-
lingual Sekani speaker, and he died a few months after my arrival.
Furthermore, while "high proportion" may be a statistically true
statement, the fact that there were only about sixty-five people in
the community meant that only a handful of adults were potential instructors.

The small size of the community was also a clue to the significant social dynamics; there were other problems at McLeod Lake
besides my difficulties in learning the language. In 1968 a huge
artificial lake (Williston Lake) had been created by damming the
Peace River at the town of Hudson Hope. The lake flooded the
Finlay and Parsnip river drainage basins, both of which had
contained Sekani traplines, and one Sekani community, Fort
Grahame. People had been physically displaced, and the flooding of prime hunting and trapping territory had created considerable social distress as well. While in McLeod Lake I discovered that Fort Ware, about 80 miles by air north of the head
of the lake, had also been affected, although in some ways not as
severely as McLeod Lake. English was also primarily spoken in
Fort Ware; I was beginning to think that doing anthropology
might have been a mistake. A lay missionary who had spent a
total of eight years among the Sekani told me at the time that his
work (translating the Bible into Sekani) was no longer possible
nor desirable since the level of spoken Sekani had continually
dropped to the point where he could only hope to record a dying
language, something he did not want to do. Since that time a
trained linguist has recorded the language. Whether this will
affect people's speech habits remains to be seen.

The implications of these recent changes for my research
among the Sekani were, I thought, enormous and not too pleas-
ant to contemplate. I had counted on conducting research into

the transition from the fur-based economy to the newer economic patterns associated with the intrusive presence of the federal government on the local level. This change was perhaps occurring in Fort Good Hope, where economic development was the topic of the day, but it looked like I had arrived about twenty-five years too late in McLeod Lake, which had been linked to the major center of Prince George by highway since 1953. Since my original hypothesis depended in part on knowing how the fur trade era social organization was linked to the traditional social categories, the lack of this knowledge meant that a new approach was necessary.

This problem, I realized, was not insurmountable. After all, some systematic form of social classification was in use by people. All I had to do was discover it. The situation into which I intruded made the elucidation of the system very difficult, however. The flooding of large portions of their territory had left many McLeod Lakers in a disorganized and confused state; no one worked at traditional occupations (trapping and guiding), let alone hunting. Their attempts to deal with the loss of livelihood caused by the flooding were made more difficult by the minimal compensation that they had received for their losses[3] and by the indifference and resignation of local bureaucrats whose job was to 'deal' with the Sekani. Neither had the economic restructuring of the region resulted in the creation of new jobs for the Sekani. They also had to cope with the influx of large numbers of White settlers into the area who came as employees of the new forest-based industries. These were largely located in the new town of Mackenzie on the southern shores of Williston Lake. The overall results of this rapid change were a dramatic increase in alcohol consumption, a high level of violence, and in general a sense that the expectation of stability and social reciprocity which normally characterizes most long-term relationships was lacking. These circumstances turned much of my notes into a repetitious record of disappointments and minor and sometimes major tragedies. For the Canadian and British Columbia governments, the Sekani had become an embarrassment. For the Sekani, the tragedy was not so easily described by common words and figures; nearly everyone had lost friends, family, the means of making a living and the sense of doing something worthwhile with their lives.

At the same time, however, it was clear that the drama around me expressed a theme of sorts, and that this pattern was in some way an expression of cultural values which had been developed in the traditional fur trade era. In other words, I had to change the focus of my research, with less emphasis on the synchronic, more on the diachronic perspective. The two viewpoints are not mutually exclusive, but it is more difficult to trace a set of ideas or a pattern through time than a trait of material culture. It was especially difficult under the conditions in McLeod Lake; no one seemed to do anything except drink, have parties and fight. There were patterns to these activities; they became clearer when I went to Fort Ware, where people spent a lot more time hunting, trapping and getting along with each other. There, it was possible to see what McLeod Lake had looked like; by no means were the two communities the same in the past, but there were patterns in Fort Ware that fitted descriptions of what things had been like in McLeod Lake. From that point, it was possible to turn to the Hudson's Bay Company Archives in order to obtain the kinds of records that were entirely absent from local sources or anthropological writings: population figures, the movement of people, the volume and kinds of trade between Sekani and Europeans, and so on. In order to see the evolutionary steps that had led to the current situation, I had to guess what the political and social configuration had been. I was largely limited to looking at the economic facts in this endeavour, since these were the most commonly available records. For example, at each point in time for which data were available I examined the relationship between changes in population levels and the practices associated with changes in the fur gathering economy. From this relationship I deduced the major social categories that had been used and combined this with all available scraps of information about political arrangements.

Leaving aside theoretical and methodological debates, I now realize that there were other ways of studying the meaning of the events that constituted the daily life of the people of Fort Ware and McLeod Lake.[4] But then I was simply too overwhelmed by the personal tragedies all around me to make consistent sense of what was left of their social relationships. As a result, this book is mostly focussed on what people think and probably thought rather than a description of what they do.

1. J.S. Savishinsky, 'Stress and Mobility in an Arctic community: The Hare Indians of Colville Lake', Ph.D. dissertation, Department of Anthropology, Cornell University, 1970.

2. Although he visited the area in 1924, the results were not published until 1937. D. Jenness, *The Sekani Indians of British Columbia*, Ottawa: National Museum of Canada, Bulletin No. 84, 1937.

3. Between 20 September 1963 and March 1965 the British Columbia Hydroelectric authority paid out a total of $36,950.00 to twenty-five people organized into twenty-two trapline 'corporations'. The figures are drawn up from an unpublished report prepared by Jack Woodward for the Legal Services Commission, 1978, Appendix 21.

4. As regards the theoretical and other debates as to how and what to examine when an anthropologist attempts to decipher what people may be thinking, I refer the reader to M. Korovkin and G. Lanoue, 'On the Substantiality of Form: Interpreting Symbolic Expression in the Paradigm of Social Organization', *Comparative Studies in Society and History* 30(3): 613–48, 1988; G. Lanoue, *Images in Stone: A Theory on Interpreting Rock Art*, Rome: Art Center, 1989, and 'Beyond Values and Ideology: Tales from Six North American Indian Peoples', *Quaderni di Igitur* 3: 1–137, Rome: Nuova Arnica Editore, 1990. The practical side of doing fieldwork among the Sekani is examined in more detail in my article, 'Breakdown and Ethnographic Consciousness: The Sekani Case', *The European Journal of Native Studies*, 4(2): 45–52, 1990.

Acknowledgements

It is almost impossible to undertake work of this nature without the help of many people, all of whom contribute different but equally necessary aid. I am very grateful to the Urgent Ethnology Programme, National Museum of Man, for providing me with funds for the field research, as did the Government of Ontario with scholarships for the nearly two years I was in British Columbia.

Much thanks are due to people in various government agencies who aided beyond mere duty: David Borthwick, Assistant Deputy Minister of Environment (British Columbia); Bob Guay, Fish and Wildlife Branch, Ministry of Conservation and Recreation (British Columbia); J.P. Kelly, Fish and Wildlife Branch, Ministry of Conservation and Recreation (British Columbia); Ken Medd, Indian Affairs Branch, Department of Indian Affairs and Northern Development (Prince George office); Rae McIntyre, DIAND (Prince George office); B.P. Saunders, Ministry of Environment (British Columbia); Dennis Tollefson, Royal Canadian Mounted Police (Mackenzie Detachment); Neil Thomas, Fish and Wildlife Branch, Ministry of Conservation and Recreation (British Columbia).

Equally helpful non-government people include M.L. Barge, British Columbia Forest Products Ltd. (Mackenzie, BC); Bentley LeBaron (Errington, BC); Debbie Hoggan, Union of British Columbia Indian Chiefs (Vancouver); Keith Jobson, University of Victoria (Victoria); Suzanne Veit, Suzanne Veit & Associates (British Columbia); Ian Waddell (Vancouver, Ottawa); Jack Woodward (Vancouver); Dave and Kay Wilkinson (Fort Saint James, BC).

I owe many debts for friendship and aid. These include many people in McLeod Lake and Fort Ware, especially Harry Chingee and family, Lester Chingee, Albert Isadore and family, Emil

McCook and family, Johnnie Poole, Louie Tomah, Elmer McCook, Herman McCook, Craig McCook, and Charlie and Hazel Boya. Bob Steventon and Anne Hogan provided hospitality and aid in Prince George. Mike and Theresa Devenny (Mackenzie), Stu and Rheta Rix (Chetwynd), Jim and Mrs van Somers (Fort Ware), Tom and Liz Holmes (Port Dover, Ont., Fort Ware), and especially Dan and Kathy Tipton (McLeod Lake), Bob and Nancy Middleton (McLeod Lake) and Father Jan Iglicki (Mackenzie) all provided friendship and aid.

Special thanks are due to Shirlee Anne Smith, Archivist, Hudson's Bay Company, for permission to use the material under her care. Professor David Turner of the University of Toronto has provided me with invaluable guidance, inspiration and friendship over the years. Professors Tom McFeat, Suichi Nagata and Peter Carstens, all of the University of Toronto, provided helpful comments on an earlier draft of this manuscript.

The cover design is taken from 'Peace River Sunset' by Robyn Hughes, 1985.

Notes on the Text

Spelling: When certain words are capitalized ("the Chief", "the Federal government", "the Band"), I am usually referring to a specific political entity as it exists in modern Canadian society; when lower case is used ("the band", "the chief", "government") I am referring to the general category. I also prefer the spelling 'Athabaskans' rather than the more current 'Athapaskans'.

Quotes: Double quotation marks are used to indicate that the word or words are cited, either from the literature or from common usages among Sekani people. Single quotes indicate a gloss, as in a translation of a term, or a particular meaning or usage of a term (e.g. 'bands' in the text refers to local hunting bands or seasonal hunting bands; the historical evidence makes it impossible to be more precise).

Prices: Prices and costs are stated in Canadian 1979 dollars unless otherwise noted.

Abbreviations Used

HBC Arch.	Hudson's Bay Company Archives
HBC	Hudson's Bay Company
DIAND	Department of Indian Affairs and Northern Development
DIA	Department of Indian Affairs
RCMP	Royal Canadian Mounted Police
B	Brother
Z	Sister
Hu	Husband
Wi	Wife
M	Mother
F	Father
e/y	elder/younger
S	Son
D	Daughter
(m.s.)	male speaking
(w.s.)	woman speaking

Map 1 The Sekani homeland

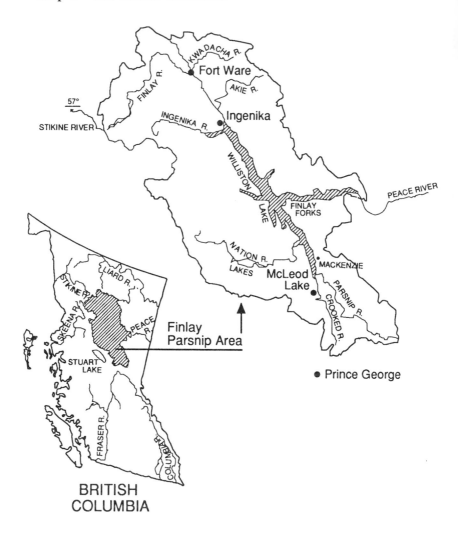

Map 2 The Sekani and their neighbours

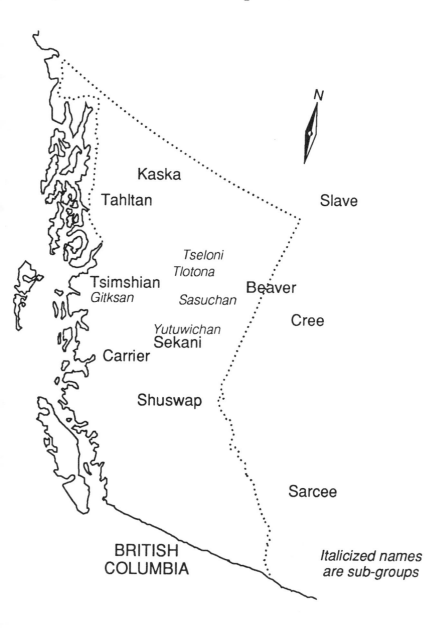

N

Kaska

Tahltan

Slave

Tseloni
Tlotona

Tsimshian
Gitksan

Sasuchan

Beaver

Cree

Yutuwichan
Sekani

Carrier

Shuswap

Sarcee

BRITISH
COLUMBIA

Italicized names
are sub-groups

Chapter 1

Introduction and Preliminary Considerations

The Sekani are the original inhabitants of the Rocky Mountain Trench area of northern British Columbia. The Trench area, the great valley formed by the easternmost and central ranges of the Rocky Mountains, was in all likelihood never the permanent home of any one group prior to the arrival of the Sekani in the middle of the eighteenth century. The Trench was not favourably endowed with game, and the Sekani, who by several accounts were Plains dwellers at one time, arrived only after apparently losing a trade war with the Beaver of the northwestern Plains and foothills. The climate is typical of the northern foothills: brief hot summers and long and intensely cold winters. Perhaps this alone would not have discouraged fulltime settlement had not transportation and travel been difficult because of the predominant spruce forest at the lower elevations. Many paths and trails in fact follow the former river bank at about the 2,200 foot contour. The Sekani had neither the raw materials nor incentive to make canoes, even the inferior spruce bark version, since there are few trees of sufficient diameter in the area. Dugouts were made from cottonwoods in the south of the region and moosehide raft were made in the north. In a word, the Sekani were great foot travellers, but necessarily limited in their ability to transport large quantities of goods and possessions. Certainly for the Carrier and Shuswap to the south, who had salmon and more game respectively, the Trench never offered an enticing invitation. The Kaska to the north lived in a somewhat less rugged, smaller scale and hence a more easily travelled landscape. And certainly the Northwest Coast people, the Gitksan Tsimshian and Tlingit, never had any reason to leave their relatively densely settled villages and salmon-laden rivers for the bleak Trench environment. The Sekani were reluctant new-comers, and, as we shall see, both the lateness and the freshness of their arrival were to play significant roles in forming their political culture.

There are also Sekani speakers who live beyond these geographic boundaries in predominantly non-Sekani communities. Today, these Sekani are not generally considered representative of the groups that anthropologists designate with the term, since they live in the midst of people with different linguistic and cultural traditions. The word 'Sekani' in this sense refers to a particular category in the Athabaskan family of languages. It means, says Jenness[1] and say some modern Sekani, "People of the Rocks", an apt description when one considers their mountainous habitat. Many Sekani simply translate the word as 'we people', since they either no longer know or have ceased to care about the traditional Athabaskan-based components of the word. Sekani know but do not use the word 'Dene' (which in Sekani would be Dunne-Tsa), which is the appellation that many northern Athabaskans prefer to use in their dealings with non-Athabaskans.

Early explorers such as Alexander Mackenzie did not use the term as such but used the more general term 'Rocky Mountain Indian'. 'Sekani' was first used in the journal of trader Daniel Harmon,[2] a fur trader employed by the Northwest Company about twenty years after Mackenzie's visit in 1793. By 1824, however, the name 'Sekani' was firmly established among the fur traders, since the explorer Samuel Black[3] used the term 'Thecannies' to refer to all inhabitants of the Trench. This suggests that the term had some currency among the Sekani even then.

Today, there appears to be a strong sense of tribal identity attached to the term. People have no difficulty in distinguishing a Sekani from a Gitksan or Carrier. In practice, however, the Sekani usually place limits on who is a Sekani and who is not somewhere around the village level. They recognize that there are "other Sekani" and speak about tribal-type unity in confrontation with Europeans and other Indian groups (not a small consideration, since today many Indian groups must sometimes face the possibility that their demands are opposed to those of other Indian people), but rarely do anything about it. The strength of this level of self-definition can be attributed partly to attempts by the Canadian federal government at bureaucratic consolidation as much as to the modern indigenous conception of 'tribe'. The primary reason for this strong but limited sense of self-identification, however, is the Sekani tradition which emerged as a result of participation in the fur trade. In other words, all Sekani acknowledge the existence of a category 'Sekani' used as a marker of tribal differences. All Sekani agree that the term refers to people who are now historically linked, but there is little agreement as to how and when this historical affiliation came into existence. It is not only that such definitions clash with received anthropological knowledge (if this were the case, then there would be very little problem), but that the irony of having an all-encompassing definition which is severely limited in practice is known to the Sekani. Indeed, such contradictions mark most of their history as a people.

Documented occupation of the Trench area has been continuous since earliest European contact in 1793. There are at present three Sekani communities in the area. Sekani people predominate in the settlements of McLeod Lake, Ingenika and Fort Ware. These three communities lie more or less in a straight line when travelling from south to north along the Trench. The total distance between the two extreme points is about 230 miles. Fort Ware has been the site of a permanent trading post since the 1920s, according to local tradition, although no documentary evidence can be found to verify this.[4] Since 1954, the settlement has been serviced by a variety of independent traders. The community of Ingenika, however, is the recent creation of people who fled the floodwaters created by the damming of the Peace River in the 1960s.[5] Ingenika is not an Indian Reserve set aside by the government, unlike the other two communities. The inhabitants of Ingenika have the use of a Reserve south of their present location, but they have abandoned this in favour of the 'illegal' squatter community. Although there are three major Reserves in the Trench[6] and there are three Sekani communities, only two villages are on legally recognized Reserves. This convoluted and delicate state of affairs has political implications for the Sekani. Since no treaty has been signed between the federal government and any Sekani group in the Trench,[7] services provided to the Sekani by the federal government are rendered as part of Indian Affairs policy. In any event, Reserves are small, as is typical of the Province of British Columbia, and contain little more than enough land for the people to build their homes. The Sekani, therefore, have been tied into a larger economy since 1805 and continue to be dependent on a variety of government programmes and policies, as well as the plans and demands of private industry, for such basics as access to forest land for timber for house construction and fuel, and for hunting and trapping land.

Although it is to be expected that some similarities exist, each of these three communities has faced different problems associated with the flooding and has reacted to them in unique ways. The similarities are today outweighed by the individual circumstances which have emerged as a result of the flooding. Although little information was collected on the situation in Ingenika, McLeod Lake was at the centre of the political storm generated by the flooding of the Trench. Fort Grahame, an old settlement halfway between Fort Ware and McLeod Lake, ceased to exist as a community. The inhabitants were dispersed. About two-thirds moved to a new Reserve south of the newly born lake near the equally new town of Mackenzie, while the remainder went to live in Fort Ware. By default, McLeod Lake is the community where most of the effects of the flooding are visible today. It is far enough from the former river course that it was not flooded, but it is close enough to be strongly affected by the founding of the town of Mackenzie and subsequent arrival of White settlers and industries.

McLeod Lakers have had to face the trauma of the dispossession of their land and resources. One result has been considerable emigration as social and economic conditions have worsened. Logging and mining companies threaten to create very similar conditions and an equally bleak future for Fort Ware. In 1979, for example, the Cyprus Anvil mining company established a camp about twelve miles from Fort Ware in order to conduct tests on an ore deposit (plans for the mine were shelved when ore prices fell a few months later). Both British Columbia Forest Products and Finlay Forest Products have large tracts of land allocated to them for future development. A map in a government office in Victoria shows that the width of the region to be logged extends from the western bank of the Finlay River to the first mountain range to the west, and latitudinally from Williston Lake in the south to a point roughly sixty miles north of Fort Ware. Logging will almost certainly be at the expense of the continued exploitation of animal resources in the region and will undermine related activities such as guiding if McLeod Lake is any indication of what is in store for Fort Ware. Fort Ware residents look to McLeod Lake to see the effects of uncontrolled development, and the picture they see is grim. Many Fort Ware people have mixed feelings about development as a result. It is a commonly held belief that development is in itself not bad, but uncontrolled exploitation of resources would create the type of social distress found in McLeod Lake.

These are some of the conditions and problems facing the modern Sekani. These are not problems in the sense that we regard pollution or nuclear war as problems. Whereas we worry about these and other conditions of modern life, most people manage to lead their daily lives with little or no ill-effects from the issues that occupy the editorial pages of our newspapers. The Sekani do not have the luxury of carrying on, however. They feel and indeed act as if the flooding of the lake, the arrival of White industries and the bureaucratic flood tide aimed at 'helping' them are overwhelmingly disorientating and threatening. As a group, the Sekani never had a very large margin of survival in the past. They seem to have an even smaller chance of continuing to live as a self-identified and relatively independent people today. And yet they have survived. Victims of the fur trade, poverty and government indifference, they have something at their disposal that allows them to continue living lives that, until fairly recently, did not differ very much from those of their ancestors of 150 years ago. This monograph is about that 'something'. Whatever it is, it is not because the Sekani were or are more threatening and aggressive than their neighbours, nor were they cowards. They did fight and win battles against other people when they needed land for hunting or trapping. Yet they have generally preferred not to fight, not because of some moral scruples, I think, but simply because it was very difficult to organize dispersed mountain nomads into some coherent entity. More than anything else, the Sekani seem to have developed several features in their political thought that allow them to act in ways that people in other band societies find very difficult. Today, however, some of these traits hold negative consequences. There is no real enemy that anyone can identify with certainty; there are only victims.

Over the years the Sekani have apparently changed a great deal in surface details, especially in the size and composition of their groups and networks. Despite such changes, however, there has been a great deal of continuity. Not all of the changes have been imposed from outside. Some have emerged from within. The Sekani continue to act within the confines of their cultural tradition, especially within those aspects of their tradition which deal with their manner of establishing bonds between people. One result of this continuity is the recurrent emergence of particular forms of social and political action, whether the context is provided by the European mercantile fur trade or by the recent presence of modern extractive industries such as logging. The way in which the Sekani establish linkages with people, expressed by the notion of brotherhood, has increased the importance of particular types of networks and social categories such as the trapping partnership, the phratry, the patronymic category, gender-based social categories and pan-Indianism. These networks find expression on all levels of social life: the hunting group, the local and regional bands and the tribe. The effect of the forces which led to the development of the various definitions of brotherhood will be examined.

Flexibility and Adaptation

What emerged from my research is evidence of a Sekani tendency to keep constant certain factors of their social organization despite some drastic changes associated with pressures imposed from the outside. This can be characterized as a tendency towards cultural continuity in some selected areas, since the Sekani were no more or less successful in controlling their social evolution than were most people faced with the same pressures; only the combination of forces and the final effect are uniquely Sekani.

Sekani adaptation to outside influences over which they have little control can be best described by two words: cautious pragmatism. They have moved to modify some of their own social arrangements to fit the new order and have exerted pressure to change these outside forces whenever they could. They have not ignored the new by retreating into a reassertion of old social patterns and ideologies, nor have they uncritically welcomed change. Their post-contact history can best be characterized as an attempt to hold the middle ground – to be flexible on the smaller issues but to retain the core unchanged. What matters most to the Sekani is their view that a particular relationship to the land forms the basis of their social relationships and, hence, the core of their cultural traditions.

It is not that explicit codes of private and collective ownership were absent among the Sekani but rather that their beliefs incorporated a well-defined guiding principle of brotherhood. The circumstances surrounding their occupation of the Rocky Mountain Trench had made the use of certain strategies necessary. As the Sekani developed and applied these strategies they appear to the observer as a people who remain unchanged in their attachment to ways of using the land in order to define themselves as a group. Had the Sekani resisted European intrusion with force and vigour they would undoubtedly have been crushed and not have survived to the present day as a self-defined people. More to the point, the Sekani are not predisposed to undertake this sort of resistance to intrusion.

The end result is an overwhelming pragmatism towards their own and outside societies. At the same time there is a shrewdness and subtlety of insight in their response to the fur trade. This subtlety still characterizes their world view today. This seems to be in contrast with much of the past and present descriptions of other Athabaskan people. If early ethnographers seemed to marvel at the physical and material skill it took to survive in the Canadian North, many recent descriptions[8] emphasize more esoteric aspects of Athabaskan culture. These are no doubt insightful and useful, but they do not seem to apply to or provide useful insights for understanding Sekani cultural dynamics. The Sekani have developed in another direction. Their political culture compensates in complexity for what might be lacking (or simply hidden to outside observers) in their religious thought or speculative philosophy.

For the ethnographer this pragmatism has one immediate result: it leads the Sekani to discount explicit lessons from history. Does the type of society exist which we studied in school where the village elders quietly contemplate matters of social and cosmological importance to the delight of visiting anthropologists? Perhaps, but the Sekani are not that society. Yet at the same time their subtlety is engaged when they anticipate the future. Some things have remained unchanged and it is this living presence of the past that is used as a guidepost in evaluating the present. There is no need, therefore, explicitly to preserve the past in the form of folktales and oral traditions that today would be mere disembodied echoes. The past surrounds and shapes the future for the Sekani in the form of the cultural associations implied by the continued use of land.

Other Viewpoints

Many years ago June Helm wrote that Athabaskans were noted for a "minimality of culture".[9] The implication was clear that there were few structurally produced constraints on behaviour.

This statement is, in part, a continuation of the debate about certain characteristics of hunting and gathering societies. Flexibility of social structure and propensity to change are usually seen as prime characteristics of this type of organization.[10] For example, Steward modified his description of band level social organization from a patrilineal/local emphasis to include composite bands after his evaluation of some Athabaskan data.[11] Membership in composite bands was seen to be controlled by several loosely defined and flexible principles. A debate on the nature of this flexibility was instigated when Service speculated that composite bands were not a traditional feature of hunting societies but were the product of social breakdowns associated with European intrusion into these societies.[12] This position was supported by Williams in his major study of band level social organization.[13]

The notion that hunting and gathering band societies are essentially flexible has dominated the literature on Athabaskan and Algonkian Indian groups. It has often been suggested that the flexibility of group formation and recruitment is a primary structural feature and that it organizes social relations in these societies. Honigmann, for example, has suggested that flexibility in Kaska social organization is linked to the personalities of individual Kaska, who appear to him to be unable to carry out a sequence of causally related activities.[14] Hence, little predictability in social relations and in planning seem to characterize their social organization. Slobodin's ethnography of the Peel River Kutchin reveals that various groupings and networks are formed using several different principles, each of which can be functionally independent of the others.[15] Groups therefore have cross-cutting membership, allowing individuals to align themselves independently of the practical goals of the group's members. VanStone notes that for the Snowdrift Chipewyan a sense of community exists despite the lack of formal organization.[16] Traditional social organization emphasizes the freedom of the individual and his family. The sense of community (the band) membership is considerably weakened by individualism and mistrust among members. Hence ties are loose and somewhat flexible.

In a more general vein Knight re-examines the relationship between animals and territoriality among northeastern Algonkians and suggests that in traditional times starvation ensued from a failure to move around within the band territory.[17] Social ties in traditional times implicitly stressed flexibility rather than rigidity, and hence fall into the same characteristic pattern as expressed by the movement of the hunting groups. Savishinsky argues that among the Hare spatial mobility has come to be a valued tradition because it relieves the social causes of stress.[18] Existing social ties, therefore, do not constrain movement or the formulation of new bonds among individuals. Nelson argues that in traditional times the Alaskan Kutchin had no notion of territorial exclusivity.[19] Such exclusivity – restricting particular areas of land for the use of one local band or individual – was impossible given fluctuations in the resource base. Resources were scattered and yet locally concentrated and were subject to marked cyclical and noncyclical variation. Sharp, on the other hand, sees flexibility as a cultural phenomenon among the Caribou-eating Chipewyan.[20] The drastic changes to which the Chipewyan have accommodated – severe depopulation due to disease, and displacement associated with participation in the fur trade – suggest that there is a high degree of flexibility in Chipewyan culture which, none the less, maintains a large measure of continuity over time. Last, Jarvenpa argues that the Chipewyans of Patuanak cannot be accurately described as always maximizing economic goals.[21] Their distribution throughout the band range is a function of other norms and ideals, although Jarvenpa does not explicitly concern himself with these notions as such; this suggests the existence and acceptance of several distinct motives.

Sophisticated arguments about Athabaskan organization have been tendered by Asch, McDonnell, Riches and Ridington, among others.[22] The latter's study of the Beaver Indians suggests that there are complex ideational structures in traditional social organization which underlie an apparently simple bilateral arrangement of kin. Here the interplay of distinct levels of categorization is as important in structuring ties as the categories themselves. McDonnell's treatment of the Kasini (northern Kaska and Southern Tutchone) demonstrates the existence of ideational constructs of social action which overlap and sometimes contradict one another. Kasini social structure appears to be flexible yet is the result of the interplay of subtle and powerful notions which continue over time. Asch suggests that Slavey notions of descent and residence are not constrained by adaptive strategies pursued by individuals. While seeking economic and material gain, people construct social relationships on the basis of ideological oppositions and analogies. This results in distinct networks and groups which cut across pragmatic groupings. Hence the flexibility which is observed on the ground is the result of the operation of ideational principles of organization which are not as yet clearly identified for the entire fur trade period.

Riches argues that for northern hunters and gatherers, including Algonkian and Eskimo people, variations in the size of groups is an indication of flux. This fluidity is related to the central problem in the social organization of these societies, which he defines as a norm of fragmentation which must be offset by means of certain mechanisms if the solidarity of the band is to be maintained. This fragmentation is the result of environmental circumstances.[23] These are best countered by creating a wide variety of ties. Hence, flexibility is the norm, although it is expressed against a background of a constant concern for group solidarity. Unlike Asch, McDonnell and Ridington, Riches locates the nexus of flexibility somewhere in the organization of production. Although sophisticated and theoretically 'sensitive', such an argument ignores the dominant role many ethnographers assign to ideology in structuring social relationships among Athabaskans.

There are, in brief, two schools of thought about the notion of flexibility in Athabaskan band organization. The first represents flexibility as the outcome of attempts to achieve some measure of material security. Social and cultural relations, therefore, merely reflect the exigencies or contingencies associated with the material conditions which characterize particular regions in the north. The second view is aptly represented by Asch when he writes, "all hunting societies, regardless of their social organization, have equal flexibility in responding to environmental conditions. . . . Hence, if one is interested in the culturally derived rules which underlie any particular on-the-ground residence group formation, it is necessary to look further then a mere stimulus–response relationship between the environment and the rules of social organization."[24] Despite this suggestion there is a pervasive notion among many scholars that no matter how 'adapted' and 'flexible' (and hence accommodating) Athabaskan band organization may have been under traditional conditions it has not fared well in recent times, which are generally characterized by massive foreign intrusion and strong economic pressures. There are many reasons that account for this attitude. Most subtle and pervasive in its influence is the notion that a process of social evolution has operated to produce a vaguely defined but none the less large gap between band societies and industrial state societies. In general, it is assumed that the latter are not as directly and strongly influenced by the physical environment as are band societies. This sentiment was reinforced by Steward in his formulation of the idea of composite band and in his description of the cultural ecology model.[25] He argued that Shoshoni adaptations to the environment, using a simple technology, were not necessarily representative of the process of cultural development in all societies. The immediacy of environmental impact, he argued, would decrease as societies increased their degree of social complexity and technological efficiency. Complex societies were more likely governed by elements of superstructure rather than by the environment.

Steward was not the first person to imply that forces of social evolution were responsible for the presence of a gradient of social development whose opposite ends were far apart due to the overwhelming influence of the environment on societies situated at the bottom of the scale. He merely reflected a generally held assumption, although he was probably the first to use Athabaskan data systematically in support of his theories. The problem of the degree of the primitiveness of certain forms of social organization has been relevant to anthropology ever since early theories were constructed to explain the contemporary existence of certain types of 'kinship' traits, such as the presence of matrilineal principles of group recruitment, even after it had been (reluctantly) admitted by anthropologists that people were not themselves primitive. The debate on evolution by Maine, Lubbock, Morgan, McLennan and Bachofen, and later by Boas and his followers, was partially limited by the manner in which the question was posed. To counter the somewhat fanciful speculations of the first group, adherents of the Boas position usually argued that Indian groups could not be used to defend the evolutionary stance adopted by the first group, since most primitives were clearly not matrilineal.[26] They could not therefore be relics of an earlier stage of human development characterized by one or several elements of promiscuity, matrilineality or matriarchy. Furthermore, the few Indian groups that possessed exclusive groups and networks such as clans, sibs or moieties were seen to rest on a more primitive foundation focussed on the family and kinship as a means of organizing social relations. In either instance the primitiveness advocated by this type of model of band society went unchallenged. The assumption of evolutionary development – and hence of Indian primitiveness – was either implicit, as in Westermark's writings, or sidestepped altogether and hence implicitly confirmed, as in Spier's, Swanton's and Goldschmidt's writings.[27]

Another constraint upon the debate about Athabaskan flexibility is the implicit connection between the nature of Athabaskan adaptations to the physical environment and Athabaskan social organization. In other words, if making a living in the Subarctic zone is difficult given the harshness of the climate, fluctuations in food supply and the simple stone technology possessed by people at the time of contact with Europeans, might we not expect that people were somewhat limited in their social and psychological development? It is a longstanding tradition in social and cultural anthropology that the lack of civilized graces among hunting peoples is due to the limitations imposed on them by the rigorous environments in which they live. Sophisticated problem solving is seen as either shrewd or ingenious, or, as some would have it, an attempt to increase leisure time.[28] No matter how ingenious these technical solutions to problems of making a living might be, they are still generally labelled as vastly inferior to ours. The debate then becomes, is or is not the environment of hunting peoples harsh? The facts have been traditionally interpreted to favour the first proposition, although some recent writers have suggested or implied the opposite, presumably in the interest of redressing the balance in favour of Subarctic hunting peoples.[29] Given this new attitude it may appear to be reverting back to the old school of environmental determinism to suggest that the Subarctic environment is indeed harsh and immediate in its impact on individuals. This, however, does not prevent people, as members of groups, from demonstrating very sophisticated attitudes in their social and psychological solutions to problems presented to them by the physical environment. It is hoped that the evidence and arguments presented here can dispel these earlier notions, at least as far as they are relevant to understanding the social dynamics of one particular Athabaskan Indian group.

As Koolage has pointed out, ethnographers' preconceived notions of culture may lead them to speak prematurely of deculturation, disorganization and disintegration.[30] This intensifies their doubts about the ability of groups like the Sekani, clearly caught in the middle of strong and sometimes conflicting forces, to deal with some of these pressures. Here I argue that flexibility of social arrangements is not a substratum that exists merely because there is no established way to turn chaos into order. Flexibility in Sekani social life is structurally produced. Details of past motives are not unambiguous, but they strongly suggest that many actions by the Sekani were attempts to enforce a certain kind of flexibility despite strong pressures by the fur trade to contain it. The peculiar circumstances of contact to which northern Canadian hunting societies were exposed affected their subsequent social development. One major fact stands out: most northern Indians were not subject to direct colonial intrusion since no settlement followed upon contact. This is not to suggest that circumstances were not difficult. Without wishing to engage in a debate about the nature of colonial domination, however, it seems self-evident that sixteenth-, seventeenth- and eighteenth-century colonialism in northern Canada – the mercantile accumulation of capital at the economic frontiers of Western society, to be technical – differed drastically from colonialism in southern Canada. There, settlement by European immigrants was an important factor. This is only now beginning to emerge in the North. The delay between initial contact and the present influx of settlers allowed the formulation of strategies which gave the various Indian groups time to accommodate to the new regime. These strategies are a continuation of past adaptations to the social environment such as, in the Sekani case, the problems associated with the nature of the contact experience with other Indian groups in the Rocky Mountain Trench.

* * *

By 'flexibility' I mean two things. First, there is the commonly accepted dictionary usage of the term which denotes two aspects: (a) fluidity, and (b) amorphousness. The instance 'a' refers to the lack of constraint imposed on future relationships by a given set of relationships in the present. No matter how precise and rigidly defined the socio-political patterns are at any given moment, fluidity ensures the ability to shift from one pattern to another without necessarily compromising the precise definition of each pattern. The instance 'b' refers to the lack of determinant form contained in the Indian notion of 'band'. Although anthropologists all agree that northern Athabaskans have some notion of community or band, there is little agreement on the structure implicit in the notion. The variety of descriptions of life in the Canadian North that is provided by anthropologists leads many writers to imply that Indian notions of band lack clarity and are only weakly expressed. This conclusion, of course, is reinforced by rapid and recent changes in the traditional band organization of northern Athabaskans. Both instances of this first usage of the notion of flexibility have emerged in the literature in light of the concern many anthropologists express about the determinant role of the physical environment.

Second, flexibility is used to refer to the movement between two precisely defined poles in a dialectical movement. The Sekani notion of brotherhood has two aspects. Each is expressed at different levels in the social structure, but at certain times one predominates. As such there seems to be different stages in the social evolution of the Sekani. In fact, however, these are merely different moments in a pattern of constant oscillation. Here, both instances of the notion of flexibility are used without regard to special notation, since movement from one to the other pole implies organizational fluidity.

In my preliminary treatment of the problem of flexibility in Athabaskan band societies I had hypothesized that flexibility of social relationships and the lack of clearly structured groups within the band was not evidence of a lack of cohesion but was rather an offshoot of contradictions within the social structure itself.[31] These contradictions, I suggested, were localized within the primary and secondary brotherhoods, following the usages and suggestions made by Turner and Wertman.[32] I saw Athabaskan social structure as consisting of domestic groups affiliated by particular types of both sibling and conjugal ties so that a certain tension existed within each domestic group between the sibling ties of the parents, which drew outsiders into one alliance, and the conjugal ties of their offspring, which drew people away from the domestic group into another alliance. The presence of one set of ties threatened the stability of the other. It was among the Hare that I had first encountered this tension, and I assumed that it was characteristic of all Mackenzie Valley Drainage Dene. Far from being universal, such tension is characteristic of the Fort Good Hope Hare because of the manner in which they actualize a particular pattern of economic relationships. Unlike Helm's earlier formulation,[33] I thought that the standard description of 'domestic group' was not a very useful analytical device for understanding Athabaskan social structure. All Athabaskans have something like a domestic group, but it is a coincidental result of the coming together of other, more important, principles.

Furthermore, I had argued that this tension could be ideologically expressed in at least two possible ways: (1) attempts could be made by members of the domestic group to minimize all ties with other groups by acknowledging only those ties that were actually negotiated and by denying the importance of those ties that were potential but not yet realized; (2) attempts to minimize the tension could be made by increasing socio-political complexity through strengthening ties to other domestic and hunting groups in the band, such that tensions within the domestic groups are subsumed within the larger unity. If the first instance prevailed then it could be expected that autonomous domestic groups would dominate the social landscape, but with only limited acknowledgment of lateral ties linking the domestic groups to one another. Relationships would tend to be short term and renegotiated every time social and economic circumstances changed. The result would be a weakly expressed sense of band unity. However, in the second case each conjugal group is permitted autonomy on the practical level of day to day realignments of social networks, but its members continually stress the importance of potential ties in formulating wide networks. The tension between actual and potential ties could, in turn, be potentially resolved on the level of ideology by including both sorts of ties within a large classification that corresponds roughly to our anthropological concept of 'band'. A sense of band unity could thus be generated and yet the very idea of unity would incorporate two structurally imposed tendencies without denying either of two possible ways of forming linkages. It is no wonder that 'band' as such could not be explicitly pinpointed by reference to one principle of unity if this second instance prevailed.

If the second instance prevailed then the sense of band unity could be expected to outweigh the tendencies towards factionalism and atomism. However, the other pole of the structural dialectic might come into play so that ideological divisions might result in a generationally expressed social hierarchy. In other words, the stronger the acknowledgement of lateral ties among the domestic groups – the stronger the sense of band unity – then the stronger might be the divisions between the sibling and partnership ties of the parental generation on the one hand and the conjugal ties of their offspring on the other, since each generation has its own unique network. There would be a strong sense of unity at the band level while the internal unity of the domestic groups would be weakened considerably.

As it turned out each of these tendencies is an inherent possibility within the Sekani system of social organization. They are not opposed to one another; rather, particular historical circumstances result in one being dominant at any one time. The other tendency is never entirely subdued, however. Tensions were most apparent within domestic groups, which, during the fur trade era, had become the dominant means of organizing people into work groups as well as being the means of creating and reproducing new social relationships. A sense of band unity, however, was strong even though ties between domestic groups had become less important. The strength with which band unity was felt and expressed was due to a number of factors basically linked to the circumstances of the Sekani's occupation of the Trench several centuries ago. These circumstances created a new sense and, indeed, a new definition of band unity that was much stronger than a mere acknowledgement of ill-defined ties that link the domestic groups together by means of cross-cutting brotherhoods (the various networks of actual and potential hunting partners). In other words, the system was much more complex – more ideationally controlled – than I had originally thought and had taken another expression than that which I had predicted.

This sense of unity gained expression through the concept of brotherhood as such. By 'brotherhood' I mean simply the sense of identity through the sameness of the public persona contained within individuals. If band unity in the long run paradoxically depends on differences in the power and abilities of members of the various domestic groups, 'brotherhood' demands allegiance to a common set of criteria. The wider the network which results, the more narrow the criteria used. 'Brotherhood' is not merely a heuristic concept on my part. It is recognized as a primary force in social dynamics by the Sekani themselves. Once in place as a more or less successful solution to the problems associated with the Sekani occupation of the Trench at the end of the last century, it has been re-applied in different guises. One by-product of the Sekani definition of brotherhood and its deployment in the creation of social networks is the possibility of a strong tension arising between men and women under certain circumstances. This has led to a clear bias in this work, since it was consequently difficult to obtain information from women, given the current social conditions.

A strong sense of the Sekani as a self-defined group on the regional level traditionally goes against the environmental requirements of maintaining flexible ties between domestic groups so as to take advantage of sudden opportunities. The flexibility of these ties has traditionally been reinforced by a continual emphasis on the importance and autonomy of the domestic group which, in the long run, can be said to generate band unity. It is the autonomy – and, hence, potential if not real differences – of domestic groups which emphasizes their isolation from one another and implicitly creates the conditions for the acceptance by each group of some central focus we call 'band unity'. Ironically, today the Sekani emphasize the autonomy of domestic groups in counterpoint to their highly developed sense of regional community, even though the strong relationship the Sekani once had to their land has been

considerably weakened. This new emphasis on the autonomy of domestic groups brings the Sekani full circle; it engages the other side of their dialectical organization and
'brotherhood' once again surfaces as a new means of linking
people whose ties to one another seem too weak to cut across
domestic group boundaries. With a sense of self that has been
strengthened by the circumstances of their occupation of the
Trench, it is not surprising that the Sekani have preferred to
solve crises by emphasizing regional unity and not the autonomy of the domestic groups and of individuals. It is part of
the Sekani experience, however, that the particular economic
and environmental pressures to which they have been subject
since first contact with Europeans have always strengthened
the other pole of the equation; the isolation of the domestic
groups has increased as a result of participation in the fur
trade, as has the relative importance of the individual.

In sum, it is not the environment that produces Sekani flexibility. It is not a lack of cultural or social complexity that produces 'weak' bonds between individuals and particular groups.
The Sekani have simultaneously accepted two elements in a
relation of opposition: autonomy in lower level relationships
and unity of the group as a whole. These two poles are, however, expressed at different levels of Sekani social life and so
are not in a relation of contradiction to one another. Social
action is not precluded, but, on the other hand, all social
action engages some tension – a tension that cannot be resolved
within this framework. Modern Sekani have a highly developed sense of self-awareness as Sekani, while maintaining flexibility and pragmatism in their attempted solutions to various
problems of social life on a domestic group basis. They have
managed this compromise by redefining band unity as 'brotherhood' and by treating 'brotherhood' in strictly ideational terms.

Although recent events have intensified some tendencies within
Sekani social organization, the contemporary structure of social
relations basically reflects the trends which were developed (or
at least, put in place) between 1870 and the turn of the century.
The Sekani concept of phratric brotherhood and its later manifestations at the end of this period – the patronymic system of social
categorization and the philosophy of pan-Indian unity – characterize both the traditional and the modern eras.

Notes

1. D. Jenness, *The Indians of Canada*, Ottawa: National Museum of Canada, Bulletin No. 65, 1932, p. 377.

2. D.W. Harmon, *Sixteen Years in the Indian Country: The Journal of Daniel Williams Harmon 1800–1816*, ed. W.K. Lamb, Toronto: Macmillan, 1957.

3. S. Black, *Black's Rocky Mountain Journal, 1824*, ed. E.E. Rich, London: Hudson's Bay Record Society, 1955.

4. I was told by the Hudson's Bay Company archivist that no documents exist. Furthermore, there are large gaps in the available historical records: the diocesan records for the area were burned in the 1950s, and Department of Indian Affairs records are sporadic until the 1960s.

5. For a summary of events surrounding the creation of the dam and flooding of the Sekani homeland, see G. Lanoue, 'Continuity and Change: The Development of Political Self-Definition Among the Sekani of Northern British Columbia', Ph.D. dissertation, Department of Anthropology, University of Toronto, 1984, pp. 356–9.

6. There are in fact more than three, but only three are inhabited. The others are small fishing stations and the like.

7. Some Sekani east of the Rockies adhered to Treaty No. 8 in 1911 but are now considered to be Beaver Indians, according to the Sekani of the Trench.

8. H.S. Sharp, 'Shared Experience and Magical Death: Chipewyan Explanations of a Prophet's Decline', *Ethnology* 25(4): 257–70, 1987. R. Ridington, 'From Hunt Chief to Prophet: Beaver Indian dreamers and Christianity', *Arctic Anthropology* 24(1): 8–18, 1977, and 'Knowledge, Power and the Individual in Subarctic Hunting Societies', *American Anthropologist* 90(1): 98–110, 1988.

9. J. Helm-MacNeish, 'Leadership Among the Northeastern Athapaskan', *Anthropologica* 2: 131–63, 1956, p. 131.

10. See R.B. Lee and I. Devore, eds, *Man the Hunter*, New York: Aldine 1968, for examples of this view.

11. J. Steward, 'The Economic and Social Basis of Primitive Bands', in idem, ed., *Essays in Anthropology Presented to A.L. Kroeber*, Berkeley: University of California Press, 1956.

12. E. Service, *Primitive Social Organization: An Evolutionary Perspective*, New York: Random House, 1962.

13. B.J. Williams, *A Model of Band Society*, Memoirs for the Society of American Archaeology No. 29, 1974.

14. J.J. Honigmann, *Culture and Ethos of Kaska Society*, Yale University Publications in Anthropology No. 40, New Haven: Yale University Press, 1949, p. 271.

15. R. Slobodin, *Band Organization of the Peel River Kutchin*, Ottawa: National Museum of Canada Bulletin No. 179, 1962.

16. J. VanStone, *The Changing Culture of the Snowdrift Chipewyan*, Ottawa: National Museum of Canada, Bulletin No. 209, Anthropological Series No. 74, 1965, pp. 80–1.

17. R. Knight, 'A Re-examination of Hunting, Trapping and Territoriality Among the Northeastern Algonquian Indians', in A. Vayda and E. Leeds, eds, *The Role of Animals in Human Ecological Adjustment*, Washington: The American Association for the Advancement of Sciences, 1965, pp. 33, 34.

18. J.S. Savishinsky, 'Mobility as an Aspect of Stress in an Athabaskan Bush Community', *American Anthropologist* 73: 604–18, 1971.

19. R.K. Nelson, *Hunters of the Northern Forest*, Chicago: University of Chicago Press, 1973, p. 274.

20. H.S. Sharp, *Chipewyan Marriage*, Ottawa: National Museum of Man, Mercury Series, Canadian Ethnology Service Paper No. 58, 1979, p. 3.

21. R. Jarvenpa, *The Trappers of Patuanak: Towards a Spatial Ecology of Modern Hunters*, Ottawa: National Museum of Canada, Canadian Ethnology Service Paper, No. 67, 1980.

22. M. Asch, 'Steps Towards the Analysis of Athapaskan Social Organization', *Arctic Anthropology* 17(2): 46, 1980. R.F. McDonnell, 'Kasini Society: Some Aspects of the Social Organization of Athapaskan Culture Between 1900–1950, Ph.D. dissertation, Department of Anthropology, University of British Columbia, 1975. R.F. McDonnell, 'Symbolic Orientations and Systematic Turmoil: Centering on the Kaska Symbol of Dene', *Canadian Review of Anthropology* 4(1): 39–56, 1984, D. Riches, *Northern Nomadic Hunter-Gatherers*, London: Academic Press, 1982, pp. 21, 50. R. Ridington, 'Kin Categories versus Kin Groups: A Two Section System Without Sections', *Ethnology* 8(4): 460–7, 1969.

23. Riches, *Northern Nomadic*, p. 97.

24. Asch, 'Steps Towards the Analysis of Athapaskan Social Organization', p. 46.

25. J. Steward, *Basin-Plateau Aboriginal Socio-Political Groups*, Washington: Smithsonian Institution, Bureau of American Ethnology, Bulletin No. 120, 1938, p. 262.

26. See, for example, J.R. Swanton, 'The Social Organization of American Tribes', *American Anthropologist* 7: 663–73, 1905. Spier, 'The Distribution of Kinship Systems in North America', *University of Washington Publications in Anthropology* 1: 69–88, 1925. W. Goldschmidt, 'Social Organization in Native California and the Origins of Clans', *American Anthropologist* 50: 444–56, 1948.

27. E. Westermark, *The History of Human Marriage*, London: Macmillan and Co., 1894.

28. M. Sahlins, *Stone Age Economics*, Chicago: Aldine, 1974.

29. A. Tanner, *Bringing Home Animals: Religious Ideology and Mode of Production of the Mistassini Cree Hunters*, London: Hurst, 1979, Asch, 'Steps Towards the Analysis of Athapaskan Social Organization'. Riches, *Northern Nomadic*.

30. W.W. Koolage, 'Conceptual Negativism in Chipewyan Ethnology', *Anthropologica* N.S. 17(1): 45–60, 1975, pp. 45, 46.

31. G. Lanoue, 'Flexibility in Hare Social Organization', *The Canadian Journal of Native Studies* 1(2): 259–76, 1981.

32. D.H. Turner and P. Wertman, *Shamattawa: The Structure of Social*

Relations in a Northern Algonkian Band, Ottawa: National Museum of Canada, Canadian Ethnology Service Paper No. 36, 1977. D.H. Turner, *Dialectics and Tradition: Myth and Social Structure in Two Hunter-Gatherer Societies*, London: Occasional Paper No. 36 of the Royal Anthropological Institute of Great Britain and Ireland, 1978.

33. J. Helm, 'Bilaterality in the Socio-Territorial Organization of the Arctic Drainage Dene', *Ethnology* 4: 361–85, 1965.

Chapter 2

A Day at McLeod Lake

This is not a typical day at McLeod Lake since, as the narrative makes clear, it is a weekend and the end of the month. People have more money and drinking is more pronounced than usual. The children are not at school. Not all the events happened exactly as described in the narrative nor are they necessarily in the sequence in which they occurred. Obviously I have had to respect people's privacy and fictionalize the descriptions of people and events somewhat. None the less, the descriptions of what people were thinking is an accurate depiction of what they said at the time that similar events took place and what they described afterwards. This book is largely about the history of a concept, the Sekani idea of brotherhood, but I realized that for someone who was not there the Sekani ran the risk of being described in terms that over-emphasized pan-Indianism and politics. I wrote this chapter to correct that impression and in the hope that a reader will be able to place the following chapters in context, to remember that the Sekani are people of flesh and blood with strong views and complex emotions despite, or perhaps because of, the fact that they live in a very small community.

* * *

There are about 60 people in the community, 25 adults and 35 children. This total includes two or three relatives who live elsewhere and are just visiting for a few days. People today (Saturday) are waking up late since there was considerable drinking the night before. It's the end of the month and some welfare and pension cheques have come in; their "pay cheques", as people call them. At about 11 a.m. Doris, Angus's wife, is going to set her net at the mouth of the stream. She has been doing this for a few days and has caught nothing, probably because it is a little too early in the season for the fish to be running. Doris doesn't always set her net in fishing season but is one of the few women who does so, even irregularly. She was raised in the bush with another tribe (as she calls them) and likes to show McLeod Lakers that she is still a real Indian, as she phrases it. Angus is proud of his wife and often invites people to his house when Doris makes bannock, which he calls Indian bread. Other women just buy their bread at the store, but Angus likes to eat "Indian food" once in a while. Angus and Doris have a big freezer that they share with their next-door neighbour, Angus's cousin Mac, where they keep the one or two moose that Angus shoots every year. They usually keep the moose meat for when Angus gets one of his cravings for real Indian food. While Doris is checking her net Angus is helping Mac fix his pick-up truck. Mac had removed the transmission and now needs help putting it back in since the truck is not up on support blocks but only jacked up about a foot.

In the next house Old Dan is awake and lighting his stove. He is very old but still very fit and alert. He goes outside, gets some wood and then decides to go to the store across the lake. The store is about a mile away by road but Old Dan prefers to cross the two-hundred yard width of this part of the lake in his little freight canoe, which he paddles like a dugout despite the width of the lake. In his youth he used to be a packer for various trading companies, including the Hudson's Bay Company, and so he is used to handling a boat. He climbs up the steep bank to the store to get his groceries. The storekeeper is also old and has known Old Dan for nearly forty years, so he has had some steps cut into the bank to ease Old Dan's climb. The trader came to Canada from the Scottish Isles over sixty years ago as a young employee of the Hudson's Bay Company. He prefers to explain that the steps were cut into the bank so he and his wife could go down and enjoy the sunset every evening, instead of admitting that he likes Old Dan's visits. Old Dan speaks little English and the trader doesn't speak Sekani, but they respect and seem to understand each other. The trader likes Old Dan's formality. Old Dan takes a long time to get his groceries since he doesn't have a list but prefers to point to an item and then ask how much more he can take after each selection. The trader administers Old Dan's government pension and writes each purchase down on a bill of sale. The trader likes doing this since it reminds him of the old days before people had cars and started going to the bank with their cheques. No one really knows what Old Dan thinks anymore, since he is over a hundred and keeps to himself. But he still paddles to see the trader nearly every day.

Two houses down Morris comes out of his house with his wife Maggie. They wander over and ask Mac if he is going to Mackenzie for groceries today. Mac points to his truck's still-unassembled transmission and shrugs. Morris lends a hand. In about half an hour the transmission is back in place and Morris, Mac and Morris's wife are in the truck on the way to Mackenzie. Angus goes fishing from the bridge over the stream leading to the lake, about half a mile from his house. He is considered a lucky fisherman and no one usually bothers going fishing until Angus has pulled in the season's first Dolly Varden. Besides, he has his own car, unlike Morris and Maggie, and so he went shopping with Doris the day before when he got his cheque from the government. His oldest daughter, Linda, fifteen years old, is cooking some food for her four brothers and sisters while her mother Doris visits her friend Gladys next door after finishing checking her net. Doris often visits Gladys for tea and a chat. Gladys, like Doris, is not from McLeod Lake, and the two women appreciate each other's company even more because of that. Gladys has been in McLeod Lake only two years or so and still feels out of place. Even after nearly fifteen years in McLeod Lake Doris likes to point out when she is angry at people that she is not one of them.

Although Doris and Gladys usually cook for their families, the custom is usually to leave food on the stove so that people can eat whenever they are hungry. Sometimes Doris forgets to cook for a few days, or she goes back to her people in the north for a week or so. Linda already knows all there is to know about a woman's tasks, especially since her mother made a point of teaching her how to cook for a family and to skin animals so she wouldn't be "like the others". None of the other girls her age know much about preparing animals, although most of them cook for their families.

When Mac and Morris come back from their shopping trip Mac decides to skin a beaver he brought back from his uncle's trapline the day before. He kept it out in the shed behind his house so that it wouldn't spoil. He asks his wife Gladys to skin it. She spreads out the beaver over some newspapers she has placed on the kitchen table and makes a long ventral incision but then laughingly says she doesn't know how to finish the job. Mac takes over and laughs at her, asking aloud why he ever married a "city Indian". Gladys is glad her husband took over the job of skinning the beaver when she sees its body lice crawling over Mac's hands. Nor does she mind being teased for not knowing much about being Indian, since the fact that she lived

for many years in the big city as a White man's wife is a source
of pride to her. Gladys is very proud of her house, which she
keeps very neat and tidy, and of her son Little Mac. Her kitchen
is deccrated with colourful posters of Canada's Food Rules given
to her by the local public health nurse. Gladys has also cut out
some pictures of flowers from a women's magazine she buys
every month. Her friend Doris doesn't read much, although their
neighbour Maggie reads a lot of romance stories from magazines. Maggie and her husband Morris have in fact gone to the
local inn where they will have a cup of coffee and some pie and
buy quite a few romance magazines for Maggie. Morris thinks
they are a bit stupid but likes buying Maggie gifts from the inn
because he wants people to notice that they are friends with the
innkeeper and his wife. Morris doesn't read very much but he
buys a comic book or a detective magazine once in a while. The
innkeeper sells a lot of comic books and romance magazines but
mostly to the local Whites. No one else from the Reserve buys
them, but when Maggie is finished reading her magazines she
usually passes them on to Doris and Gladys. All three women
say they like best of all the romantic stories that have happy
endings in which the young couple gets married.

Up on the hill Young David and his wife Lucy are also going
to Mackenzie in their car to do some grocery shopping. Like
many people with a car, they prefer to buy food once a week at
the big supermarket rather than at the local store. Because the
local store is run for very little profit by its owner, the former
Hudson's Bay Company trader who bought the store and settled
there after many years of running the Company trading post, prices are not very much higher there; however, there is less choice
than in the big supermarket. People like going to the enclosed
shopping mall in any case since they can buy other things as well
and sometimes stop for a drink at the bar. The ex-trader does not
sell alcohol, nor does the local hunting lodge; when people want
to drink they must go to Mackenzie to buy liquor or beer. People
used to goto a inn three miles down the highway, but fewer of
the older people go there now ever since young Whites started
hanging around the place. A few winters ago several people got
killed coming back from a night of drinking when a tractor-
trailer ran them over as they were walking on the highway. The
young boys from the Reserve used to go to the hotel but the
owner banned all of them when one of the boys got his chainsaw
and turned the front door to sawdust after the owner wouldn't
serve him any more beer. They don't like the owner anyway
since he was usually ruder to them than to his White customers.

Lucy's younger sister minds her six-month-old nephew, who is Young David and Lucy's child. She is seventeen and has a child of her own, but the Children's Aid society took it away from her because they said that she was too young to take care of it. She was a mother at fifteen after some young boys got her drunk at a party in the community hall. No one really knows if she misses her child or not since she never talks about it, but she prefers to stay at her sister's house minding her nephew than hang around with the young boys her age. She is very shy and rarely looks at people when she smiles. Her sister and brother-in-law like her to stay with them because she stays out of trouble and they have a baby-sitter on hand. Besides, there are only a few other girls her age in the community and some of them like to party with the young boys rather than stay at home with their families. Most children play with their brothers and sisters when they are young, but after puberty the girls tend to remain at home during the day while the young boys stay together.

Old Joe is nowhere to be seen. He has lived alone since his wife died six years ago, one of his sons was shot to death a while later by his cousin and the youngest son went to live with a friend. Old Joe drinks heavily and so no one is surprised at his absence. His boy was shot when he and Young David were taunting their cousin. The cousin was also drunk and got his shotgun but luckily missed Young David. Young David settled down after that and got work as a logger after marrying Lucy. His two uncles, Paul and Old David, are standing between their adjacent houses and having a chat. Each is about sixty and a widower, although Paul has two teenage children still staying at home. Both men occasionally work as guides for White hunters but Old David drinks a bit too much and sometimes forgets to show up on the appointed day, so he doesn't get as much work as he used to. Paul also works as a guide, and is one of the best in the region. He is a good worker and doesn't drink very much, but is very worried about his children because of the drinking and violence in the community. His youngest daughter is only fourteen and growing up to be exceptionally beautiful. She is very quiet, though, and usually stays at home with her father and sister when she's not at school. Her older sister sometimes likes to have a drink or two with the boys and encourages her sister to come along because she thinks that she is too shy. One house away Old Frank is cleaning out his gasoline stove and airing his bedding. He too lives alone; in his case he never married after an accident as a young man left him disfigured. Old Frank is considered a little bit strange by other people because he disappears for weeks at a time, usually in the bush at the hunting camp of distant relatives in another tribe. Old Frank is generally very quiet after a lifetime of living alone but he has a few close friends with whom he is always joking.

Near the entrance of the Reserve there is a cluster of three houses; the biggest is occupied by Paul's oldest son, about thirty, and his young wife Annie and their two children. Paul's son George owns a car and the Reserve's only colour television set. He works as a logger about six months a year. No one is jealous of his money and possessions since nearly everyone could do what he does and buy the same things. Most people prefer to get their government cheques and do odd jobs around the community for cash. A few young boys who started working in the mills in Mackenzie soon moved off the Reserve and haven't returned. Most people would like more money but feel safer living on the Reserve than in town where they know no one. Besides, George is very generous and likes to have a drink with his friends to be sociable, though he never lets it interfere with his work schedule. Annie is very neat and likes to do beadwork. Their house is very clean and decorated with examples of her work, which she also sells to tourists by leaving a few items at a nearby lodge. Annie's parents live in the second house directly in front, while a little way back from the first is Joe's house, which is often empty. Since his divorce Joe has lived on the Reserve but he used to live in Prince George and often goes back there for weeks at a time to visit friends.

This morning George left early to go to town to get a chainsaw repaired and hasn't come back. Annie was still sleeping and the children had crawled into bed with her. Nobody is stirring in this part of the Reserve except for Old Cecilia, Annie's grandmother. She's up and about, walking around the house stooped and muttering to herself. She occasionally goes over to one of her great-grandchildren sleeping in its crib. This is Jennie's child and Doug and Mary's granddaughter. Jennie is seventeen and had the child when she was living in town. She came back home when her boyfriend moved out of their house. Jennie's other two sisters who live at home are visiting the oldest, Susie, who lives with a White man across the lake. The young boys often go visiting Susie since she is very pretty and a bit sassy, but her boyfriend usually drives them away when he is at home because they entice her to drink. He is often away working in the bush for weeks at a time, however, and then Susie sometimes drinks and parties with the young boys from the Reserve. No one minds that Susie is living with a White man, but the young boys often complain about the lack of women on the Reserve and so they say that it's all right to visit Susie even if she's living with someone. Patty, one of Jennie's two sisters who still lives at home, also had a child taken away by the Children's Aid Society. Usually no one minds if a young unmarried girl has a baby since the girl's mother will often raise it as her own, but Patty was only fourteen and her mother thought it would too difficult to keep the child. Patty had gotten pregnant during a wild party and didn't know who the father was, and a few of the boys sometimes liked to brag that the child was theirs because it had been Patty's first experience.

Doug and Mary come back from Mackenzie and Old Cecilia helps put the groceries away. Patty and her sisters have disappeared, or perhaps have spent the night at their brother-in-law's place. Old Cecilia is muttering to herself and her daughter Mary tells her to shut up, that she's always making too much noise. Cecilia starts crying and saying that she misses her mother, her "mum", who died a few months ago. Cecilia is about seventy and no one remembers how old her mother was when she died; Mary thinks about ninety. Mary consoles her but whenever these scenes occur she knows that Cecilia will keep on crying more and more if she shows too much sympathy. Cecilia used to live with her mother in a house next to Angus and Doris but cried so much after her mother died that Mary took her in. Her husband Doug is a bit tired of having the old woman live with them but there's no other place for her to go. Doug gets irritated with his mother-in-law and Mary knows this, so she too sometimes gets angry with her mother for disturbing the peace of the house, even though she doesn't want her to leave. Cecilia often goes to Old Dan's house for a drink and to talk Sekani. Cecilia speaks English but feels more at home in Sekani, which few other people bother speaking now. Besides, Old Dan is still lively and has a twinkle in his eye. He makes her laugh when he teases her about the two of them being single. Although at her age she thinks her days of going with men are over, she likes the fact that Old Dan is still talking like a sweetheart, even if he's over a hundred and keeps her guessing about whether he's serious or not. Like some other old people, Cecilia is lonely since most young people don't have time for her except as a baby-sitter. Cecilia was married for many years but her husband died when she was in her early fifties. She was lonely but luckily her mother was still alive for her to take care of. Mary wishes that

Cecilia would go to visit Old Dan now but knows that the two of them would start drinking and Cecilia would get even more maudlin.

Doug decides not to join the argument between the two women and goes outside to work on his boat. He has been building a boat for the past few weeks and it's almost ready for the start of the fishing season. He doesn't fish a lot but likes to have a boat ready for those times when he wants to do so. Doug's mother was from McLeod Lake but his father was not, so Doug feels a little bit in competition with other men and likes to appear busy all the time. The boat's ribs have all been fitted to the 'keel', which is really only a piece of wood that temporarily hold things together until the frame is assembled, and Doug is now ready to put the plywood shell over the ribs. Then he will cover the shell with canvas and dope it so that it is waterproof. He usually builds one boat per year, for himself, and then sells or gives it away so that he can have another boat to build. Doug is a good boat builder and his boats always last longer than other people's, about five years instead of three or so. He also likes to go hunting once in a while, but usually only takes a day trip down a logging road in his car. He rarely gets anything, even though he is a good hunter, because he basically goes to have some peace and quiet rather than shoot something. He usually goes alone or with his brother-in-law and they share a small flask of whiskey to keep warm.

In the afternoon, after people have come back from Mackenzie and put their groceries away and eaten lunch, a second wave of people goes to the town. This time, some men are going without their wives. Mac, Morris and Angus travel in Mac's truck. Around six in the evening they decide to go home after having spent an hour at the bar. There they met Old Frank, who had hitch-hiked into town a few hours before. He is incoherently drunk and getting kicked out of the bar by the manager for causing a disturbance. Old Frank is in fact quiet but doesn't want to pay for a bottle of beer that he says he didn't order. The waiter doesn't understand him very well and isn't very polite, though Old Frank doesn't seem aware of the fact. Mac and Morris pack him into the pick-up truck and head back to the Reserve but decide to put him in the back when Old Frank is sick in the cab. About ten miles from town they realize that they forgot to buy beer for the night. They go back but the liquor store is closed so they have to buy beer from the bar. The price is higher but they don't mind paying more. However, they don't like buying their beer at the bar since they say that the manager doesn't like Indians and sneers at them every time they come in. They think that it isn't fair, since a lot of Whites also buy liquor from the bar after hours and are probably more drunk than they are (they have to drive back to the Reserve twenty-eight miles away, so generally go earlier in the evening when there are fewer police patrols on the highway). Mac is a good driver and proud of his new pick-up truck, so he doesn't want it impounded by the police if they catch him drinking while driving.

They return to the Reserve without incident. Often there is some trouble since most Indians don't have much money or can't get credit and so they can usually only buy old cheap cars that often break down. They aren't maintained very well in any case. When they break down and the repairs can't be done at home they are usually just abandoned. Most men are good drivers but a few of the younger men have had their driving permits suspended after drinking and driving. The trip takes about a half an hour and Morris and Angus have had a couple of beers each. Mac isn't drinking but is laughing at everything Morris is saying. Morris is witty and can make good puns in Sekani, English and Cree. No one besides Morris understands Cree, but when he speaks it they all agree that it sounds like a pretty funny language. Mac is suspicious about his friend Morris's ability to speak Cree since this sounds very similar to dirty words in Sekani, but he thinks it's funny all the same. They laugh and joke about Old Frank in the back, who should be shivering from the chilly wind but is instead sleeping with his mouth open despite the bumpy ride. When they get to the Reserve Old Frank wakes up and goes home. No one will see him again for about four days.

Mac's wife is waiting for them with Angus's wife Doris. They each have had a beer, only one, but are mad at their husbands for not having brought them to town. They start yelling at them about being no good, especially after Mac's wife Gladys catches sight of the mess in her husband's truck where Old Frank was sick. Gladys is usually timid but doesn't like it when the men drink too much and are sick. The men just laugh but decide to go to Morris's house since they know that Gladys and Doris will not follow them there. At Morris's house his wife Maggie is cooking some food for their child. She ignores the men as they come in and sit down heavily on the couch. It is a small house and the living room and kitchen are really the same room. Most of the houses on the Reserve are small with the same kitchen-living room arrangement and one or two bedrooms. There isn't much privacy in the houses but most people don't mind. It's hard to refuse someone hospitality when they come around to visit, but at times like this Maggie wishes there was a room where she could shut herself away from all the noise. The Band Council is always building new houses, so there is enough room available, and quite a few people have a house all to themselves. When Morris worked for the Band Council he used to complain that building new houses all the time encouraged people not to maintain the houses they already had, but Morris stopped working for the Council and got himself a new house when he got married and needed the space.

Maggie feeds little Jonathan, puts him to bed and goes out without a word to the men, who have been joined by two of Mac's nephews, Louis and Paul. She walks up the road to visit her father but he is not alone as two of her younger brothers intend to have a party in their father's house with their friends; her father, Old Patrick, has lived alone since his wife died six months ago. He is a bit slow after a severe accident he had a few years ago while drunk, but likes to play with his grandchildren. He was going out when he saw his son arrive with three friends and some beer. Maggie accompanies her father to Mac's house. Old Patrick sits in the corner and his grandchildren start teasing him and laughing when he starts smoking one of his hand-rolled cigarettes. He holds the cigarette between thumb and forefinger and draws the smoke so deeply that his cheeks collapse. His grandchildren howl with laughter and call it Indian smoking, since their father doesn't seem to smoke in the same way. He just holds the cigarette in his mouth the way they see White men do. They like their grandfather but since he doesn't speak and dresses funny with a hunting cap on his head like the other old men they think of him as old and Indian. They go to school with White children and the teacher never calls them Indian or lets other children call them Indian in class. The other children never mention it in any case, even in the schoolyard at recess. For the young, to be Indian is a confusing category. They are proud of it but cannot define it very clearly. Neither can their grandparents, at least not in English, but then the grandparents don't feel the need to define Indian like the young people do. Maggie smiles at her nieces and nephews and goes to the kitchen, where she sees Doris and Gladys. Doris and Gladys don't feel particularly close to Maggie, but tonight they are all alone since their husbands are drinking at Maggie's place. Besides, there aren't any other married women nearby. The other women their age from the entrance of the Reserve and the top of the hill rarely visit them or each other. They offer Maggie a beer. They have had a few drinks each by this time and warm up to Maggie quickly.

People are dropping in at Morris's as the evening wears on. David from up the hill has come down, weaving slightly and slurring his speech. A little later Paul's son George drives by, looking for his wife Annie. He says that she has disappeared and is going to get a beating since she's drinking and the children are alone. He doesn't like to leave his children with Annie's mother and grandmother Cecilia because when Cecilia and her daughter stay together too long in the same room they always start to argue. Annie is having a drink with her sister across the road, but George doesn't think of looking there even though Annie visits her sister often. There are now about a dozen people in the small living room and all have been drinking heavily for a few hours. Morris's wife Maggie comes back home and starts screaming at her husband to get rid of all these people; she doesn't like her house to be full of drunks. Morris answers that it's his house and these are his friends and that no one is drunk except her. Gladys and Doris are standing outside the open door looking in but not especially looking for their husbands. They came with Maggie because Maggie was mad and determined to reclaim her home and they thought there might be trouble. Gladys is smiling a little at this confrontation between Maggie and Morris, but she is generally smiling anyway. She has prominent cheekbones and is a very handsome woman, but her husband chipped one of her front teeth and his cousin once hit her with the stock of his rifle when they were both drunk so she has a large scar on her forehead. She decides to help Maggie out by telling her husband to come home. He says that he wants to stay. Then Doris gets mad, but Angus keeps joking with the other men that they should go looking for women "to jump". He looks at Doris and laughs when he says this. Angus has already told Mac and Morris many times that he doesn't go around looking for other women, but Doris is very jealous anyway. Finally Gladys gets really mad and starts calling Angus names. Angus stops laughing and tells her to shut up if she knows what's good for her. Doris is silent; she doesn't come from the area and is still timid in front of people whenever there is a confrontation. The men often make fun of her since she is older than her husband. He sometimes protests that his friends shouldn't laugh at his wife, but he generally laughs when he is telling his friends to be quiet. Doris doesn't like drinking very much and only does so when Gladys comes over with liquor. She likes Gladys but wishes that she wouldn't drink so much because she knows it makes Angus mad. Angus drinks too but she knows he's the type to laugh and joke and not fight.

Tempers are rising when Jimmy walks in. He is Old Patrick's and Cecilia's brother, also a widower. None of his many children live at home. He was with Old Patrick and Old Patrick's wife Liz the night when Liz died of a knife wound that no one is sure was inflicted or accidental. Everyone falls quiet when Jimmy walks in. Jimmy is very drunk and is staggering; usually he walks very straight and is a graceful man. People feel angry about Liz's death as this is still unexplained, but they are also a little afraid of Jimmy because of what they think he did to her and because of what they know he did to another Indian man who was visiting the big city from the north and met him when he was drunk. Jimmy got mad for no particular reason and attacked the man with a broken beer bottle. This frightens people even more, since they know that Jimmy does things for reasons that even he isn't aware of. He is a very good carpenter, though, and sometimes people ask him to fix their houses or to make things for them. He always works conscientiously when he doesn't drink, but people still don't like him very much because he is unpredictable and tends to drink by himself, which few other people do. When he enters Morris's house Jimmy starts muttering that he didn't do it. No one had said anything before, but after this comment young Frank starts arguing with him. Young Frank had dropped in about an hour before. He doesn't usually drink with Mac, Morris and Angus but instead normally starts the evening visiting his brothers and a few White friends and only later does he come to where other people are drinking, either at Morris's or at Angus's house. He accuses Jimmy of killing Liz but no one, including young Frank, can think of a reason why Jimmy would have killed his sister-in-law. Jimmy has been considered a bit dangerous and even crazy since his wife died and he started chasing much younger women, but Liz was old and not very pretty and she and Jimmy always got on well, especially after Liz's husband Patrick had become a bit slow. The police did not arrest Jimmy for Liz's death and people are even more confused because of this. Young Frank is a good speaker, but Jimmy is very experienced in holding his ground. He speaks eloquently and his posture changes. He draws himself erect and stops swaying. His hands never leave his sides. Jimmy is not talking about the night Liz died but about what a man has to do sometimes even if he doesn't know why. He talks about luck, about when he was a soldier in the war and never got wounded although all his friends died. He tells Frank and the other young men that they don't understand how to behave like real men. When Jimmy speaks Frank doesn't really understand what he is talking about, but the older men do and they fall silent. Frank thinks Jimmy is evasive but Mac, Morris and Angus look at each other and away from Frank and Jimmy. Frank is convinced that he has been insulted when Jimmy said that the young men aren't real men. He's young and strong and likes to boss people around. He's a good worker and sometimes makes lots of money working as a logger.

Frank gets mad at his inability to catch Jimmy out in a lie and throws his last card down. He says that Jimmy's family has always been crazy and so it isn't surprising that Jimmy would kill someone for no good reason. Jimmy falls silent and his eyes blaze. There are a few other people present who belong to the same patronymic category as Jimmy and they naturally protest that young Frank and everyone in his family is always shooting off their mouths because they think they are better than the other people on the Reserve. A younger man gets up; it is Jimmy's oldest nephew and Angus's cousin. He is a little older than Frank. He starts swearing at Jimmy, though not threatening him. This younger man also has a reputation as a dangerous person when drunk, but Mac, Morris and Angus don't respect him very much because they know that there is another side to Jimmy: the Jimmy who works, who used to be a very good hunter, who is extremely lucky at setting traps when he wants to and who gives plenty of warning when he is mad. They know that this other man is none of these things. Even though Mac and Morris are related to young Frank, they respect Jimmy. Even if Angus and Jimmy's nephew are cousins, Angus is a bit ashamed of him. None of the three really know what to do if Frank and Jimmy start fighting, but all three know that if Frank and Angus's cousin do so they will clear them both out of the house to prevent Morris catching hell from Maggie if all the furniture gets wrecked. Jimmy gets up and announces that he going home. This stops things from getting completely out of hand, but young Frank is even more frustrated because he wanted to provoke Jimmy into a fight. Young Frank has a personal grudge against Jimmy which he won't talk about, but people know that young Frank really dislikes Jimmy and is always trying to ridicule the older man. And most times, just like tonight, he is unsuccessful and ends up looking a little bit like Jimmy described him, arrogant and uncontrolled.

The party breaks up and the men go home with their wives, while the unmarried men leave together to continue drinking and to look for girls. Later that night one of Annie's sisters, Rita, will be chased by the boys while she is walking home from a party she went to off the Reserve, but she will run and hide in the outhouse, where she eventually falls asleep. The boys seem to be more interested in teasing her than in seriously running after her, but there is no telling what they could do if they caught her since they often egg each other on and what starts as teasing can end up as rape. Some of the girls don't mind the teasing too much because they like being with the boys and seeing them fight among themselves and tease each other about the girls, and even Annie's sister had willingly submitted to these boys more than once, but tonight she was tired and mad since she had spent the evening listening to Annie complaining about her White boyfriend. At times like this Rita isn't fond of the boys nor of men in general since they can be cruel in ways that women, in her experience, are not. She had seen her mother say some very nasty things to her father when both of them had been drinking too much but she knew that her mother's sharp tongue rarely showed itself unless her father started accusing her mother of running around with other men. Rita was pretty sure that her mother didn't do this but sometimes her mother did act coy with other women's husbands and this would get her father mad. Still, she thought that her father shouldn't get so mad at her mother for things like that because he didn't understand that being a young and pretty Indian girl was doubly difficult because many White boys made vulgar comments and touched young girls when they didn't want to be touched. Rita thought her mother was neither young nor pretty but maybe that made things worse for her. She didn't know what to think but she knew that she wanted to avoid the boys tonight. She had heard about the argument at Morris's house between Jimmy and Young Frank and knew that Young Frank would be angry by now and probably infecting the other boys with his bad mood. That same night Annie's cousin almost got caught by the same gang of boys but she ran to a nearby house where she was sure they wouldn't dare follow her. It was 2 a.m. and she fell asleep on a spare bed. The boys all went to a friend's house. They sometimes argue and fight among themselves but tonight they just laughed and continued drinking and joked about chasing the girls and scaring them until they got tired and fell asleep on the various mattresses on the floor.

Chapter 3

Population and Economy

Drastic changes in the political and economic domains have created a difficult environment for the Sekani. The flooding of the Trench area has led to the loss of a great deal of Sekani hunting and trapping territory. Along with the floodwaters came increased provincial and federal government activity at the local level. As traditional social bonds become increasingly irrelevant to everyday life, people have replaced the weakened matrix with another organizing principle, namely, the universalist idea of pan-Indian brotherhood. When immediate conditions worsen and people are forced to lessen their involvement in everyday practical affairs, they increase their involvement in the more abstractly defined domain. One result is an apparent widening of networks. This is particularly evident in the political dimension, since politics is seen as a forum which expresses and attempts to resolve anxieties about contact with the outside Euro-Canadian world. The other side of the picture appears ironic; people seemed unconcerned with establishing durable ties with each other despite their strong sense of identification with the idea of the community.

The lack of identifiable and definite patterns expressed on the mundane levels at first suggested that activities were undertaken to satisfy individual whims and practical requirements without regard to a 'traditional' social and cultural matrix. In fact, the work histories of people in Fort Ware and especially in McLeod Lake did not at first reveal any pattern of association. This first, and false, impression was particularly easy to accept in the case of McLeod Lakers, who rarely engaged in any sort of long-term cooperative activity. In Fort Ware, however, people still formed cooperative partnerships; these patterns of relationship and their associated categories might hold a clue to what, I thought, had been lost at McLeod Lake. There were enough similarities between the people of the two communities on the cultural level to make this a reasonable assumption. Before examining these patterns in the next chapter, however, there are a few significant characteristics of Fort Ware social organization and economy that are worth keeping in mind, especially the tendency to maintain a particular pattern of work activity and the relationships that this implies, despite the fact that funds must be transferred from the money (welfare and jobs) sector. In other words, the people of Fort Ware maintain 'traditional' patterns (in the sense that these are informed by a sense of tradition) by making money in other activities that are not part of nor necessarily consistent with such patterns. On the one hand, it is not surprising that people who consider themselves hunters continue to hunt; on the other, it must be remembered that they have alternatives in the labour market and are aware of the trade-off. The people of Fort Ware are aware of economic profit and loss, of the consequences of investing time in particular activities and not others, and so on. These decisions, however, are informed by a different context than that which usually gives meaning to these terms. Clearly, people are trying to validate and maintain a particular way of life in light of pressure to change.

There are other features of Sekani social and economic life which make sense only when seen as recurrent themes within a traditional culture, especially the dimension of bonding which I have called 'brotherhood'. Two traits which imply the notion are attitudes towards migration and the continued emphasis on hunting and trapping despite poor returns and the presence of alternative ways of making a living. Both characteristics are expressive of a particular type of social bond in which patronymics are the significant markers of the boundaries involved. There are two major and pertinent considerations here. First, Sekani attitudes towards emigration reflect their concern with maintaining the patronymic category as a viable basis for forming networks. Their attitudes towards the continued use of the land base affords them an opportunity for preserving this social context as a significant basis for social action. Although the Sekani express their concern with emigration and the land in terms of the well-being of the community and not in terms of maintaining a system of patronymic-based associations as such, this aspect of their social structure remains none the less important in the organization of the bush economy and in patterns of emigration. The second point is that purely economic considerations appear to play very little part in forming or sustaining ideas about emigration or land use.

In this chapter I will examine the demographic aspects of emigration insofar as population dynamics are linked to the structure of the local economy and the social structural aspects of brotherhood. The evidence comes mainly from Fort Ware, where there is a well-defined economic dimension to everyday life. In McLeod Lake, the absence of such a sector makes it difficult to see what role the economic concept of scarcity plays in migration and in the organization of labour; in other words, testing the proposition that adherence to a particular principle of association comes from tradition rather than necessity requires some sort of control in the form of a set of options which people can select.

Interlude 1: Population in the Past

Travellers' and traders' accounts such as those left by Simon Fraser, Alexander Mackenzie, Daniel Harmon and Samuel Black are the only sources of information on population levels at the time of contact (1805) and shortly thereafter.[1] Despite limitations on interpreting the data imposed by the brevity of their respective sojourns in Sekani country (with the exception of Harmon, who lived many years with the Carrier, about fifty miles southwest of McLeod Lake), these writers suggest that very few Sekani lived in the Trench area at the turn of the century, perhaps about 200 or so. A century later, Haworth and Morice suggested similar numbers.[2]

No mention is made of epidemics in the Hudson's Bay Company records, although it is likely that hunger exacted a slow but steady toll upon the population. One traveller reported (no doubt mistakenly) that Fort Grahame women were adept at controlling the birth rate and that this and disease accounted for a steadily decreasing population.[3] However, Jenness, who at least stayed with the Sekani for three weeks in 1924, specifically states that infanticide and abortion were unknown, nor does he mention the presence or effects of disease, although the numerous references to debilitating hunger in the Hudson's Bay Company records suggest weakened physical resistance.[4] Other references to epidemics in the region (then called New Caledonia) nowhere mention the Sekani.[5] Given the relative stability in the population and the absence of accounts of epidemics, it seems clear that the Sekani were disposed to limit their number by other means. To what extent they were 'aided' by war and disease in the past is certainly still open to investigation, but the situation is clearer for the contemporary period.[6]

Interlude 2: The Dynamics of Change

There are no clear guidelines in the literature on what happens in cases of contact between Westerners and 'tribal' ('non-Western' is generally meant) peoples, partly because accounts are so fragmentary in some cases, partly because there is contradictory evidence in others. The effect of cultural domination of a 'tribal' people is generally considered to have disastrous effects upon population levels, among other things.[7] However, it is not at all clear that this was the case for the Sekani, as I have suggested. No epidemics were noted, nor did trade appear to have produced demographically dramatic effects such as war. In fact, the arrival of European trading companies appears to have decreased the intensity of conflicts between the Sekani and their neighbours, as we shall see in Chapter 6. Much by way of warfare was linked to competition for European trade goods, directly or indirectly, so the arrival of the Europeans probably mitigated this tension somewhat. In any case, losses sustained through such conflict were probably minimal (with one exception mentioned below). Despite Sekani traditions of bloody battles with the Cree to the south and to the east, there is nothing surviving in the Hudson's Bay Company records that can verify these accounts.

Accounts of other Athabaskan situations are not of much assistance. Krech has argued that epidemics associated with contact are moderated by several factors, nor was the environment necessarily characterized by continuous fluctuations in resources in pre-contact times.[8] Still, the locus of change for Krech is in the social organization and here, he argues, developments are dramatic. The Arctic drainage Athabaskans in general are said to have adopted a bilateral-bilocal type of social organization, which is taken as an indicator of greater flexibility and social mobility.[9] Helm, who has consistently favoured the view that bilaterality has always prevailed among these groups, argues that there is no evidence of severe depopulation normally associated with post-contact epidemics among the Mackenzie river Dene.[10] Post-contact epidemics simply replaced pre-contact infanticide as a limiting factor in population growth. In sum, both of these authoritative writers see population growth rates as important aspects in deciphering Athabaskan social organization, despite their disagreements over contact conditions. On the other side of the coin is the archival evidence gathered by Krech, which shows that when disease struck it tended to strike all groups simultaneously and with short-lived but tangible devastation.[11] Indeed, epidemics raged among the Carrier, as Morice has shown, and among the Beaver in the first twenty years of the nineteenth century.[12] But both Janes and Sharp argue that Mackenzie Basin and Chipewyan peoples, respectively, have remained unchanged in basic features from at least early contact times to the present day, notwithstanding drastic depopulation in the Chipewyan case (up to 90 percent, according to some estimates).[13] Even the fur trade was a double-edged instrument of change, since it both maintained and promoted dispersal of people according to traditional patters of movement.[14] This stands in opposition to the common interpretation that involvement in the fur trade leads to a reduced involvement in traditional patterns of resource exploitation.[15] Even in the case of the Chipewyan, early-contact-period subsistence patterns are described as consistent with post-contact economic conditions.[16]

Clearly, we are facing varied and often conflicting approaches to Athabaskan – and Sekani – demography and social change. Be it as it may, the Sekani demographic picture remains relatively stable during the last century. This fact, coupled with the unclear picture painted by theories that look to the economic base for a motive force for change, suggests that other, non-materialist forces may be at work in preserving the population stability of the Sekani. This is made even more apparent in the modern context, when it could reasonably be hypothesized that the recent influx of money would have allowed increases in population as living conditions improve. An analysis of the modern economic sector reveals how some measure of conservatism is enforced by the Sekani; some money from the 'modern' sector is channelled into 'traditional' pursuits.

Interlude 3: Historical Trends in Population Growth

Although federal government aid has been available to the Sekani since the 1920s (mostly in the form of very limited relief in times of duress), its very minimal role did not affect people in any significant way for thirty years or so. It is only since the 1950s that government transfer payments, including subsidized housing, welfare payments, social assistance to the elderly and impaired, and funds for education and health care at the local level have been introduced. Despite the conventional wisdom that birth rates and hence the total population should increase as a result of these measures, there does not appear to have been any drastic demographic change over the last two centuries. Although the data are far from irrefutable, it appears that infant mortality has decreased in recent years.[17] The data in table 3.1 reveal that Fort Ware has an unbalanced age–sex ratio, with 92 out of 160 residents under the age of twenty-one. The same information is presented in table 3.2 for the McLeod Lake Band, although here the small size of the community makes general comments an unwise proposition.[18]

Despite a high rate of emigration and an abnormally high death rate,[19] the population is relatively young, with forty out of eighty-

Table 3.1 Age–sex composition, Fort Ware, August 1979

Age	Male	% of total	Female	% of total
0–5	9	5.6	13	8.1
6–10	10	6.2	15	9.3
11–15	11	6.8	14	8.7
16–20	8	5.0	12	7.5
21–25	6	3.8	6	3.8
26–30	6	3.8	4	2.5
31–35	3	1.9	5	3.1
36–40	7	4.3	5	3.1
41–45	3	1.9	0	0
46–50	4	2.5	2	1.2
51–55	2	1.2	4	2.5
56–60	0	0	0	0
61–65	3	1.9	2	1.2
66+	5	3.1	1	0.6
Total	77	48.0	83	51.6

Table 3.2 Age–sex composition, McLeod Lake, August 1978

Age	Male	% of total	Female	% of total
0–5	5	6.0	4	4.8
6–10	4	4.8	1	1.2
11–15	5	6.0	5	6.0
16–20	7	8.4	9	10.8
21–25	9	10.8	5	6.0
26–30	6	7.2	4	4.8
31–35	1	1.2	1	1.2
36–40	2	2.4	0	0
41–45	1	1.2	1	1.2
46–50	1	1.2	0	0
51–55	2	2.4	2	2.4
56–60	4	4.8	0	0
61–65	1	1.2	0	0
66+	2	2.4	1	1.2
Total	50	60.0	33	39.6

three people under the age of twenty-one.[20] I have already alluded to the remarkable stability in population figures for the Sekani as a whole. Although it is not clear from the evidence what role was played by natural factors such as disease, it is evident that today selective emigration is important in both communities. Here I propose to examine the facts and figures in a little more detail.

Population statistics from police and census reports are not available for the period before 1858.[21] However, these figures generally agree with the numbers culled from other sources. An examination of the available census figures[22] reveals a few small peaks and valleys. Between 1858 and 1970 the population was relatively stable. In 1858 a number of 151 was recorded, but this did not include all of the people who later traded at Fort Grahame, founded in 1870. Undoubtedly some of these northerners were included, as the Hudson's Bay Company records sometimes imply, since they likely traded at McLeod Lake, but others undoubtedly traded farther north with Indian intermediaries. In 1894, ninety-five people lived in McLeod Lake. It was only sometime between the 1944 and 1955 censuses that the population reached the mark of one hundred. Fort Grahame, with ninety-nine people in 1894, reached the same milestone between 1924 and 1929. The total population varies from 194 recorded in 1894 to a high of 455 recorded in the 1970 census.

These post-war figures are probably more at variance with the facts than the early non-census figures and official statistics from before the Second World War. Because census figures reflect membership in the political units called 'Bands' rather than the communities themselves, we have no way of knowing how many people actually lived in communities after the early 1960s. Before this date, given the relative lack of change in the economy and in Sekani relations with the outside, the official figures are more likely to reflect real conditions. With apologies for the number-juggling to come, the number of Sekani who live in the Fort Ware and McLeod Lake area must be deduced from the figures listed for the political units called Fort Ware Band and McLeod Lake Band. Emigration has drastically increased in McLeod Lake since the 1953 construction of the highway between McLeod Lake and Prince George to the south. Fort Ware, on the other hand, has remained more or less isolated to the present day. For example, the town had 160 residents in 1979, including a few non-status Indians who are not on the official Band list, which included 199 people. In McLeod Lake, on the other hand, only fifty-three people lived on the Reserve itself, while 141 lived off-Reserve. Of these 141 off-Reserve Band members, thirty can be added to the McLeod Lake total since they lived within the twenty-mile radius which marks the boundary of significant interaction. If only the total number of residents is considered, there are 243 people living on-Reserve and 150 living-off Reserve, for a total of 393 people in both communities. The official 1970 total of 455 people can now be modified and placed in context. If 150 of 393 people, or roughly three-eights, lived off-Reserve in 1978–79 then in 1970 it could be expected that about 282 Sekani (roughly five-eighths of the Band totals) were living in McLeod Lake, Fort Ware and points between. Since emigration has been fairly constant from McLeod Lake since the mid-1960s, it would be reasonable to suspect that the same proportions would obtain for this period as well.

Now the range of variation is clearer and it is significantly less than the recent official figures suggest, from 194 in 1894 to 282 in 1970. The early figures undoubtedly represent a period when the Sekani did not emigrate to cities in large numbers, and all reports suggest that a figure of 194 represents the number of people actually counted in 1894, not only those who were 'registered' with the 'Band' (two meaningless concepts back then). If anything, the early figures are probably too low, since there must have been a few people absent in the bush when the count was made. Certainly the phenomenal increase between 1924 and 1929 represents the gathering of more accurate data rather than a drastic jump in the birth rate. In short, the adjusted figures for the last quarter century suggest that some mechanism has offset the gains from relatively improved health care which has resulted in a higher infant survival rate. Although the death rate is relatively high for McLeod Lake, this is not the case for Fort Ware. There, a stable number is maintained through selective emigration.

Present-Day Population Dynamics

By 'selective' is meant that individual choices reflect community influence on particular categories; emigrants are not randomly spaced throughout the social structure or community. In the long run, the selection process works at the level of the family, such that all the members of a particular patronymic category leave the community within a relatively short span of time. This can be seen in particular residence histories. One McLeod Lake household,[23] for example, moved from the Reserve around 1958, although they remained within the twenty-mile radius that marks the boundary of interaction with the community. Over time a split emerged in the household (which included kin other than offspring), such that the parents increased their participation in community life on the Reserve while their children developed close ties with neighbours and people outside the twenty-mile boundary. One link was with people from a community about seventy miles away, another with people in a community eighty miles distant. As the children grew up these ties became stronger; a few of the children married people from these other communities. Of the four marriages contracted by the children, only one was with a resident of McLeod Lake.[24] The father of these children had two brothers who were residents of McLeod Lake and who were in the midst of dissolving their own households. Their wives had died a few years before and all the children except two (one in each household) had left home. Some of the children who had left had married people outside the community or had developed close friendships with children in the first, off-Reserve, household while occasionally living there. The parents of the off-Reserve household encouraged the close friendship between their own younger children and their nieces and nephews because they saw them as strengthening their links to the Reserve community, while the on-Reserve children saw these ties as a way of avoiding some of the negative aspects of living in the community (their fathers both drank). Ironically, while both sets of motives can be well served by strengthening particular ties within the same network, the end result will be the extinguishing of that particular patronymic in the Reserve community when the two older men retire from any sort of active social life. This will further encourage the children of these men to solidify the associations they have already developed with their off-Reserve cousins and, by extension, with their cousins' contacts outside of the community circle.[25]

Links between patronymics are also important in Fort Ware. Several years ago, for example, three brothers lived together. One moved to a Tahltan community about 150 miles away and married a local woman.[26] One of the two remaining brothers died, and the widow married the surviving brother. This marriage was not particularly well received in the community. Although it is not unusual for a widow to marry her brother-in-law, the circumstances of the second brother's death raised some eyebrows; the man had been shot at a drinking party involving his brother and a few other people. The resulting gossip certainly played a role in encouraging the deceased man's children to visit their uncle in Tahltan country. One of these three brothers obtained a job in the Tahltan community. This enabled his younger brother to visit more often and to increase the length of his stays. For one reason or another he kept getting into fights with local Tahltan, so his stays never lasted for a very long time initially. When he and one of his brothers got a little older they also started getting rowdy in Fort Ware. Eventually someone in the town threatened to shoot the older of the pair. Although many people were sympathetic to the brothers' troubles because of their 'difficult' childhood (although they would not call it that; people say that the older brother was "angry" at his father's death),[27] their behaviour was deemed potentially dangerous and therefore intolerable. Because the brothers sensed that Fort Ware residents were becoming less patient, the two switched their allegiance from Fort Ware to their uncle's Tahltan home. The older brother, at least, was of a marriageable age but unable to find a spouse in Fort Ware. He established a household in the Tahltan village. He started describing his stays in Fort Ware as "visits", rather than the other way around. His younger brother started accompanying him to the Tahltan community. Their mother died two or three years later, and after the funeral the younger of the two never returned to the community. The father is alone, the last of his patronymic category. He is an old and broken man (though he was to make a desperate attempt to have his son reintegrated into the community; see note 34, this chapter).

A Fort Ware man is married to and lives with a woman from Ingenika. Three other men with the same patronymic (his parallel cousins) have emigrated from Fort Ware, probably to the city, but their present whereabouts are not known to anyone in the community. Two women from the same patronymic category have married non-Sekani. Although it is not the largest, this has the highest number of emigrants of any Fort Ware patronymic network. Another network has the same number of off-Reserve representatives, but these people are very recent arrivals in Fort Ware, settling there after the flooding of Fort Grahame. They have few ties to other Fort Ware residents. The first patronymic network, however, has clear northern origins (many Fort Ware people believe that they are "from the north", though they are not explicit as to the lines of connection with their neighbours, the Kaska). In brief, the patronymic networks with the highest number of members outside the community tend to disappear no matter how many representatives live in the community. Tables 3.3 and 3.4 present a summary of the evidence concerned with patronymic affiliation in Fort Ware and in McLeod Lake, respectively. In McLeod Lake only two same-sized patronymic networks have more than one member household living on-Reserve. A third is as large as either of these two but consists of only one household living off-Reserve.

The Process of Control

These few examples demonstrate the social pressures involved whenever people make decisions about residence and affiliations. The fact that a single member of a household may choose to live off-Reserve is not immediately imbued with any particular significance by members of the community. During the last thirty years or so many people have lived away from the Reserve for a time and have later returned to the community; nearly 30 per cent of adult men over forty have lived away from the community for at least six months, according to interview data. At some point, however, a person must make a final decision: stay or leave. Whatever the choice, other members of the patronymic tend to follow suit since the presence of a relative outside the community makes the opportunity to leave somewhat easier and the possibility of obtaining locally the social and economic requirements for a start in life somewhat harder. The type of pressures brought to bear by other community members informs a person of his (rarely her, as we shall see) chances of successfully becoming a full-fledged member of the community. Individual choice thus becomes reconciled with general community sentiments. The final result may be the extinguishing of a patronymic category in the community.

There are ten patronymics associated with McLeod Lake Band. Representatives of only seven of these are found within the community, with five of seven represented by only one person or household. Members of the other three patronymics live outside the twenty-mile radius from the Reserve that I selected as the limit of interaction for McLeod Lakers. These other people have little or no contact with members of the core community. The situation is slightly different in Fort Ware because of the lower rate of emigration. A summary of the evidence is presented in table 3.5, while table 3.6 presents a summary of the historical evidence from the Hudson's Bay Company records.

Table 3.3 Changes in patronymic membership, Fort Ware

Patronymic	No. adults total[1]	Females emigrated	Males emigrated	Females married off-Reseve	Males married off-Reseve	Residents
Abou	10	–	3	2	1	4
Charlie	5	–	–	–	–	5
Davie	1	–	–	1	–	1[2]
Massettoe	11	–	–	1	–	10
McCook	18	1	–	–	–	17
Pierre	8	–	–	–	–	7
Porter	2	–	–	–	–	2[4]
Poole	16	–	–	–	3	13[3]
Seymour	8	–	–	–	–	8
Tomah	2	–	–	–	–	2[5]
Boya	2	–	–	–	–	2[6]

[1] Adults over eighteen years as of 1 January 1979.
[2] One male adopted by member of Seymour patronymic.
[3] All three married women from Ingenika.
[4] Conjugal pair only.
[5] Ingenika man married Fort Ware woman.
[6] Conjugal pair.

Table 3.4 Changes in patronymic membership, McLeod Lake

Patronymic	No. adults total[1]	Females emigrated	Males emigrated	Females Married off-Reserve	Males Married off-Reserve	Residents[5]
Alexis	–	1	–	–	–	–[2]
Chingee	23	1	2	2	1	17
Fisher	1	–	–	–	–	1
Frank	1	–	1	–	–	–[3]
Inyallie	17	2	2	2	4	7
Isadore	9	–	1	1	2	6
Lebrun	2	–	–	1	1	–
Solonas	25	2	5	3	1	14
Tylee	2	–	–	–	1	–[4]
Toodick	2	1	1	–	–	2

[1] Adults over eighteen years as of 1 January 1979.
[2] One child listed in Band records; location unknown.
[3] Sole representative; location unknown.
[4] Conjugal pair.
[5] On-Reseve or within a twenty-mile radius; see text.

Table 3.5 Patronymics in use, McLeod Lake and Fort Ware, 1978–1979

Fort Ware	McLeod Lake
Abou	Alexis
Boya	Chingee
Charlie	Fisher
Davie	Frank
Egnell	Inyallie
Massettoe	Isadore
McCook	Lebrun
Pierre	Prince
Poole	Solonas
Porter	Tylee
Seymour	
Toodick	

Table 3.6 Patronymics in use, McLeod Lake, 1893–1895

Chingee
High Yaller (High Yallie)
Isadore
Pierre
Solonas
Two Dick (Toodick)

Note: Names in parentheses are alternate spellings or versions given in the documents.

Source: HBC Arch. B119/a/6.

Interlude 4: Origins

Of the ten names found to be associated with residents of McLeod Lake, only six can be established as being used at the turn of the century. It is not clear, however, if the strictly lineal features of patronymics had emerged by that time. In the original Hudson's Bay Company records, men were listed by what appear to have been personal names, while women were usually listed by their relationship to a man who was 'established' in the Company's books ("Mrs. David"). These personal names appear to be the basis for the later patronymics. The information collected in the Hudson's Bay Company records matches the information I collected.

Although documentation is lacking for Fort Ware, Fort Grahame is well represented in the Hudson's Bay Company records. Some former Fort Grahame residents now live in Fort Ware, as do the descendants of the more northerly nomads who are referred to in the records as trading at Fort Grahame. Of the ten patronymics listed in the 1979 Fort Ware Band list, only three are listed in the Hudson's Bay Company records which survive from 1893 to 1894: Pool (Poole), Davie and Toomah (Tomah).[28] (The current spelling is given in parentheses.) Two other names are mentioned in the records: Azony (Izony) and Hunter. Their descendants today live in Ingenika.

If the residents of Ingenika are included (as former residents of Fort Grahame), then five of ten patronymics are accounted for in the records from the turn of the century. The others, however, are not so easily traced. Porter is the name of a man who arrived in Fort Ware from Lower Post about a generation ago. McCook is the patronymic of a White hunter who lived in the area about sixty years ago who married a Sekani woman. Charlie is mentioned in various records but may not be associated with present-day holders of the name since it was very common in the contact era. Abou is found in birth and marriage registries from the 1940s, so the original bearer of the name arrived in Fort Grahame or Fort Ware sometime between 1895 and 1945 (a gap during which no records survive). The name, says Honigmann, is associated with the Nelson Indians (the Tselona Kaska); there may be a connection.[29] Massettoe is the final name on the current list. A Tlingit named Old Massettoe came to Fort Grahame from Teslin Lake in the west, although the dates are uncertain.[30] Contemporary Sekani either do not remember particular lines of connection or say they have been there "forever" when asked about their ancestors.

There are two other surnames in use in Fort Ware. One is Boya, a man from Lower Post who married a Fort Ware woman. His father's sister had married a Fort Ware man a generation ago. Egnell is the patronymic of a man who lives a short distance from Fort Ware across the Finlay River. Honigmann states that there was a Hudson's Bay Company trader by that name at Lower Post in the 1890s, although the name was spelled Agnell at the time.[31] The current holder is a non-status Indian, although the people of Fort Ware do not make this distinction. Both of these names are not yet included in the official Band list. In sum, some continuity between the last century and the present can be established for many but not all of the Sekani. This implies a fairly constant turnover of people, a high degree of emigration and immigration.[32] Although not significant in itself, the relatively high rate of immigration and subsequent adoption of a common identity focussed on the community (in the past, presumably a band identity) implies a certain flexibility and, more important, that some efficient mechanism to forge a common identity existed. This despite the fact that, as we shall see, the Sekani had very definite ideas about their rights of ownership to what they claimed as their homeland.

The Control of Social Resources

In the contemporary period, one of the ways in which some people are included and others excluded is the allocation of housing. Housing is an important resource that helps a young man attain full adult status. Hence, housing is a social resource, and the allocation of housing is the means whereby community sentiments can act directly upon individuals. If housing is denied to a young person, then that person's chances of forming successful and strong ties with others will be seriously impaired. If a man is a member of a large patronymic network, he can use these ties as a base from which he can gain experience on the trapline and perhaps the use of a house for his family. He need not ask the Band for aid. If his network is small, then he must necessarily ask the Band to help him. Underlying these considerations lies the overwhelming possibility that without suitable housing a man is unlikely to be in a position to marry. Without marriage he will never become a senior partner in the hunting partnership networks, though no one will ever take away his right to work alone or with his wife (if he does manage to marry) on his trapline, if he can obtain one.[33] But the fact remains that without a wife, a man is in more difficult straits as far as inheriting rights to a trapline is concerned, not to mention developing close ties with people of his age and capabilities who are disposed to help him in sharing the risks of trapping. In brief, Band resources can help a man without a large pool of potential partners by substituting some of the things that make a man a desirable partner. Hence, people with small patronymic networks can be encouraged to stay in the community. Those without Band help must seriously consider the option of emigration if their patronymic networks are small. At some point, both motives overlap since people feel little obligation to help anyone who is unpopular or a reluctant worker, no matter what his surname may be.[34]

The stock of houses is limited in both communities, although the amount and its significance varies. Houses are usually partly prefabricated two-room wood frame buildings, though many Fort Ware people have successfully lobbied the Department of Indian Affairs to give the Band the cash equivalent so that log houses can be built.[35] McLeod Lake, with a higher rate of emigration, has more available houses than Fort Ware, though these are not all in good repair. None of the houses in either community have running water and the government prefabricated houses soon get very cold in the winter, perhaps because of insufficient insulation or the fact that they are built with cheap materials and so shrink and warp in peculiar ways, letting in draughts. The actual amount of housing, however, is not as important as might be expected in emigration decisions. People willingly live under what might generally be called crowded conditions, while others live alone in their houses. Nearly all the people of Fort Ware have some houses or cabins on their traplines and these are of course much smaller and less comfortable than their houses in town. Yet no one ever complains about crowding or cold when on the trapline. In the town, crowding is rarely recognized as a sufficient reason for obtaining housing from the Band Council, although it might be used to justify politically a particular decision by the Band Council, a decision that depends in fact on many other factors. Obtaining a Band house, therefore, is a sign of community approval and not of 'physical' need.

If crowding is more social than spatial, then so is the allocation of housing more political than practical. While the political power an individual may have does not affect the outcome of allocations, neither is the power of the Chief and Council members paramount. The final decision seems to emerge from a consensus, usually arrived at in general Band meetings. A Band meeting is used as a forum in which to announce a designated theme as a criterion for selecting which community members will be encouraged to stay and which will be encouraged to leave. Any theme as such, under these conditions of general scrutiny, will have to pass muster with the majority of people. Hence, the Chief is an important organizational fulcrum within the community but acts essentially as a formal promulgator of what people have already been thinking and saying.

Interlude 5: Political Decision-Making in the Recent Past

The earliest records that survive date from 29 June 1974. For the meetings of which there are records (about twenty in all), the pattern is clear: the Chief speaks for a few minutes on the general problem which must be addressed and then proposes a motion that deals with the problem. He always depends on his family and other close kin to get motions moved and seconded, although this is not the crucial issue here since all motions are followed by a long process of discussion and accommodation of various interests which may not be easily reconciled one to the other. For example, on 1 June 1976, the Chief specifically announced that houses ought to be given to older people who were poor and sick. Hence, no houses were to be allocated to young people, a very important and sensitive limitation given that older people are less likely either to want to or be able to move from the community, while for younger people the availability of housing is likely to play a much more important role in decisions about emigration. In fact, the minutes reveal that a house was to be given to a single woman and her aged father while a young married man's request was passed over. In this case, the young man had recently arrived from another community from the north. He was welcomed by virtue of his marriage to a Fort Ware woman, but (as it was said nearly ten years after the fact) it was "too soon" to give this man a house. He had to prove himself, it was said, but another and probably more important reason for denying him a house (then and

every following year) is that the man was regarded as an exceptionally good hunter and hard worker; he built his own house with some
help from his father-in-law, an ex-Chief who was highly respected
and a member of the same large patronymic category as the current
Chief. In one sense, by marrying into a large patronymic category
whose members are in a position to help him, the young man automatically lost his marginal status despite the fact that he was not an
official member of the Band.

The meeting of 9 December 1977 is more significant since that year
it was decided to build twenty houses on the Reserve. In this case, the
large number of houses, instead of decreasing the focus on integration
into the community, resulted in a clear debate in which inclusion into
the community was a central theme. More houses, in other words,
lessened the possibility of invoking other subsidiary reasons such as
crowding as a means of limiting counterproposals to what the Chief
felt was just. Giving someone a house (or, of course, withholding
Band help) is so immediate a measure in people's emigration decisions that inclusion is rarely directly alluded to; the result is too
final. When there are only a few houses to be allocated, there is no
reference to outside ties or the personal desirability of the candidate
in the debate. With more houses available, these issues can become
public since everyone knows that the time between the debate and
actually moving into a house is at least one year; in this situation
decisions are therefore far from final in any particular case. The
1977 list of potential recipients contains no names of people with
outside affiliations whatsoever. These people were all members of
patronymic groups with more than one representative in the community. All the candidates for housing were married and already
had active partnerships with other band members. The debate became more acrimonious when the allocation of an already existing
house was discussed and grew so sharp that no decision was taken
until a subsequent meeting. One eventual recipient of a house
(there were only five built in all) was already married and had any
well-developed ties in the community. People, in other words, chose
a relatively safe candidate.

Housing and Control Summarized

These scant notes suggest that living space by itself is never a
criterion in the allocation of housing when the available stock is
limited. Single people sometimes received houses, while men
with large families living in cramped quarters were denied. Living
space became an issue only when a person's suitability in other
areas had been settled, whenever there was a choice between
otherwise suitable candidates, in other words, because of an
increase in the housing stock. In general, people from large patronymic groups (and certainly not only the Chief's; the politics of
power plays little role here) tended to get houses, even though
their membership in large networks almost guaranteed them a

head start compared to people with few relatives. Houses were also given to people with good prospects of starting families; in other words, they were getting married or had recently gotten married and were active hunters in partnership with senior men. This more than anything else explains the 1976 rejection of the young northerner with a large family who had married a Sekani woman. Although admired as an able hunter, he was somewhat too able. Unwilling to become a junior partner since his senior partners would invariably have benefited from the partnership more than he would, he was treated as if he were already settled, despite his recent arrival. In sum, people who are marginal by reason of their lack of ties within the community and/or the presence of ties outside the community will be ignored and therefore encouraged to leave by denying them what everyone acknowledges is a crucial resource for a young man about to get established.

The Economy of Fort Ware

Economic necessity does not appear to play a large role in forcing people to leave, nor are people attracted by the relatively large sums which are now available from the Government or private industry. The same population density is characteristic of very different economic regimes. In 1894, for example, the year of lowest recorded population, there was a high rate of dependency on country food despite limitations in resources (a point examined in Chapter 7). On the other hand, 1979 was marked by a dependency on store food even though bush resources were relatively plentiful. There was also an assured supply of money with which to purchase goods.

Although I have used terms like "relatively plentiful" in reference to the general state of the economy, I do not want to convey the impression that the Sekani are rich or even well off. They are not. Compared to many contemporary Indian groups they are relatively poor. Living conditions are still occasionally very harsh, and there are many times when food is not abundant. Still, people are much richer than they were throughout the period of the early fur trade, a time often described in the Hudson's Bay Company records as characterized by hunger and generally poor health conditions. It would be more accurate to say that there is a limited but reliable amount of money in the local economy on which people can count. Table 3.7 shows the sums that entered the community in the form of social assistance (welfare) payments.

On average, nineteen people receive welfare each month. The total is $78,237.84 per year, or about $6,520.00 per month. This is not the major source of income, however. About $30,000 per year enters the community from guiding and related activities, although this figure is an estimate based on interviews with local guide-outfitters. The revenue from trapping during

Table 3.7 Social assistance payments, Fort Ware

Date	Amount ($)
April 1972	4,302.00
January 1973	5,585.00
July 1977	6,077.00
August 1977	6,878.00
November 1977	6,454.48
December 1977	6,934.48
March 1978	5,724.48
May 1978	6,825.48
June 1978	6,925.48
July 1978	7,280.48
August 1978	7,675.48
September 1978	7,575.48

Source: Fort Ware Band Office files.

the 1976-7 season (October to May) was $17,705.00 This was an incomplete figure; actual income from trapping was probably $20,829.00, if the lower figure is indeed only 85 per cent complete as the Department of Indian Affairs believes (most Sekani trappers keep no records). The available data on trapping income for one year are presented in table 3.8, though there were probably 100 castoreum (beaver scent glands) and ten black and grizzly bear pelts not included in the official figures kept by the local trader and the Department of Indian Affairs. These bring the total estimated income from trapping to $29,000.00. In addition, as much as $75,000.00 enters the community from the Band Council, usually for construction of houses and cleaning of the Reserve. About $31,680.00 per year comes from the Canadian government Family Allowance payments plan. Total community cash income is therefore about $244,000.00 per year, or about $1,524.50 per person per year (calculated in 1979 dollars).[36]

Estimating expenditure is rather more difficult. Food at the local store cost about $200.00 per month per adult if not supplemented generously by country food. This does not include other goods which people often purchase at the store. Although the trader did not reveal his exact income (there was some

Table 3.8 Fur harvest,[1] Fort Ware

Species	Average value ($)[2]	Harvest[3]	Revenue ($)
Beaver	39.17	177	6,713.09
Muskrat	6.30	35	220.50
Mink	34.49	30	1,034.70
Otter	61.33	6	367.98
Coyote	60.83	1	60.83
Fox	63.29	–	–
Wolf	107.35	–	–
Weasel	1.98	14	27.72
Wolverine	166.33	2	332.66
Skunk	5.61	–	–
Fisher	148.31	1	148.31
Marten	31.96	311	9,939.56
Lynx	214.29	3	642.87
Bobcat	207.01	–	–
Squirrel	1.47	814	1,196.58
Raccoon	29.72	–	–
Black Bear	62.88	2	125.76
Castoreum	unknown	unknown	unknown
Total			$20,810.56

[1] Season ending April 1979.
[2] Average British Columbia prices; from BC Fish and Wildlife Branch files.
[3] Observed during fieldwork and from records kept by local trader.

resentment in the community about his prices), I estimated his annual sales to be very close to $200,000.00 per year. An unspecified amount of money (though considerably less, perhaps $10,000.00 to $20,000.00) leaves Fort Ware when people charter aeroplanes to go to Prince George or Mackenzie. In general, therefore, people spend everything they earn. If they had more, they undoubtedly would spend more on trapping equipment and the like. This does not mean, however, that they are motivated in any way by a desire to accumulate money or goods. People appear to be indifferent to either prospect. Money is saved for certain necessary goods like guns, snowmobiles and ammunition, but usually these are bought on credit through the store. Since credit is ostensibly 'free' (the interest is hidden in the higher cost of goods), there is little incentive to increase income only to buy particular items with savings.

Fur Trapping and the Market

Fur trapping is an important component of the economy in Fort Ware, but an analysis of investments and returns suggests that it may be more important as a social activity than as a source of income. The data suggest that trapping is not a market oriented activity. Table 3.9 summarizes returns for two traplines for the 1978–9 season, while the costs of operating a trapline are presented in table 3.10. The prices noted are estimates drawn up by the trappers themselves; both trappers are highly regarded within the community for their abilities.

There are other necessities which are not included in the list but which are indispensable none the less. Traps may cost $900.00 for a minimum set of forty-five, although the present trend is to shoot furbearers rather than to trap them.[37] In addition, trappers need ammunition, power saws, snowmobiles and gasoline ($4.00 per gallon even in 1979). Some of these items are 'capital costs' and do not figure in a yearly tabulation; others have alternative uses. None the less, costs are high because the list of necessities has grown every year.[38] Today, people would not consider going to the bush without cookstoves, lanterns and washtubs. All of these items and considerations suggest that traplines rarely yield profit, if they ever do at all.[39] Fish and Wildlife officials, fur buyers, local White trappers and my own conclusions agree: Sekani traplines are capable of much higher yields. According to some estimates, the optimum yield may be as high as ten times the present level listed in table 3.9. The only debate is about the degree of underuse, not its presence.

Table 3.9 Returns for two traplines, Fort Ware, 1978–1979

Species	Line 1 number	Price ($)	Line 1 return ($)	Line 2 number	Line 2 return ($)
Beaver	4	39.17	156.68	19	744.23
Marten	54	31.96	1,725.84	10	319.60
Mink	6	34.49	206.94	2	68.98
Wolverine	1	166.33	166.33	–	–
Ermine	–	1.98	–	2	3.96
Muskrat	–	6.30	–	4	25.20
Otter	–	61.33	–	1	61.33
Squirrel	–	1.47	–	31	45.57
Total			2,255.79		1,268.87

Notes: Prices are BC averages,
          Figures for returns are from local files kept by van Somer's store.

Table 3.10   Construction costs for one trapline cabin, Fort Ware

	Item	Price ($)
4	Windows	180.00
14	5" Stovepipe	21.00
1	5" Elbow	2.00
8	8" T hinges	16.00
1	Cookstove	40.00
6	Rolls roofing paper	90.00
2	Airtight heaters	170.00
1	Roll plastic	30.00
12	Sheets 5/8" plywood	300.00
10 lbs	2 1/2 " nails	15.00
50 lbs	8" spikes	75.00
	Total cost of materials used:	$939.00

Source: Fort Ware Band Office files, from a document dated 1977.

For purposes of comparison, table 3.11 is a list of all purchases made by a McLeod Laker in 1902. This was a typical shopping list for the time. Not only did the man supply himself for trapping, he obviously bought a fair portion of his family's quarterly (according to the internal evidence in the ledger) store-bought durable goods. These items cost 124.5 Made Beaver, a unit of trade which meant that the trapper had to pay about eighteen prime beaver pelts for these goods. The cost of running a modern trapline, about $1,839.00, represents about fifty-eight prime beaver pelts in 1979 dollars, or about twenty-eight pelts for supplies alone. This is during a time when fur prices were at their highest levels since the 1930s, whereas the earlier prices were from a time when conditions were very difficult in the Trench area. In 1915 the cost (in 1915 money) of bringing goods to Fort Grahame was $0.10 per pound; in 1979 (in inflated 1979 dollars), $0.16 per pound, a clear saving in real terms, but the amount of goods bought has increased by severalfold. In sum, costs are greater and returns are lower in real terms.

The impact of modern technology has not appreciably altered returns from trapping. If the new technology were used to its full capabilities, returns would be substantially higher than they are at present. Several White trappers in the region, using the same technology as the men of Fort Ware and using an identical length of trapline, were able to make about $40,000.00 per year with a new profit of $10,000.00. These trappers do not over-trap, since in many ways they are more closely watched by the Fish and Wildlife branch of the government.[40] Snowmobiles are a case

Table 3.11 Typical debt, McLeod Lake, October 1902

Item	Price[1]
125 lbs flour	25
²/₅ cartridges 45.70	4
5 lbs powder	2 ½
1 pair football hose	1 ½
12 lbs rice	4
2 bottles painkiller	2
25 lbs sugar	10
2 lbs salmon[2]	3
16 lbs bacon	8
2 lbs apricots	1
1 overalls	2
3 lbs tallow	1
16 salmon[2]	2
1 file 8"	½
2 lbs shot	1
1 hat black cowboy	8
1 undecipherable	2
1 pair boys' overalls	1
1 lb chocolate	1
7 lbs tea	7
12 lbs beans	4
4 tins lard	6
1 4-pt. white blanket	8
1 shirt "best"	4
100 caps	1
2 undecipherable	1
1 flannel shirt	1 ½
1 bar soap	1
2 lbs apples	1
1 ⅓ lbs powder	2
2 lbs raisins	1
1 tin coffee	1
1 tin syrup	2 ½
8 salmon[2]	1
1 boys flannel shirt	1 ½
1 1 ½-pt white blanket	2

[1] Prices expressed in Made Beaver (MB). One MB equalled seven large beaver pelts; one black bear pelt equalled 15 MB.

[2] Traders often included more than one listing of a particular item because there was no agreed upon shopping list. A person traded according to his diminishing balance of credit.

Source: HBC Arch. B119/a/10, fo. 41.

in point. Most households in Fort Ware have at least one. These have been increasingly popular during the past ten or fifteen years or so. Recently, however, a few of the older trappers have decided to return to using dogs for winter transportation. Dogs seem cheaper, say some hunters, but there is more work involved in maintaining them. Although snowmobiles cost more, they can generate much more income for the trapper, if that is indeed the motive behind their use. However, it is patently obvious that this is not the case. In brief, snowmobiles are worth the extra investment if a higher return is what the hunter wants. The fact that snowmobiles are increasingly regarded as prestige items rather than mundane tools is no surprise. Many young men with only marginal involvement in trapping and winter hunting are the most eager buyers of snowmobiles.

As is often the case, there were some inadvertent consequences of this flirtation with the new technology. First, much of the canine breeding stock was left unwatched. Hence, hunters are sometimes unable to resupply themselves with good dogs. Second, and more important, is the seeming lack of interest in trapping by many young men. There are many factors involved here, but the flirtation with the market mentality that accompanied the introduction of snowmobiles undoubtedly played a part in this change, as did the introduction of Band-sponsored wage labour. Snowmobiles made it very easy for a trapper to reach his minimum goal; too easy, in fact, since many would not bother to take their families out with them to the bush for the entire trapping season. Hence, many young men have had limited exposure to bush life compared to their fathers. And although the older men are interested in maintaining the tradition of partnerships by recruiting younger men into existing networks, there is a limit beyond which these social considerations cannot be easily accommodated. If young men are so unskilled that they are a complete liability on the trapline, they will be passed over since no one wants to work for free, or rather, the earnings a young man makes as a junior partner usually pass into the household pool, and so a mature trapper would essentially be giving money to one of his equals if he were to take on a relatively unskilled partner. It is not so much the money that is lost as it is the money that will not be earned if the senior partner cannot work to his full capacities because of a reluctant or unskilled junior partner. This is more important today when men go out to trap and hunt with their partners and not with their families, since a junior partner is in some ways replacing his partner's wife's labour. He is responsible for the camp and preparing the skins trapped by the senior man.

All of this implies that trapping is not a completely market oriented activity. The data presented in Appendix II do indeed show that returns from trapping have not varied dramatically over the years, despite the gaps in the evidence. For example, the marten harvest varies between 522 pelts in 1824 in 448 pelts in 1978. Beaver shows more fluctuation, with variation between 153 pelts in 1908 and 1,345 pelts in 1830. The annual average catch for those years in which returns were available (a total of twenty-one) is 323.6 marten pelts and 825.7 beaver pelts. The higher number for beaver includes a phenomenal and unexplained six-year period from 1826 to 1831 in which nearly two thousand pelts per year were harvested. If these are excluded, then the average beaver harvest is 337 pelts per year. These returns are illustrated in figures 3.1 and 3.2.

The data contained in tables 3.12 and 3.13 demonstrate the relationship between prices and furs of all species in the region (the Finlay-Parsnip Management Area) from 1965 to 1974. This excludes Indian-owned traplines, since the government report from which the figures are drawn was based on evidence volunteered by the trappers themselves. Indian trappers rarely keep accurate records, at least for Fish and Wildlife bureaucrats. Still, it is clear that for non-Indian trappers (who are allegedly

Table 3.12 Returns[1] by species, Finlay–Parsnip area[2]

Year[3] Species	1966	1967	1968	1969	1970	1971	1972	1973	1974
Beaver	536	180	502	241	416	323	348	317	331
Coyote	4	3	3	4	5	4	7	4	1
Ermine	184	42	106	38	10	48	23	47	18
Fisher	11	3	9	11	9	17	12	80	7
Red Fox	2	0	1	2	1	8	3	4	1
Lynx	46	8	5	0	1	13	11	65	58
Marten	159	79	217	225	354	233	133	284	284
Mink	73	24	63	61	66	74	31	74	46
Muskrat	241	34	170	241	149	176	146	116	174
Otter	24	1	12	14	12	23	14	23	46
Squirrel	261	75	173	221	31	478	85	161	139
Wolf	2	0	0	5	0	2	1	3	7
Wolverine	11	5	11	10	8	11	8	19	16

[1] Returns include all traplines reporting for the years listed but exclude Indian returns.
[2] Corresponds to Finlay–Parsnip drainage basin.
[3] Indicates year-ending.

Source: J.P. Kelly, 'A Historical Review of the Interest and Management of Fur Trapping in North Central British Columbia', Victoria: British Columbia Fish and Wildlife Branch, Department of Recreation and Conservation, 1975.

Table 3.13 Furbearer prices, British Columbia, 1966–1974

Year[1]	1966[2]	1967[2]	1968[2]	1969[2]	1970[2]	1971[2]	1972[2]	1973[3]	1974[3]
Species									
Beaver	15.40	12.73	15.05	18.40	15.09	12.55	17.18	18.11	16.83
Coyote	11.22	6.62	6.69	13.52	13.01	12.70	15.64	29.49	31.39
Ermine	1.35	0.97	0.85	1.01	0.69	0.57	0.64	0.72	0.40
Fisher	15.33	11.41	12.41	18.67	21.09	26.59	29.35	33.93	49.14
Red Fox	10.58	5.69	7.73	12.80	11.03	11.79	15.97	32.83[4]	46.40[4]
Lynx	37.35	27.77	29.43	31.16	25.93	27.32	38.07	86.10	93.92
Marten	11.47	9.05	8.56	8.31	8.10	7.90	8.33	15.07	16.31
Mink	14.33	11.48	12.51	13.54	9.81	7.83	11.78	12.01	12.96
Muskrat	1.75	0.97	0.91	1.33	1.21	1.34	1.76	2.38	2.72
Otter	24.96	18.22	20.40	26.98	27.82	27.82	33.54	57.46	42.03
Squirrel	0.63	0.61	0.56	0.45	0.41	0.32	0.56	0.93	0.87
Wolf	22.40	17.97	22.64	27.78	23.24	20.03	30.40	57.26	82.56
Wolverine	24.96	24.83	31.46	39.56	38.42	59.04	71.46	94.41	82.98

[1] Year-ending.
[2] Price from Canada Yearbook.
[3] Price from West Coast Fur auction.
[4] Includes all subspecies of fox.

more responsive to market forces) fur harvest are usually price-inelastic. Figures 3.3 and 3.4 illustrate this relationship for beaver and marten, respectively. Supply factors such as those linked to environmental changes – either man-made such as logging, or natural periodicity – seem to be the dominant agent in explaining this relationship.[41] Prices, of course, are set by the market through the annual fur auctions throughout Canada, and the prices are set after a trapper has committed himself to the trapline. In sum, market forces play little role even in decisions made by trappers who are interested in maximizing incomes.[42] It is little wonder that the Sekani do not respond to the possibilities inherent in the newer technology, especially when they say that high income is not one of their goals. It seems clear that in the past the Hudson's Bay Company tried to enforce a tighter market-oriented trade but it was unsuccessful, as we shall see. It also seems clear that with the advent of a more competitive trading system and, most importantly, other sources of money, the Sekani can continue to pursue hunting and trapping in a way that is consistent with non-economic motives.

Figure 3.1 Moose, marten and beaver harvest, McLeod Lake, 1824–1848

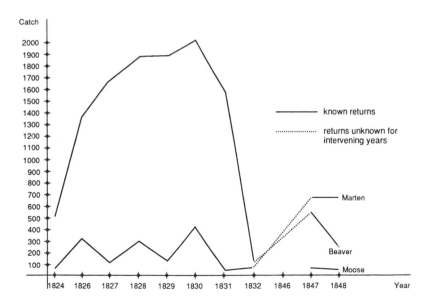

Figure 3.2   Moose, marten and beaver harvest, Fort Grahame and Fort Ware, 1892–1978

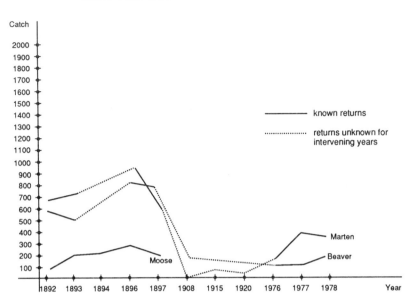

Figure 3.3   Supply and demand of beaver, Finlay–Parsnip drainage basin, 1965/1966–1973/1974

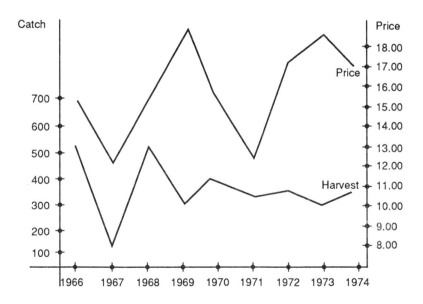

Figure 3.4 Supply and demand of marten, Finlay–Parsnip drainage basin, 1965/1966–1973/1974.

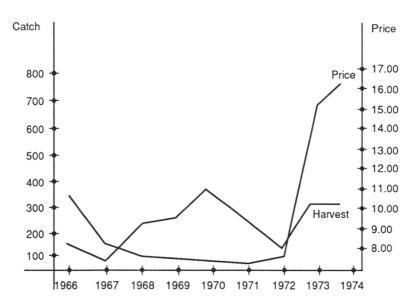

Conclusion

If, as Asch notes, the fur trade depends on price differences between the value of goods sold and the prices of furs on the market, then it is clear that trading can continue without provoking important social structural changes as long as the difference exists.[43] If the difference collapses, then the dependency of the trapper on European goods can cause hardship. Hunters who wish or need to continue participating in the fur trade may therefore be unable to do so.

The Sekani have circumvented or at least delayed this trade-off by using cash from other sources to finance their reduced participation in the fur trade, in the sense that they no longer depend on the fur trade to make a living. In fact, only one-eighth of the income of Fort Ware residents is from the sale of furs. It seems that the fur harvest has been reduced so as to minimize the loss of cash from other sources which is poured into the activity (costs outweigh returns by one or two hundred dollars per trapline per year, although this is hard to calculate more precisely since costs are not as easily recorded as returns). The fact that people none the less continue to trap points to the presence of a non-economic rationality. This is not to say that there have been no changes in Sekani attitudes towards hunting and trapping. Indeed, a new and somewhat practical attitude is emerging in many aspects of economic behaviour. In fact, that such a concept as 'economic behaviour' can be used at all in this context is itself a mark of change from the days when hunting was a way of life, not a way of doing things restricted to one domain. Still, the question must be asked why the Sekani hunt and trap at all, especially in such a way that the traditional system of partnerships is maintained. Surely the simple habit of tradition is insufficient to explain the continued interest in a way of life which the Sekani readily admit is uncomfortable at best and dangerous at worst. The question and its answer is particularly relevant in the context of Fort Ware, where real alternatives exist. At the very least, this continued interest in maintaining active networks of a particular kind must relate directly to a desire to maintain a way of life which is, to the Sekani, evidently being undermined by the forces of modernization. The evidence that population levels are relatively stable in the historic period and that there is today an identifiable process by which particular resources are defined as essential and then allocated or withheld also suggests that there is something that, if not entirely 'traditional', is not completely congruent with a market-oriented mentality. In order to understand the rationality behind these attitudes more fully it is necessary to examine Sekani social relationships in the historical context in which this rationality evolved and to examine how the system of partnerships is part of an ongoing systematic tradition which is linked to the Sekani idea of brotherhood.

Notes

1. D.W. Harmon, *Sixteen Years in the Indian Country: The Journey of Daniel Williams Harmon 1800–1816*, ed. W.K. Lamb, Toronto: Macmillan, 1957. S. Fraser, *Simon Fraser, Letters and Journals 1806–1808*, ed. W.K. Lamb, Toronto: Macmillan, 1960. A. Mackenzie, *The Journals and Letters of Sir Alexander Mackenzie*, ed. W.K. Lamb, Toronto: Macmillan, 1970. S. Blacks, *Black's Rocky Mountain Journal, 1824*, ed. E.E. Rich, London: Hudson's Bay Record Society, 1955.

2. P. Haworth, *On the Headwaters of the Peace River*, New York: Scribners, 1917. A.G. Morice, *The Western Denes, their Manners and Customs*, The Canadian Institute, Proceedings for 1888–1889, vol. 7, 1890, p. 112.

3. This kind of evidence cannot be taken too seriously, since a casual traveller would not be in a position to know anything about infanticide or birth control methods other than what the local trader told him. Haworth, *On the Headwaters*, p. 71

4. D. Jenness, *The Sekani Indians of British Columbia*, Ottawa: National Museum of Canada, Bulletin No. 84, 1937, p. 55.

5. A 1915 government report mentions a "mysterious epidemic", although the internal evidence in the letter indicates that this is second-hand information; DIAND 1915. An 1850 measles epidemic decimated the whole of New Caledonia, writes Father Morice from Fort Saint James, but its virulence and the weather prevented it spreading farther north. A.G. Morice, 'La femme chez les Dénés', *Proceedings, International Congress of Americanists*, 15th Session, vol. 1, 1906, p. 382. Morice elsewhere suggests that Dene birth rates were more or less equal to non-Dene groups, but that the infant mortality rate, although higher relative to other Athabaskans, was lower than in some other American Indian groups. Unfortunately, he does not specify the causes of this reduced mortality rate, nor does he provide figures. None the less, the fact remains that nowhere does he mention epidemics and fluctuations in population among the Sekani. See A.G. Morice, *The History of the Interior of British Columbia (formerly New Caledonia) from 1660–1880*, London: John Lane, 1906 p. 307.

6. Another view on Trench demography comes from a trader named McLean, stationed in Fort Saint James sometimes in the 1830s. He wrote: "It has been remarked by those who first settled in the district of New Caledonia that the Indians are rapidly decreasing in numbers since their arrival – a fact which does not admit of doubt: I myself have seen many villages and encampments without an inhabitant. But what can be the cause of it? Here there has been neither rum nor smallpox." Although McLean had lived in McLeod Lake for a time, he does not seem to be speaking of the Sekani here, since they had no villages or encampments to speak of at the time. McLean, says Morice, was a brutal man who used any method at hand to increase the trade in New Caledonia, including the use of rum (his statement notwithstanding). See J. McLean, *Notes on Twenty-Five Years Service in the Hudson's Bay Company*, London: Richard Benrley, 1849). Morice, *The History*, p. 296.

7. E. Service, *Primitive Social Organization: An Evolutionary Perspective*, New York: Random House 1962. A.G. Bailey, *The Conflict of European and Algonkian Cultures 1504–1700*, New Brunswick Museum Series No. 12, 1937. D. Jenness, *The Indians of Canada*, Ottawa: National Museum of Canada, Bulletin No. 65, 1932.

8. S. Krech, 'Disease, Starvation and Northern Athapaskan Social Organization', *The American Ethnologist* 5(4): 710–26, 1978.

9. Ibid., p. 724. Bilaterality as a form of social organization which favours social and spatial flexibility among Athabaskans has been argued primarily by Osgood and by Helm. See C. Osgood, *The Distribution of the Northern Athapaskan Indians*, Yale University Publications in

Anthropology 7: 1–23, New Haven: Yale University Press, 1936. J. Helm, 'Bilaterality in the Socio-Territorial Organization of the Arctic Drainage Dene', Ethnology 4: 361–8s, 1965.

10. J. Helm, 'Kin Terms of the Arctic Drainage Dene: Hare, Slavey, Chipewyan', *American Anthropologist* 62: 279–385, 1960.

11. S. Krech, 'The Influence of Disease and the Fur Trade on Arctic Drainage Lowlands Dene, 1800–1850', *Journal of Anthropological Research* 39(2): 123–46, 1983.

12. See footnote 12, Morice, 'La femme chez les Dénés', p. 126.

13. R. R. Janes, 'The Athapaskan and the Fur Trade: observations from Archaeology and Ethnohistory', *Western Canadian Journal of Anthropology* 4(3,4): 159, 1975. H.S. Sharp, 'The Caribou-Eater Chipewyan: Bilaterality, Strategies of Caribou Hunting and the Fur Trade', *Arctic Anthropology* 14(2): 35–40, 1977.

14. Janes, 'The Athapaskan and the Fur Trade', pp. 344, 345.

15. See, for example, E.B. Leacock, *The Montagnais 'Hunting Territory' and the Fur Trade*, American Anthropological Association Memoir No. 78, 1954.

16. Sharp, 'The Caribou-Eater Chipewyan', p. 40.

17. Two local Oblate priests stated that all pertinent church records had been destroyed. Only a partial record survives in the care of the local Catholic priest (then Father Jan Iglicki) in Mackenzie, BC.

18. I used a twenty-mile radius as the cut-off of effective interaction in deciding on who could be considered as a resident of McLeod Lake. Even if the off-Reserve people within this radius are excluded, this would not change these data by more than 10 per cent.

19. There were about thirty-five violent deaths between 1962 and 1978, although this could not be verified in the local records.

20. The higher numbers of older men compared to women may be linked to the nature of relationships between men and women, a point examined in the next chapter. In several cases widowers stated that their wives died as a result of accidents which were alcohol-related.

21. The information is presented in Appendix I. This information was largely compiled by B. Steventon, who graciously allowed me to examine his unpublished data. This was supplemented and corroborated whenever possible by my own examination of DIA and RCMP reports and HBC records.

22. The figure of 151 for the population of McLeod Lake in 1858 must have been reduced somewhat by the founding of Fort Grahame in 1870, since this post was specifically intended to draw people to it who previously came down from the north to trade at McLeod Lake.

23. Although the number of households varied considerably during my stay, there were thirty-five at the time in which I drew a map of the community. A 'household' refers to a house which is occupied, which at the time varied in size between one and nine people.

24. This marriage was considered "too close" because the spouses are parallel cousins. In traditional terms it is expected that people would regard this as too close a link, since the spouses would have addressed

each other by sibling terms. Modern usage follows the usages of the Catholic Church, which forbids cousin marriage of any sort.

25. Unlike the Fort Ware situation, emigration from McLeod lake cannot be linked solely to efforts to keep the population below a particular threshold. The flooding of the Trench area has undermined many of the traditional forms of continuity. Emigration no doubt represents a reaction to social breakdown. I managed to talk to only a few people who had left McLeod Lake, and they basically spoke in similar words. The thirty-five violent deaths between 1962 and 1978 are all attributed by McLeod Lakers to the effects of alcohol-induced violence and to tensions associated with the flooding.

26. I have no information on this man's motives since I never managed to interview him.

27. 'Anger' in this sense is not directed at anyone in particular but refers to a disturbance in the equilibrium that often characterizes everyday life.

28. HBC Arch. B249/d/3; B249/d/9.

29. J.J. Honigmann, *The Kaska Indians: An Ethnographic Reconstruction*, Yale University Publications in Anthropology No. 51, New Haven: Yale University Press, 1954, p. 26.

30. Y. Harris, interview with Frank Abou, Fort Ware, BC (1983) (personal communication).

31. Honigmann, *The Kaska Indians*, p. 45.

32. From the published and archival sources mentioned above and from interviews with people a non-Sekani origin can be verified for one-half of the patronymics and about one-third of the people of Fort Ware. About one half of the patronymics are associated with descendants of non-Sekani or with people from outside the region. The bulk appear to be from the north, probably from the group which Honigmann identifies as the Tselona Kaska. Many Fort Ware people suspect that they are of northern origin but could not provide details except in cases when immigration was recent. See J.J. Honigmann, *Culture and Ethos of Kaska Society*, Yale University Publications in Anthropology No. 40, New Haven: Yale University Press, 1954, p. 34; note 35, below.

33. The few men who are in this position usually obtained their traplines from their fathers, whereas men with wider partnership networks have more choice: through their fathers and through their fathers-in-law. Hence, a list of men who have not inherited traplines directly from their fathers is most likely a list of socially prominent men rather than marginal members of the community. Because some of the details of trapline ownership and inheritance were considered confidential, I cannot reveal the identities of the people listed in table 4.2 (trapline ownership, see following chapter). There is a correlation, however, between patrilineal/patrilateral (e.g. B to B) inheritance, small size of patronymic network and social and political prominence.

34. It is noteworthy that housing is sometimes explicitly denied on the same basis as it is granted, namely, to include some and to exclude others. During one meeting I attended a man proposed his son as a

candidate for receiving a house. This young man was the same as the one who had developed close ties with people in a Tahltan community. He was married and had a child. He wished to return to Fort Ware, however. His name, proposed by his father in the son's absence, brought about some snickering at the meeting. The Chief put on his chairman hat and decided that the motion was out of order since housing was not yet the subject of discussion. When the time came, the man repeated his proposal. He argued against the nomination of another man who, the Chief had told me before the meeting, was to receive the house. Since the man had made a public issue of it, he was told that his son was not a suitable candidate. The Chief, ever diplomatic, suggested that the father did not know that the son was planning on leaving Fort Ware in any case for a few months' work, and hence it was inappropriate to give him a house at this time. The fact that many young men leave Fort Ware for the same length of time as this young man had is no indication, in their respective cases, that they are not to return at some point. In this particular case, however, it was felt that the man had made his choice. This was slightly ironic, since the Chief's candidate for a new house was in the same situation. In fact, it was argued in the meeting that this particular young man needed a house in order to encourage him to stay in the community. This was not really necessary, however, since his father lived alone in a large house and was willing to have his son live with him. Nevertheless, he had a member of a well-represented and re-spected patronymic and had strong partnerships with other men in the community. The unsuccessful candidate did not.

35. These are about the same size as the wood frame houses but are usually much more comfortable in the winter. They are also more private and prettier and can be adapted to individual requirements. The prefabricated houses are of course all the same size, though people usually try to modify them by removing or adding internal division walls as they need them. The Band bought a tractor with which to haul trees cut for houses. As is often the case in these kinds of endeavours, people immediately put the tractor to use hauling wood for heating. People also received some Band money for cutting down and trimming the lumber for log cabins. All in all, the self-managed projects usually bring much better results to the community than those in which some government department makes decisions hundreds or thousands of miles away from the situation.

36. Since households change in composition quite quickly, an esti-mate of annual household income would not tell us very much about long-term trends. This takes on added significance when it is remem-bered that at least eleven of fifteen people between the ages of forty-one and sixty in Fort Ware are outsiders or the descendants (within two generations) of outsiders. This includes people who have arrived in Fort Ware during the last sixty years. This information comes from state-ments made by the people of Fort Ware and from sparse church records. At worst, it is too low an estimate. Stated another way, six of twelve pat-ronymic groups are known to have entered Fort Ware from another

community in recent memory. This includes at least twenty-seven adults (those over twenty years of age as of 1 July 1979). In sum, it appears that immigration is just as important in Sekani demography as emigration.

37. Shooting furbearers allows greater flexibility than trapping since it requires less commitment of time, money and effort. Shooting is also better suited to a person who wishes to work alone. It is indicative of a lessened reliance upon trapping as a source of income, as well as a sign of the weakening of partnership bonds between hunters.

38. The high cost of goods in Fort Ware is due to the high transportation costs from Mackenzie. The average cost is $0.16 per pound, although it is higher in winter, when goods are flown in. Another factor in high costs is the interest rate which must be added to all goods. Since people pay through credit and interest is charged the trader by his suppliers, he must pass this cost on to his customers. I calculated that the trader carried his customers an average of three months each, which added 5 per cent to the cost of goods.

39. A social planning consultant reached much the same in the way of conclusions after analysing the situation in Fort Ware. B. LeBaron, 'Fort Ware Resource Uses', unpublished paper prepared for the Fort Ware Indian Bank, Fort Ware, BC 1979, p. 16.

40. John Kelly, 'A Historical Review of the Interest and Management of Fur Trapping in North Central British Columbia', Victoria: British Columbia Fish and Wildlife Branch, Department of Recreation and Conservation, pp. 11–102.

41. No studies have been done of the White trappers in the region. Some state that they are market-oriented. This makes sense, since most of them trap full time and have no real alternative but to maximize their income. Many say, none the less, that trapping represents a way of life as much as a means of making money. many are from the south and seeking freedom (as they put it) from a regular routine. Whatever may be the case, they do not form partnerships of the same kind and significance as do the trappers of Fort Ware. They tend to be isolated from one another and certainly do not live in one community.

42. The maps in Appendix VIII of my dissertation indicate the distances covered by the Fort Ware Sekani in their search for food and furs. The distances are substantial and are an additional demonstration of a continued interest in using the land.

43. M. Asch, 'The Economics of Dene Self-Determination', in G.A. Smith and D.H. Turner, eds, *Challenging Anthropology*, Toronto: McGraw Hill-Ryerson, 1979, pp. 344, 345.

Chapter 4

Lower Level Relationships

In the last chapter I have shown that patronymic networks are important in emigration and hence in maintaining the population in the regional band within a threshold of about 200 people. The number of people has remained more or less constant during the historic period, despite what appears to be a steadily increasing birth rate in recent years. Although it would be wrongly imposing a system-oriented foresight on the Sekani to suggest that an individual decides to emigrate so that a relatively unchanging number of people allows traditional forms of association to be maintained, the fact remains that a stable population does permit particular patterns of association to continue, and that these patterns are traditional in the sense of being informed by a belief in maintaining some sort of coherency in political organization. Patterns of association, whatever they might be, do not as such depend on a critical population threshold, but on a person's everyday particular balance between people and land. In this chapter I will examine other aspects of associations between patronymics, especially as they reflect traditional political beliefs in some way. In the previous chapter I mentioned that, faced by the disillusionment and confusion produced by the recent loss of their land, people in McLeod Lake gave the ready impression that there was little that was systematically organized in their lives. Fort Ware, less directly affected by the flooding (only to the extent that former residents of Fort Grahame moved there), seemed by comparison a good window on the past; men in Fort Ware still hunted and trapped in appreciable numbers and, more important, seemed determined to keep doing so despite increasing job opportunities in logging and a growing flow of cash from government transfer payments.

Yet the contrast with McLeod Lake was not as clear as I had thought it would be. Although trapping and hunting partnerships between men were common, even this seemed unfocussed and random because of the way in which such ties are formed. People have a tendency to blur the distinction between actual and potential partnerships; the latter is a very large category compared to the former. Past potential links which were never actualized are forgotten as insignificant. The individual hunter, not surprisingly, tends to remember what he did, not what he could have done in a different set of circumstances. At any one time, if we take any given generational block as a simplified way of representing relationships, what people can do in the present depends very much on what their fathers did in the past. What they can do is much more flexible than what they actually choose to do; what anyone 'could' do, given the extent of the networks, can easily be translated as 'almost anything'. Yet this flexibility in the present generation depends very much on creating a static image of the previous generation's possible partnerships. In other words, possibilities for action and alliances are very wide at any moment but once choices are made the pattern gels into a somewhat more restricted history that tends to condition future choices. The reality is more complicated because the Sekani 'generations' are social, not age categories as such, and, unlike neat diagrams in textbooks, people have the unfortunate tendency to be born just about any year instead of in neat twenty-year cycles. None the less, there are some definite patterns, and it became apparent that these are related to a person's membership in one of several categories and that inclusion into a category is based on something more than simple pragmatic considerations.

Partnerships as such are particularly important in economic life, but economic factors are not necessarily the most important regulators of linkages. None the less, economic activity is the most obvious feature of everyday life and forms the basis for the system of social classification. In this chapter the evidence relating to this system of classification will be examined, beginning with the 'kinship' terms. These terms are systemic only insofar as they indirectly reflect various social processes that are part of an ongoing dynamic. As such, they are more properly labelled 'relationship terms' rather than 'kinship terms'. In the Sekani case kinship – shared biological ties – has little to do with the terminology used to describe relationships despite some overlap with a genealogically-based system. Although only a handful of Sekani use the traditional terms (in Sekani) today except for a few examples which apply to the immediate family, these still provide a clue to the organization of daily life. More importantly, they point to dichotomous features of Sekani social organization that are linked to the evolution and expression of the concept of brotherhood.

The Classification of Sekani Nomenclature

I would like to stress at this point that I found no evidence of differences in male and female usages of the terms. Were such differences present they would have had little bearing on this work, since it is primarily an examination of the mode whereby associations and partnerships are formed between men. Throughout my research I tried to be consistently empirical, that is, I avoided imbuing the existing partnerships with a previously discovered kinship term. I would never ask, for example, "do you call X by the term Y?" Rather, I examined every instance of partnership in terms of the denominations provided by the people themselves, in the form, "what do you call X?" Most of the people interviewed were men. However, in those few cases where women participated in hunting and trapping activity, no differences were observed in the usage of terms. The only logical conclusion is that such differences – minute, albeit interesting, even in the late 1920s and 1940s when they were recorded by Jenness and Honigmann – have collapsed in the last thirty years, as has the generalized distinction between elder and younger siblings and cousins that these authors noted.

A list of the terms collected by Jenness is presented in table 4.1, along with a list collected by Honigmann around 1954 from a Fort Ware resident.[1] I collected the third and much sparser list in 1979. Fort Ware people say that the terms have not been commonly used since the beginning of this century. Although it is unlikely that their use lapsed eighty years ago, there is little doubt that they have not been used since the era of massive government intrusion in the North during the 1950s. This is in part linked to the recent emphasis by the Sekani on establishing English as a first language.[2]

Jenness argues that consanguinity regulated marriage among the Sekani.[3] This, and his relentless biological orientation in the translation of the terms themselves, indicates that he believed that the Sekani model of relationships was basically bilateral. In addition, the absence of cross and parallel cousin distinctions is consistent with features found among many Athabaskan groups which, in modern descriptions (though not in Jenness's time), are sometimes labelled bilateral.

If the system were consistently bilateral, then certain regularities

Table 4.1 Sekani relationship terms, 1924, 1954, 1979

Term[1]	English[2]	Term[3]	English[4]	Term[5]	Content[6]
1 settane	my eB, my yB my male cousin				
2 hotige	my eB, my elder male cousin	udiiga	my eB; if older than ego, FBS, MZS, MBS; BS(w.s.)		
3 asidle	my yB, my younger male cousin; BS(w.s.)	istitla	my yB; if younger than ego, FBS, MZS, FZS, MBS; BS(w.s.); HuZS(w.s.)	sechit'le	my B, my FBS
4 se'tise	my eZ or yZ, female cousin				
5 sade	my eZ, my elder female cousin	sedade	my eZ; if older than ego, FBD, MZD, FZD, MBD; BD(w.s.)	sedates'e	my Z, my FBD
6 esdje'	my yZ, my younger cousin; BD(w.s.)	isd(ii)e	my yZ; if younger than ego, FBD, MZD, FZD, MBD; BD(w.s.); HuZD(w.s.)		
7 abba	my F	aba	my F	aba	my F
8 ane	my M	ana	My M, MZ (also called Sowe)	sema	my M
9 esta	my paternal uncle my step-F	isda	my FB, MHu	usta'	my FB, MB

#	term	gloss	term2	description	abbr.	meaning
10	sase	may maternal uncle				
11	abedze	my paternal aunt			adada'e	my FBWi, my MZ
12	songwe	my step-M	sowe	my MZ (also called ana); my FWi		
13	seskege	my children				
14	setchwe'	My D, step-D, BD(m.s.) ZD(w.s.)	setue	my D, BD(m..s.); WiZD(m.s.); ZD(w.s.) (also called Sedaze)	setw'e	my D
15	setchwa'	my S, step-S, BS(m.s.); ZD(w.s.)	setcua	my S, BS(m.s.), WiZS(m.s.) HuBS(w.s.)	sechwe	my S
16	sazi	ZS, ZD(m.s.)	(s)edzaze	my ZS, ZD (also called setue); WiBS(m..s.)		
17	ase	my grand-F	istiia	my MF, FF		
18	asu	my grand-M	etsuun	my MM, FM, MZ; WiM(m.s.); HuM(w.s.)		
19	asa	my grandchild				
20	ese	my F-in-law	atse	my WiF(m.s.); HuF(w.s.)	ad'tse	my FeB, WiFB
21	esu	my M-in-law			ad'tsu	my WiM
22	senaze	my S-in-law	sinaze	my DHu	sanase	my DHu
23	setcha	my D-in-law	setca	my SWi (also applied to grandchildren?)		

				my ZHu		
24	klaze'	my B-in-law, Z-in-law	klaze			
25			senawu	my Wi	pan'e	my Wi
26			setawu	my Hu		
27			isla	my HuB, WiB, ZHu (also called klaze)	usla	my WiFBS, WiFB, FBDHu WiZHu
28			abea	my WiZ(m.s.), BWi(m.s.)		
29			ekla	my HuZ(w.s.), BWi(w.s.)		
30			seda	my sweetheart		

[1] *Source:* D. Jenness, *The Sekani Indians of British Columbia*, Ottawa: National Museum of Canada, Bulletin No. 84, 1937, pp. 50–1.

[2] *Source:* Ibid, pp. 50–1; terms used by both sexes unless otherwise specified.

[3] *Source:* J. Honigmann, *The Kaska Indians: An Ethnographic Reconstruction*, Yale University Publications in Anthropology No. 51, New Haven, Yale University Press, 1954, pp. 80–1, fn.

[4] *Source:* Ibid., pp. 80–1, fn.; terms used by both sexes unless otherwise specified.

[5] Collected in Fort Ware, 1979.

[6] Collected in Fort Ware, 1979; people were given a list of names of everyone in the community and asked what term they applied to each person.

in usage could be expected to surface. In other words, a given equivalence in usage can be expected at any genealogically equivalent point. For example, it could be expected that BS/BD (m.s.) would be the same (equal) as ZS/ZD (w.s.). That is, the terms used by female speaker to address or refer to brother's son or brother's daughter would be the same terms as used by male ego to refer to sister's son or sister's daughter. This would follow in a bilateral system since the genealogical distance between the persons involved is the same in each case. This does in fact occur in the first of the two lists, which can be expected to be closer to the 'traditional' system than the third list. But the expected relationship ZS/ZD (m.s.) = BS/BD (w.s.) does not hold; female ego uses terms for BS/BD that are equivalent to those used for younger brother and sister. Even if sex of speaker is not taken into account, then the expected relationship BS/BD = ZS/ZD (male speaking) does not obtain. Nor does it hold for a female speaker, although the terms are co-equal (BS/BD = ZS/ZD, male or female speaking). All of these dry equations point to the fact that the pattern exhibited by the Sekani relationship terms is not bilateral and therefore not based solely on genealogical connections.[4] On the other hand, we find that S/D (m.s.), = S/D (w.s.), which is consistent with a genealogically-based system. Although S/D = ZS/ZD indicates a genealogical 'error', the pattern is systematic in that it holds for both male and female speakers. Terms on the second ascending and second descending generation levels, however, are consistent with both genealogical distance and sex of speaker. These regularities are usually signs of a bifurcate-merging bilateral system, although not invariably so. For the Sekani the divergence from the strictly bilateral pattern occurs in the first descending generation, where BS/BD (m.s.) are distinguished from ZS/ZD (w.s.), and ZS/ZD (m.s.) are distinguished from ZS/ZD (w.s.). Hence, we find that BS/BD (m.s.) = ZS/ZD (w.s.), but that BS/BD (m.s.) does not equal ZS/ZD (m.s.) or BS/BD (w.s.), but that B/Z (w.s.) = BD/BS (w.s.). These traits are usually signs of a lineal tendency in the system of classification.

One distinguishing feature of Sekani relationship terms is the equivalence in terms, for male and female speakers, between children of same sexed siblings and children of opposite sexed siblings in the first ascending generation. This also holds for the first descending generation for male speakers, although a woman addresses children of her male siblings by the special terms *asidle* and *esdje'*. These terms are also applied to a woman's own siblings; they are not used reciprocally by her nepotic kin, however. This may point to the role of generation in regulating the usage of terms, at least for women. It definitely calls into question the apparent solidarity of the domestic group of origin for brothers and sisters. A formal analysis of the terms is not powerful enough proof, however, to sustain this conclusion. We shall see how the identity conferred by the domestic group does in fact play an important role in structuring relationships.

Contemporary English usages of relationship terms do not reflect the oscillation between bilateral and lineal features which is characteristic of Sekani terminology.[5] English usages tend to be consistent with a bilateral/genealogical pattern, with a few exceptions. There is no differentiation between first and second cousins and there is merging on the second and third ascending generation levels; old people tend to be addressed as and referred to by the terms 'grandfather' and 'grandmother' regardless of their ties to the speaker. Even in English there were a few exceptions to the genealogical pattern. One person distinguished parallel from other cousins by using the term 'first cousin'. Another called his parallel cousin 'brother'. Although suggestive, these usages were too infrequent to allow any solid conclusions to emerge.

Despite the overt bilateralism in English usages, modern Sekani terms are not so consistent. For example, men use the term *uslah* to refer to WiFB on the first ascending generation and to WiFBS, WiZHu and FBDHu on their generation level. *Uslah* in fact refers to actual or potential trapping partners regardless of their generation. However, older men depend more on links traced through their sisters rather than those traced through their wives. There is no term in the modern version of their terminology which corresponds to the old term *klaze*, 'sister's husband' (and possibly his collateral kin as well). This suggests that while there are two major categories of partnerships, as we shall see, only one of them is assigned a position in the modern terminological system.

At the same time the equivalency between cousins and siblings has been partially preserved on the patrilateral side by both men and women. This is reflected in the content of the term *sechit'le*, 'my brother and my father's brother's son' and in the content of the term *sedates'e*, 'my sister and my father's brother's daughter'. This correlates with the pattern of lineal inheritance of patronymic surnames which is now in use. On the other hand, the fact that matrilateral and patrilateral terms contain some equivalences argues against the development of strong matrilines or patrilines.

In sum, an examination of the traditional set of relationship terms reveals that the Sekani did not possess what is usually called, in the literature, a 'standard' pattern. It is clear that both lineal and bilateral features can be identified. The significant feature associated with bilateral classification is its expansionary tendency in the formation of networks. Lineal features, however, express a tendency to favour exclusive and somewhat rigid networks. This is particularly evident in the use of patronymics by the Sekani. The modern use of English terms reveals no particular continuation of traditional lineal features, while modern Sekani terms, although few in number, do evoke these dichotomous tendencies.

Patronymics

The lineal features of Sekani social classification are reflected in the continued use of a patronymic naming system. By patronymic is meant the category of people who share the same surname, inherited patrilineally, and changed by a woman on the occasion of her marriage. Patronymics as such were introduced as a means of identification sometime after the turn of the century. Available church records show that the process was complete by the late 1920s and early 1930s, although it is not at all clear when the process started since trading records are sparse from 1895 to 1925 and non-existent after that date.[6] The presence of many French surnames in the North obviously reflects the influence of the Oblate order, many of whose early members came from France. VanStone argues that patronymics were adopted so that accurate band lists and other government records could be maintained.[7] Surely, however, patronymics were adopted for different reasons from the Sekani point of view. They must have played a specific role in their system of social organization. Their use as a bridge between Indian society and White bureaucracy therefore may be only coincidental, since there is little reason to suppose that the Sekani or any other Indian group willingly accommodated themselves to the bookkeeping exigencies of the Hudson's Bay Company. In Fort Ware and to a lesser extent in McLeod Lake people draw upon members of this category in order to form ties that go beyond the network given by birth. Its influence is so important that it is used as a means of regulating access to certain strategic resources such as housing and, more importantly, to traplines. At the same time the patronymic network does not act as a corporate group. Its members do not jointly own property and only in exceptional circumstances do they demonstrate any tendency towards political or economic solidarity.

In the last chapter we have seen that the allocation of housing shows the Sekani concern with not only having wide patronymic networks but with transcending these immediate connections by forming ties with people outside the network. When people do so they create cross-cutting affiliations which tend to weaken their allegiance to the domestic group of origin and, by implication, to their patronymic network. Somewhat ironically, however, the way in which people gain access to traplines points to a completely opposite tendency. Instead of reaching out beyond a particular network, the disposition of traplines tends to urge people to limit their associations to the domestic group of origin. Here, however, we must distinguish between theory and practice. Traplines are, in theory, allocated according to simple and direct patrilineal inheritance. In practice, the allocation of traplines reveals some of the same ambiguities we have seen in the structure of the relationship terms and in the provenance of people. All say they are Sekani, yet many have non-Sekani origins. With traplines, all say that they pass from father to son, but the facts are rather more complicated. Traplines are of particular importance in Fort Ware, not only as a symbol of the land and all that this implies but as a real base for economic survival. It is not surprising that the ability to hunt and trap effectively (again, defined as a social rather than individual ability) is an important marker of a man's adult status.

There are twelve traplines in use in Fort Ware; none are regularly used by residents of McLeod Lake. Two of the twelve are not contiguous with the other ten but are owned by former Fort Grahame residents. They are located south of the other traplines. Many of the traplines had once been owned by White trappers who lived in the region (though not in Fort Ware itself). These lines were purchased by the Department of Indian Affairs as they came available to be turned over to the Sekani. The Departmental files are not clear when this policy was initiated, but government employees believe that it was initiated in the early 1950s. Such purchases were intended to stop the continual encroachment by Whites on Sekani land, an encroachment which had been inadvertently encouraged in the first place by the bureaucratic structure of the government. Apparently White trappers simply registered a line in their name in one Department

(Natural Resources or the previous equivalent), which did not know what the other (Indian Affairs) was doing with its trapline policy. As a result, many Indian traplines are still 'new'. Hence, it is difficult to speak of strict patrilineal inheritance when the trapline has not yet passed out of the hands of its original owner or in cases in which the owner's son is not yet the legal keeper of the trapline since his father is alive. Patrilineal inheritance is also ignored when a man has no sons or if his sons are already established as junior partners on other traplines by the time their father is ready to 'retire'. When young men affiliate themselves to more experienced men as junior partners, especially through marriage with the owner's daughter, they stand an excellent chance of inheriting the man's trapline. In cases when patrilineal inheritance is not an assured fact but remains an ideal, the Chief can intervene. There is only one documented instance of this happening, however.[8]

The same selection pressures which can be used to exclude can also be used as a means of bringing someone into the community as a participating member.[9] As in the case of housing, getting a trapline from one's own patronymic network or domestic group of origin is not particularly crucial in deciding who is and who is not a member of the community. There are cases where Fort Ware residents without their own lines were passed over in favour of outsiders. The power of the Chief is crucial here, although I should stress once more that no Sekani Chief would consider using 'power' which was not sanctioned by general community consensus. Although no data exist from McLeod Lake, the Fort Ware data are presented in table 4.2. Fort Ware residents do not remember the exact details of the disposition of tracts of land which were used before the imposition of a government registry system.

Partnerships

Table 4.3 contains a list of partnerships that were active during my stay in Fort Ware. It is obvious that not everyone forms partnerships as such. It is also obvious that a man may have more than one partner and that he will therefore trap (and sometimes hunt) with different men at different times. He will do this without jeopardizing his other relationships. There are degrees of closeness between partners, so that some partnerships engage feelings of friendship while others do not. Pragmatism and friendship are simultaneously engaged in most partnerships,

however. The most interesting fact which emerges from the data is that many partnerships proceed through a shared affinal link rather than through a consanguineal link.
Of a total of twenty-six relationships identified, one can be ignored because of incomplete data. Of the twenty-five which

Table 4.2   Trapline ownership and transfers, Fort Ware

Line	Connection	Details[1]
1	none	Transferred at request of Ft. Ware Chief from deceased Ingenika resident.
2	F to S	Purchased for Indian use by Indian Affairs Branch from White trapper; no date recorded.
3	F to S and D	Purchased from White trapper in 1938; subsequent transfer registered in 1976.
4	B to B	Last transferred in 1961.
5	MB to ZS	Transfer resulted in line being placed under Ingenika jurisdiction.
6	B to B	Ingenika line now owned by Ft. Ware resident.
7	F to S	Last transferred in 1951.
8	F to three D and one DHu	Originally transferred from White trapper. Subsequent transfer in 1958. Now only used by DHu.
9	F to S; then B to B	Originally owned by F, two S, and two unrelated partners.
10	none	Transferred from White trapper in 1953.
11	F to S, DHu and DHu's partner	Transferred from White trapper in 1950.
12	Partner to partner	No known affinal or consanguineal relationship; transferred when one of two original owners obtained his own line.

[1] Obtained from interviews and Indian Affairs Branch files.

Table 4.3 Trapping partnerships, Fort Ware, 1978–1979

Senior Partner[1]	Partners	Relationship[2]	Details
M. Abou	Ray Abou Gordon Abou George Abou	BS/WiS BS/WiS	Married BWi after B's death.
H. Charlie	Melvin McCook	BWiZHu	
A. Massettoe	Jerry Smaaslet Mitch Smaaslet Tommy Poole	FZHuBS FZHuBS ZHu	J. and M. Smaaslet are sons of a woman who left Ft. Ware.
P. Seymour	Jerry Seymour Willie Poole Louie Tomah	WiS/S ZHuBS	No known ties between L. Tomah and P. Seymour.
F. Charlie	Duncan Pierre		No known ties.
G. Massettoe	Charlie Boya	MBS	
P. Massettoe	Joe Egnell	DHu	P. Massettoe also traps with Wi.
J. Massettoe	Alec Massettoe		Relationship not clear.
D. McCook	Arnold McCook Elmer McCook	S S	
John McCook	Craig McCook	S	
M. McCook	Joe McCook	B	M. McCook had recently returned to Ft. Ware after long absence. J. McCook died 1979.
A. Pierre			Traps alone or with members of household.
J. Poole	Duncan Pierre	WiZHu	
M. Porter	F. Porter M. Porter H. Poole	S S WiZS	Latter junior partner only works occasionally with M. Porter.
J. Seymour	F. Seymour	MS/B	They are step-brothers with loose partnership.
A. Charlie			Traps largely with members of household.

[1] May not be the legal owner of a trapline.
[2] Slash (/) indicates alternative affinal or consanguineal ties.

remain, twelve were either with sons or with other members of the domestic group (there is a link with wife's domestic group of origin that is implicitly acknowledged as a means of developing a potential partnership). They therefore represent very weak ties, if any, to other domestic groups. What is somewhat surprising in light of the literature on Athabaskan trapping and hunting patterns and considering the nature of the Fort Ware community is that only two adult men trapped with their brothers. Of these two, one is a man who returned to Fort Ware after an absence of many years. His older brother no longer had any other active partnerships since he was too old, and in any case he had never married. His former partners – his other younger brothers who stayed in the community – have long since developed other ties and registered their own traplines. The other case of fraternal partnership is intermittent, and depends on the older brother's professed interest in inculcating a taste for trapping in his younger brother. The older brother had at least one other viable partnership of the regular (non-patronymic) type, while the younger brother had none. Both brotherly pairs, therefore, are at the opposite ends of the age scale – one man of the older pair was in his seventies, while the youngest of the other pair was in his teens. These two cases, therefore, are more the exception than the rule. The bulk of the remainder represent people who trace a tie either through their respective groups of origin, or between members of the domestic group of marriage of one of the partners.

There are two types of social ties that are important and recognized by the Sekani in attaining adult status. The first type of tie involves the social and economic networks of which a person is a member as a result of a particular inherited patronymic identity. This is the only type of tie which children and youths can claim. Adults, in turn, are expected to marry and form ties to people outside of their patronymic category. This second set of links largely supplants the first as a person matures, without, however, extinguishing them. People with fewer patronymic ties experience some difficulty in forming ties of the second type. Without considerable hunting experience and without adequate living quarters, they are often undesirable as junior trapping partners or as spouses. If the community wishes, deliberate efforts can be made to encourage them to stay by providing them with at least one requirement, housing. If the effort is not made and if people experience difficulty in forming the second type of tie, then they may have little choice but to consider seriously leaving the community.

Furthermore, the manner in which traplines are allocated does not really contradict the Sekani concern with forming wide-ranging ties that go beyond the limits of the patronymic network. A patrilineal bias is simply one facet of the allocation of resources. The formation of one set of ties presupposes the existence of the other. The two are interdependent, although a man with wide networks may no longer need his patrilineal inheritance. But it is there none the less. This patrilineal bias is reflected in the Sekani terms which are remembered, though not used, today. *Sechit'le, sedates'e* and *ad'tse* (terms 3, 5 and 20 in table 4.1) draw an equation between ego's siblings and his patrilineal parallel kin (FBD and FBS). Equivalent terms for the matrilateral side have not survived. Furthermore, another patrilateral kinsman, FeB, is equated with a man's wife's brother rather than with his mother's elder brother. On the other hand, some bilateral merging is preserved in term 9, *usta'*, where father's brother is equated with mother's brother. Term 11, *abedze/adada'e*, equates father's brother's wife and mother's sister, which also suggests bilateral merging at first glance, but a real bilateral equation would link mother's sister with father's sister.[10]

The wide range of the networks created by reference to the rigidly lineal system of patronymic identification is mirrored by the exclusivity associated with the formation of wide-ranging and hence flexible partnership ties. These ties are flexible in that there are no proscriptions applied in the selection of potential partners. The only explicit proscription is the ban on limiting these partnerships to people already within the patronymic network. Partnerships represent an attempt to widen a person's networks, but the manner in which they are formed reveals that the Sekani are also concerned with maintaining the solidarity of the domestic group over time. Hence, the apparent flexibility of partnerships is merely restricted in another dimension.

To sum up, there are at least two important processes at work which affect the size and social composition of the community. The presence of acknowledged ties or the links that a given person can be reasonably expected to develop are the major factors which decide on a person's exclusion from or inclusion into the community. The fact that personal popularity plays a minor role does not mean that goodwill cannot be evaluated, nor that it is forgotten when it comes time to allocate houses and select partners. Nor does it mean that goodwill is not important in mundane affairs, as if people carry on their lives purely within the regimentation of social structural principles. It means only that the two areas can be treated separately, with little overlap between them. The ability to form partnerships is a mark of adult status and is certainly taken as a sign of good character. The social control of disruptive behaviour is a different process than the control of status through housing and relationship. The allocation of housing involves positional control, while other forms of sanctions are more personal.

A summary of a man's life cycle can be presented based on the evidence presented here. Men who have negotiated successful marriages tend, at first glance, to form alliances with members of their spouses' domestic group of origin. They rarely actualized ties based on a shared patronymic identity. However, a significant proportion of ties are traced through a man's sister rather than through his wife. There were four linkages noted which pass through a sister and two which pass through wives. A sister's husband is preferred over wife's brother as a junior partner. Wife's sister's husband is a potential partner in one case and wife's sister's son is another. There are thus two counterpoised options which are open to Sekani men. A senior trapper uses links based on his domestic group of origin – ties traced through his sister – while a junior partner without ready access to a trapping territory will depend on ties traced through his domestic group of marriage; his wife's relatives, in other words. The cycle which develops during a man's lifetime has three phases. When he is young he will use those ties based on his domestic group of origin to form an alliance with someone in a domestic group outside of his patronymic category. A man will then often choose to trap with his wife's brother again, someone outside his patronymic category. When he is older he may use these ties to obtain a trapline, although it is more frequent for traplines to pass from father to son or from father's brother to brother's son.[11] As a senior trapper a man enters the last phase of the cycle. He will use his ties to solidify his position and hence attract a junior partner, preferably his younger sister's husband. A man comes full circle, in one sense, as he grows older. First relying on his domestic group of origin to establish himself when young, he branches out through contacts traced through his wife and then ultimately relies once again on his domestic group of origin.[12]

Marriage

Some of the structural features of Sekani society that have been
discussed above emerge in relations between men and women
and, specifically, in the domain of marriage. Domestic groups
reflect lineality as well as the openness which marks their non-
patronymic ties. Although domestic groups act as politically and
economically autonomous units, a man's partnerships necessarily engage some sort of tension within his domestic group, since
marriage links a man to his wife's domestic group of origin, especially his wife's brothers. Nor does a man weaken his affiliation to his own domestic group of origin after his marriage;
instead, this domestic group ceases to exist as a group after a
man marries. The networks and patterns survive, however. Since
tension within domestic groups is in part caused by the fact that
people have different patronymic identities, it is reasonable to
suppose that it has existed ever since patronymics have been in
regular use as an important social category.

There is little doubt that in the past marriage was exogamous
relative to the hunting group (the 'band'). The limit of the exogamous boundary was, as we shall see, variously extended and
contracted to suit particular political conditions. For the moment,
this fact implies that men exerted a certain degree of control over
women, at least as regards the selection of a spouse. Suffice to
say at this point that this generated a certain amount of tension
between men and women or, to be more accurate, that it was
symptomatic of the different social identities conferred upon
people. Nor would it be inaccurate to say that a certain amount
of tension still exists between men and women, as can be seen
in the high rates of spousal violence that will be examined in the
next chapter. This tension emerges in though is not caused by
the gender-based division of labour. Men spend the bulk of
their time with other men, as women do with other women.
Besides work, men also spend some time gambling and drinking together. They change their behaviour in the presence of
women in the sense that these activities normally stop when
women are around. Many men view the tension between the
sexes as strengthening the bonds which link one partner to
another; men are sometimes drawn together because of tension
in their relationships to women. The 'competition' for women
rarely results in hierarchical boundaries being established;
quite the opposite, in fact. For example, there is a lot of
joking about sexual relationships, though men do not openly
talk about their wives in this way. There are some extra–marital

affairs; only rarely do these cause tension. The general attitude is that such things should not be talked about since they threaten to disrupt friendships and partnerships. Hence, by conducting their relationships on an egalitarian basis men effectively mask any underlying tension.[13] In brief, men have a tendency to recognize an implicit boundary that divides them from women, a kind of male solidarity in their dealings with them.

To a certain extent these newly defined boundaries between men and women are reflected in the lower rates of marriage, especially in McLeod Lake.[14] Standards of fidelity after marriage have also apparently changed. Jenness mentions that the penalty for infidelity by the woman was death; jealousy was openly displayed.[15] Today no stigma is attached to men for sexual encounters before marriage, but discretion is expected after. This apparently tolerant attitude is partly the expression of the notion that infidelity is unimportant as long as no important social bonds between men are broken.[16] The notion of control and power is important, especially in the realm of social behaviour. Hence, a man who cannot 'control' his wife will appear weak and will find it difficult to relate to other men as an equal. Yet divorce is virtually unknown, although some couples lead more or less separate lives while continuing to live together.[17] Infidelity ceases to be a concern when the couple is older and ties are well established.

Modern Sekani marriages are to some extent still governed by the wishes of the fathers of the prospective brides.[18] To some extent the influence of fathers over daughters passes to one of his sons after he is married. In effect, a man may act as head of two households, his own and his father's, especially if he is the youngest son. This influence is sharply limited but clear none the less. It tends to be strongest in cases when the youngest son has established his own household and still has unmarried younger sisters living in his father's house. A younger son has an interest in making sure that his sister's marriage will favour his chances of acquiring good partners in the future, since his older brothers will likely have 'used up' the social resources of the patronymic network. In all cases a man 'rules' by suggestion and tries to enforce his wishes, when he can, by means of the limited economic services he continues to perform for his domestic group of origin even after his marriage.[19] Still, a sister performs much the same tasks in the household (chopping wood, fetching water) and others as well (cooking, looking after siblings or, more likely in this situation, offspring of older siblings) and so has a certain amount of leverage of her own in any such disputes. This, combined with the traditional value placed on individual autonomy and the fact that many younger people are more and more economically independent, virtually guarantees her the right to marry any man she wishes. Neither men nor women wish completely to break the pattern of choices they and their parents have made, however, so nearly everyone acknowledges the implicit politics of marriage before the rupture point is reached. There is tension but rarely does it erupt into confrontation.

These inter-family ties and tensions are the modern equivalent, or descendant, of the period of initial matrilocality, as described by Jenness,[20] that was typical for older Sekani. There are several points that can be summed up quickly. First, initial matrilocality was practised in order to cement good relations with the bride's family. Second, the bride's father still retained some control over his daughter after her marriage. This was acknowledged by her husband when he undertook to perform bride service to acquit himself of this indirect control.[21] Third, the newly married couple sometimes chose to stay with the bride's parents after the period of bride service was completed. These considerations all point to the delicate balance in relationships between various domestic groups which is involved in marriage, relationships in which women are vital markers of the bonds between people. Today, such bride service is unknown in formal terms, although men still display interest in the social implications of matches.

In contemporary Sekani society there are no hunting groups as such, only networks. These resemble the older 'bands' only insofar as some partnerships persist over time. The interest which men display in alliances is an expression of the important role women play in defining these networks. The men seem to be interested in maintaining patronymic network exogamy, to judge from their comments when, in a few cases, it was ignored. Since men often hunt alone with other men and not within a temporary association of domestic groups, they rely on each other a great deal, possibly as much as or even more than they ever did in the past, despite the cushion provided by other sources of income and by modern technology. Therefore, it is just as important today as in the past that partnerships be stable.[22] There is another consideration that impinges on the question of tension between men and women. Boundaries around families are stronger than ever, in the sense that there is little else in the way of local level relationships, so it is even more crucial that whatever links exist between these semi-autonomous units are not undermined by contingent events. The importance of marriage in relation to partnerships has not decreased, despite a reduction in the number of people who actually hunt and trap. Partnerships still represent a dominant form of economic activity, but they are as socially important as they ever were in defining what is, for the Sekani, the core of their society. Insofar as partnerships cross patronymic boundaries and depend on marriage ties, men still have a vested interest in controlling women's choices.

Male control over women is in part reflected in the rules governing sexual encounters. To judge from the old account, modern standards have changed drastically over the years. Mothers, states Jenness, once kept close watch over their daughters.[23] Today relations are much more casual. Pregnancy is now viewed as the "fault" of the woman instead of as a prelude to marriage. This change is also reflected in the fact that it is now possible, let alone conceivable, to make a charge of promiscuity against a woman. Women can now survive alone with their children thanks to government transfer payments. The rate of marriage has dropped dramatically in the last several years, according to available church records.[24] In fact, the local women are "too close", say some men. Hence, there is uncertainty about the limits of the exogamic boundary. 'Too close' in this sense refers to sexual behaviour more than to genealogical closeness per se. Still, it is rare for women to be as promiscuous as some men imply. The important point in this regard is that there is a stereotype which is accepted as part of the discourse that describes relationships between men and women. Promiscuity is neither a traditional behaviour nor was it ever the moral standard. Its emergence in the realm of popular discourse points to an increase in ambivalence between men and women in modern society.

Now that the traditional activities of hunting and trapping are largely carried out without women's help (though of course there are all sorts of other tasks which women normally do while staying in the community), a new role has emerged for women in the context of the community. If women are in one sense relatively unimportant in economic terms – especially in the era of government transfer payments – they are perhaps more important as symbols of the changes which have emerged to accord with the new regime. It is no accident that women now say, in Fort Ware, that they cannot go to the bush as often as they once did nor for as long a time as in the past because their children are attending school. Given the importance of education as a symbol of progress and its implications for integration with the

White world, women are increasingly regarded as responsible for the reproduction of the domestic group. It is no surprise that the ambivalence of integration and education are matched by the tension between men and women. Today the main social point of reference for Fort Ware women is the world of the village and children, whereas men still define themselves as hunters who engage in active and direct relationships with each other. The social unit which engages their attention is smaller than that of their wives and sisters and involved in an entirely separate sphere of activity. Although a gender-based division of labour has always characterized the fur trade economy, men and women were seen as unequally participating in a common endeavour. Now hunting 'bands', highly modified and barely recognizable as overlapping networks of partnerships, continue to exist without women, but women are the links between partners.[25] Women are increasingly thrown together into a new category which is not entirely of their making, but which they are recognizing as their unique role.

Conclusion

An examination of 'traditional' Sekani kinship nomenclature reveals both lineal and bilateral features, although a glance at modern English usages suggest that only the bilateral features have survived. The inheritance of patronymics, however, still follows patrilineal lines. Sekani social behaviour also reveals features which can be linked to both a lineal and bilateral type of 'kinship' universe. Bilaterality is usually associated with great flexibility in the formation of ties. This surfaces as a tendency to form associations beyond the limits of the patronymic category. On the other hand, an examination of the partnership system reveals that exclusivity is also favoured. This exclusivity is manifested as a tendency to favour ties traced through a man's own domestic group of origin even after he is married and well established as a hunter. Hence, the domestic group continues as the network of reference even after it has virtually ceased to exist as a cohesive and recognizable group.

In sum, the Sekani have a well-defined pattern of ambiguity in their social life, and this pattern is as paradoxical as the phrase "well-defined ambiguity" is oxymoronic. The Sekani, for example, also favour patrilineal inheritance in theory and in fact, with its concomitant restrictions of the resultant networks. At the same time they favour extending ties widely but, paradoxically, they accomplish this by reinforcing ties that link a man and his sisters in the category 'domestic group of origin'. Hence, lineality is stressed, albeit in a weak and somewhat ambiguous manner. The dialectical qualities of Sekani social life are also manifested in the relations between the sexes. The formation of networks through partnerships and marriages engages the Sekani definition of the self insofar as men continue to define themselves as hunters. In doing so they engage at least two distinctions, since there are two types of partnership links between men: junior and senior partners linked through ties traced through relationships based on the domestic group of origin and those based on ties traced through the domestic group of marriage. Furthermore, this antagonistic closeness is also expressed in the change in a woman's surname at her marriage. This reinforces the autonomy and solidarity of the domestic group of marriage while subordinating the importance of the woman's necessary contribution to its survival as an independent entity – a survival which ironically initially depends on a man forming ties with other men through his wife.

An increase in the supply of money has affected the relations between men and women, although this change has not been revolutionary by any means. Women stay in the community and form a self-recognized residential core. Men are more committed to the bush and even use money from other sources to finance this continued participation. Hence the genders play separate roles, or at least the differences in power between men and women that the older men alluded to are being maintained. There is a gender-based tension which, while not caused by the influx of money and other recent changes of this type, is certainly associated with the modern sector. None the less, the presence of lineal and bilateral features in the traditional nomenclature suggests that the tension that is engaged in relationships is linked to an older cultural tradition.

The apparent inconsistency between the use of a modern English bilateral terminology and modern social practice with its many non-bilateral traits can be resolved by noting that the patronymic category includes at least one affinally traced partnership category which has no English equivalent (*klaze*, ZHu). In sum, the Sekani have readily adopted English usages because they have adopted an English 'kinship' trait, patronymic surnames. This reflects their continued interest with establishing partnership ties, and although the importance of the patronymic category is obvious in this regard, no immediate reason from the modern data suggests itself to account for its importance.

The lineal and bilateral tendencies within Sekani social structure indicate the simultaneous presence of two distinct and opposed tendencies. These traits are not sufficiently explainable by strict reference to the current system of social relations and economic conditions. Furthermore, it is likely that the tension between men and women, the simultaneous presence of two opposing strands in the social structure and the continued reliance on non-bilateral and non-genealogical categories used in the formation of networks all point to a strong and continued presence of an older cultural tradition. It is a tradition that has perhaps emerged in some ways in a more abstract form, as pan-Indian brotherhood. And, as we shall see, this tradition can be located in a more coherent form in the history of contact and confrontation with other surrounding tribal groups in the nineteenth century.

Notes

1. An effort has been made in table 4.1 to compare the three lists where possible. Jenness's list contains a typographical error in term number five which has been corrected. No information is available on how Honigmann collected his list. Father Petitot's dictionary, published in 1876, is another source, but the Montagnais ('Mountain') Indians referred to are likely not Sekani ('people of the rocks') but a branch of the Slavey. See J. Michael, 'Les Chitra-Gottineke: essai de monographie d'un groupe Athapascan des Montagnes Rocheuses', Ottawa, *National Museum Bulletin* 190: 49–93, 1963. J.J. Honigmann, *The Kaska Indians: An Ethnographic Reconstruction*, Yale University Publications in Anthropology No. 51, New Haven: Yale University Press, 1954; D. Jenness, *The Sekani Indians of British Columbia*, Ottawa: National Museum of Canada, Bulletin No. 84, 1937, p. 52.

2. English is the everyday language of Fort Ware and McLeod Lake. The situation is surprising because of the relative isolation of these communities.

3. Early unresolved problems in the classification of Athabaskan kinship nomenclature can be traced back to Spier, who in 1925 proposed the Mackenzie Basin Type, in which parallel and cross cousins were not distinguished. The creation of this new category was inspired by attempts to classify kinship systems by their cousin terms, originally proposed by Morgan. Jenness made no attempt to categorize the Sekani classificatory system, other than labelling it "simple". Much of his information on the Sekani came from A.G. Morice's work, *The Western Denes, their Manners and Customs* (The Canadian Institute, Proceedings for

1888–1889, vol. 7, 1890), although there is no real evidence to suggest that Jenness failed to collect his own list of terms. Unfortunately Jenness translated the terms into what he regarded as their English equivalents without specifying the genealogical positions that each term could encompass. The implication remains, therefore, that Sekani terms are much like English (bilateral) terms. Although Murdock apparently used Jenness as his source, he drew very different conclusions than what the cautious Jenness had implied. Murdock described the Sekani as possessing bilateral descent – which is not accurate – with Hawaiian cousin terms (the Sekani do merge cross and parallel cousins). He claims they had no clans or "demes", no moieties or kindreds, a bilateral extension of the incest taboo to all first cousins and some sororal polygyny. All of these latter data are more or less consistent with Jenness. Just how the Sekani are supposed to have defined social boundaries is hard to say, however, since they seem to have been accorded very little with which to work. Furthermore, while commenting on Sekani terminological patterns, Murdock fails to note the interesting and certainly odd Sekani pattern in which women differ from men in their use of terms for nepotic kin. This, plus his insistence on the lack of kindreds (there is a clear association between societies with Hawaiian terms and a ban on first cousin marriage on the one hand and the presence of kindreds on the other) leads one to wonder just how closely Murdock or his assistants read Jenness. Honigmann's conclusions were just as general as Jenness's though not as demonstratively wrong as Murdock's. He points out that the taxonomic pattern exhibited with Sekani terms is related to particular social structural features commonly associated with bifurcate merging terminologies: the levirate, sororal polygyny and sister exchange as the dominant form of marriage. Sister exchange is also correlated with the terminological identity between brother's children and husband's sister's children. I have been unable to find any evidence, however, for sister exchange, either in the literature or among Sekani informants. See Honigmann, *The Kaska Indians*, p. 83. J. Helm, 'Kin Terms of the Arctic Drainage Dene: Hare, Slavey, Chipewyan', *American Anthropologist* 62: 279–385, 1960. L.H. Morgan, *Systems of Consanguinity and Affinity of the Human Family*, Smithsonian Contributions to Knowledge 17: 1–590, Washington: Smithsonian Institution, 1871. G.P. Murdock, *Social Structure*, New York: Macmillan 1949, pp. 230, 371. Jenness, *The Sekani Indians*, p. 37. Morice, *The Western Denes*. L. Spier, 'The Distribution of Kinship Systems in North America', *University of Washington Publications in Anthropology* 1: 69–88, 1925. Honigmann, *The Kaska Indians*, p. 81 footnote.

4. By this is meant the Sekani idea of genealogy, which follows the generally accepted biological facts.

5. On motives and forms of changes in Sekani and English, see G. Lanoue, 'Language Loss, Language Gain: Cultural Camouflage and Social Change Among the Sekani of Northern British Columbia', *Language in Society* 20(1): 87–115, 1991.

6. J. VanStone, *Athapaskan Adaptations: Hunters and Fishermen of the Subarctic Forests*, Chicago: Aldine, 1974, p. 87.

7. Ibid.

8. A line was purchased by the Department of Indian Affairs sometime in 1961. It was then re-assigned to a Fort Grahame/Ingenika resident. He died in 1976. Two Ingenika residents attempted to obtain the line by applying to the Department. Their connection to the deceased is unknown, but they did share the same patronymic and one referred to the deceased as his "uncle". However, both were partners with a third man who already owned a trapline. Their claim was disallowed. The Chief of Ingenika wrote to the Department and suggested that the line go to a "relative". This presumably meant someone in the deceased man's immediate family. The Department usually re-assigned traplines on this basis in any case. The person who was nominated by the Chief at Ingenika was not interested, however. This fact must have been known to the Chief, who was apparently trying to keep the line under the jurisdiction of Ingenika despite the lack of an obvious heir. The Chief then pressed the case of the two whose initial claim has been refused. The line was re-assigned to a Fort Ware resident "in consultation with the Chief". The man was a recent newcomer who had married a Fort Ware woman. He was highly regarded in Fort Ware by other hunters, especially because he was a "good worker". After his marriage he had immediately formed several strong partnerships in the community.

9. It is noteworthy that conflict is handled by separate mechanisms and not by denying access to traplines and houses as punishment. If someone is consistently branded as a troublemaker, people may do several things. They may expel the person by means of a direct order by the Chief and Council (I only know of cases of men being expelled; women also leave, but they apparently anticipate unacceptable situations more than men). This is for a predetermined time. They may also ask the police to step in. If, on the other hand, a person breaks a civil law which is not part of community values, people will protect a person by refusing to cooperate with the police. Since there are no police permanently stationed in Fort Ware, the absence of corroborating witnesses (apart from the plaintiffs) makes it impossible to lay any charges or to press these charges if they are laid. Third, people may choose to kill an offender. I collected no direct evidence, but there was talk of this measure being used in several cases in the past. In this case (and in the cases of all homicide; this information I collected directly) the decision is left up to an individual and sanctioned (or not) by the community after, not before, the fact. This tradition makes all killing a dangerous event, regardless of how many "good" reasons the killer (and usually his family) accumulate, since revenge is always a real possibility.

10. Following Sekani logic, FZ represents a link which FZHu could use to press some sort of claim on Sekani-owned resources, while FBWi is the counterpart tie which the Sekani can use to press claims on resources owned by FBWi's group. By recognizing FBWi as part of 'their' group (whether this is the patronymic network or the Sekani as a whole), potential claims by FBWiB or FZHu are weakened.

11. This is also reflected in the preponderance of links traced through a primary consanguine relative. There are nine such links, traced through either a brother or through sons.

12. It is difficult to locate unambiguous expressions of some of these opposed tendencies in modern Sekani terminology, unless the absence of a corresponding term for DHu (sanase) is taken as evidence of an older man's concern with maintaining his domestic group by bringing young men into it. Ego's SWi, therefore, is more important to S than she is to ego, because the partnerships which ego's son forms through his marriage help establish his independence from his father. Ego's daughter, however, brings people into partnership with her father. Similarly, the wide range of partnerships associated with uslah – people linked to ego by virtue of his marriage – reflects the importance of partnerships formed in a man's early productive years.

13. This is another clear example of the guiding role of Sekani ideology, which is in striking contrast to the accepted 'wisdom' in which men compete for women. See, for example, M. Harris, Culture, People, Nature, New York: Harper and Row, 1980, p. 489.

14. In McLeod Lake, for example, the last marriage was contracted in 1974. Since that time at least four children have been born outside of any marriage or permanent union. There are several permanent unions in which there are children but which are not legal marriages. The Sekani are, for the most part, traditional Catholics and now see marriage in legal terms; that is, within the church. In Fort Ware, there were two households where the mothers had never lived with a man. According to informants and to the literature, this would not have been possible in the past. Some Fort Ware people blame the Canadian government, which provides money to women in this situation, for this state of affairs.

15. Jenness, The Sekani Indians, p. 54.

16. Too few cases of infidelity were known to allow any conclusions to emerge. Two cases were often talked about by Fort Ware residents, however. Both involved the death of one spouse, although neither death was of an unfaithful partner. Nothing but the fact that these people had been killed could be verified (including the circumstances of their deaths). Possibly these cases are remembered and talked of because of the social drama involved in each case, not because of the infidelity per se.

17. The newly emerging division between men and women resembles the general traits of many other northern Indian communities. Helm and Leacock offer a five-part typology of settlement patterns in the subarctic, in which the male/female split is one of two major traits which are presently emerging. This is related to the decline of the fur trade and to the infusion of government subsidies that replace lost trapping income. This is accelerated, imply Helm and Leacock, by government-subsidized housing which encourages people to choose semi-permanent residence in a community rather than life in the bush. They do not say why this should be a factor in the change, however,

since there were Sekani-built homes that people used as temporary shelters before the government started offering subsidized housing. See J. Helm and E.B. Leacock, 'The Hunting Tribes of Subarctic Canada', in E.B. Leacock and N.O. Lurie, eds, *North American Indians in Historical Perspective*, New York: Random House, 1971, pp. 362, 363.

18. One noteworthy case involved a young Fort Ware man caught in a triangle formed by his wishes, his mother's and those of his "sweetheart" (the usual Sekani term). The mother strongly disapproved of his prospective match on the grounds that the girl was involved with another man. None the less the marriage went ahead with the blessing of the man's father, who had the last say in the matter.

19. This includes giving meat from the hunt, collecting and chopping firewood for winter use, but rarely does it include gifts of money.

20. Jenness, *The Sekani Indians*, pp. 54, 55.

21. The setting up of a household is less important than the social and political implications of his marriage. Hence, it is easy to understand why Morice describes Sekani marriage as a lackadaisical affair. Morice, 'La femme chez les Dénés', *Proceedings, International Congress of Americanists*, 15th session, vol. 1, 1906, p. 274.

22. There is only one case within the last several years of a Fort Ware man going elsewhere to find a bride. He did not stay long in his in-laws' village, however. If this is any indication, young men spend little or no time in the household of their intended spouse. Some men have mentioned that they spend a long time in a foreign village in order to become "accepted", but they do not specifically refer to their future wife's family.

23. Jenness, *The Sekani Indians*, p. 52.

24. From 1940 to 1949, eight marriages were recorded; from 1950 to 1959, seventeen marriages were recorded; from 1960 to 1969, three marriages were recorded; from 1970 to 1978, two marriages were recorded.

25. In only one case did a man go trapping with his entire family and never with a partner. This man does not live in the community itself, but several miles away. Nor does he possess legal Indian status, although this counts for little in comparison to the fact that he was allegedly involved in a serious dispute with a Fort Ware resident several years ago. Since he has little interaction with other residents, I did not include him in table 4.3. Another man without partnerships is in a different position. He is well liked and respected by other residents, but several factors are at play here. First, he is a former Fort Grahame resident who was displaced by the flooding. His trapline (which was not flooded) is at the northernmost tip of Williston Lake, at the southernmost extent of Fort Ware territory. This distance may be a factor. Second, he prefers to trap alone with his family. In fact, he basically lives on his trapline and visits Fort Ware. He maintains partnerships with men in Ingenika. He did most of his trading for supplies at Ingenika. These factors suggest that he is not part of the Fort Ware community as such.

Chapter 5

Political Culture and Its Expressions

There seems to be a convention in scholarly work that an argument can be carefully crafted in response to particular contentions in the literature or it can address more implicit issues that are sometimes called 'conventional wisdom'. This may be in response to the fact that the field is too ebullient to contain a commonly shared language of discourse among its practitioners. Or, alternatively, the writer may find that his thesis is cast in too unconventional a manner to address particular arguments within the field. The more unconventional the argument, in other words, the more the writer may feel constrained to address larger philosophical issues that may be the only points of shared experience his audience recognizes. When dealing with situations of capitalist eruption in previously tribal areas, somewhat like the Sekani case, the urge to address the issue of how the juggernaut of competitive monopoly capitalism operates on the fringes of the larger market economy can become overwhelming since, as conventional Marxist theories tell us, the internal contradictions of capitalism are more obvious as the normal mediating mechanisms fail to find ideological support in the local popular culture. Hence, for a long time we were presented with, if not books and articles, doctoral theses that made the requisite obeisant trip down the path of structural Marxism: studies of how peasants adjust their 'mode of production' to accord with capitalist requirements, of how African cultivators and New Guinea highlands tribesmen are little more than peasants and capitalists after all since they are, respectively, either oppressed by market conditions or successfully manage their meager resources with a view to increasing their capital stock of pigs. Such arguments are neither right nor wrong. They are simply viewpoints of lesser or greater usefulness in understanding what happens when change is sudden and dramatic. We know, in other words, that alienation is a normal product of capitalism and so we would strain credulity if we were to interpret recent increases in alcoholism, homicide, child abuse and the like as anything else than examples of what happens when normal 'superstructural' mechanisms of adjustment are no longer meaningful when people are presented with a new and ineluctable but none the less historically determined economic regime. On the other hand, it is clear that people have some control, no matter how constrained, over the forms and meanings involved in changes of this type. To describe the psychology of oppression, if that is indeed our initial definition of the situation, may require a different starting point if the analysis is to move beyond already well-accepted banalities. The problem of ethnographic description (meaning, 'explanation according to commonly held conventions') is deeply attached to what the observer believes to be the appropriate model of social and cultural dynamics.

That the current political culture of McLeod Lake and Fort Ware is clearly linked to the dynamic of the recent and very drastic changes in the local economy is obvious. The flooding of large areas of hunting and trapping territory, the creation less than thirty miles away of a new community of 5,000 workers devoted to stripping the land of its trees, and the imposition of a local branch of the federal bureaucracy – in brief, all of the changes associated with the incorporation of the southern Sekani into the Canadian economic frontier – have resulted in the breakdown and re-ordering of social categories and networks in McLeod Lake and, to a lesser extent, in Fort Ware. Given the obviousness of the situation, it would be tempting to treat capitalist hegemony as the given and see how it adapts to a local environment, its protocol for social relationships interpreted and otherwise given a meaningful form in an alien cultural and ideological context. Even the details of the upheaval lend themselves to such a viewpoint. One particularly significant trait in this context is the emergence of pan-Indian sentiments in McLeod Lake; this and other related changes are fairly typical of many other Indian groups in Canada facing similar economic circumstances. None the less, it is noteworthy that the process I have labelled 'breakdown and re-ordering' has, to a surprising extent, been consistent with Sekani political traditions. While not entirely lacking merit, the adoption of a ready-made model of social and cultural change would therefore hide the functioning of a long-term evolutionary dynamic that, in the end, corresponds very little to categories and processes of change as anthropologists usually understand them. Most prominent among these traditions has been the idea of uniting people by using the notion of brotherhood; by positing identity based on a category that is not immediately tied to everyday conditions, in other words. Before examining this tradition more closely, its contemporary expression should be examined in more detail.

The Local Context

The first evidence of universalism in McLeod Lake arose during my attempts to elicit terms of relationship. Since the McLeod Lake community is so small, virtually all people within the same generation level are related to one another, if we use 'related' as meaning the sharing of identifiable consanguineal links. While people do not use relationship terms that publicly acknowledge the consanguineal net (any one person divides the community into two halves, 'friends' and 'family'), their English-language usage of relationship terms does not distinguish first from second cousins. Consequently, nearly everyone in the category 'family' stands as cousin to one another. It soon became apparent, however, that genealogical closeness within the acknowledged 'kinship' network and its implicit unity was by far not the only significant expression of universalism among the Sekani.

Descriptions of economic activity and ideological rationalizations, in the sense of 'accepted ways of proceeding', were also vague as to internal boundaries. For example, trapping in McLeod Lake is a minor activity by almost any set of standards, whether measured by time expended, money invested, returns generated or efforts at planning. None the less, people consistently stated that anyone could trap or hunt anywhere, at any time and with anyone as a partner. "Everyone" received a share of the meat from a kill, people insisted. Universalist answers of this type were also offered when questions were asked about alliances between people, about obtaining permission to use land registered to another person, and even when questions were posed about the ownership of various parcels of land. It was clearly stated that no one could stop any other person in the band from hunting on another's trapline; some even said that people could trap anywhere, although these people were not themselves trappers. People were said to be subject only to those regulations issued by the Fish and Wildlife Branch of the provincial government. Ironically, as people well know, these regulations apply to everyone. Although people no doubt wholeheartedly believed in these sentiments and despite the fact that much of this complex

is strongly evocative of traditional expressions of personal autonomy, the fact remains that there was little in the way of any
activity which could contradict or gainsay these statements.
Although there were plenty of moose in the vicinity and nearly
everyone had access to a freezer for the storage of meat, and
despite the easy access to the bush by way of logging roads,
there was little hunting by members of the community during
my stay.

Despite this seeming lack of differentiation, universalist sentiments have not given rise to a consistent political programme
that reflects a concern with unity, either within the community
or with other Indian groups. At first I thought this might be due
to inconsistencies in these sentiments when they are taken as a
coherent body of thought. People had, I thought, unsophisticated
responses to the very complex problems they faced. The lack of
discriminatory criteria in statements like, "People used to share
everything before the Whites came", and "Indians were all com-
munists before the Whites came", I took at first to be simple
mindedness. Only later did I realize that these blanket condemna-
tions of Whites and the accompanying panaceas (for example,
"we'll go and live in the bush and shoot any White who comes
after us") were more or less deliberately left vague. This was
later clear when the seriousness of the militancy behind these
statements was taken at face value, but at first this philosophy
seemed like an attempt to diffuse their problems by placing them
in a larger and somewhat vaguer context.

Pan-Indian sentiments are linked to southern political ideas
which filter into McLeod Lake by various means. One source of
these intrusive doctrines was readily apparent: the education,
political activity and sympathies of some of the younger members of the community exposed them to pan-Indian literature
from the United States.[1] These ideas were usually commented
upon favourably and provided a context for discussions of particular difficulties. Younger politicized people tended to espouse
a pan-Indian political stance as a ready-made goal. Although
much of the material in these publications does not specifically
expound pan-Indianism, the content serves to focus attention
on the importance of political action within government insti-
tutions. Hence, there is a new idea in the air; not only do problems arise from contact with the outside world, their solutions
require an engagement beyond the confines of the community.
To the extent that their content serves to generate discussion that
would be difficult in older forms of discourse, these periodicals
are not critically evaluated by the McLeod Lake Sekani who read

them. They provide a viable explanation and validation of recent events, given the increasingly obvious limitations of traditional political responses and the blatant similarity between conditions in McLeod Lake and the conditions of Native people in developing countries. The parallels between the recent reversals of the Sekani and those experienced by other groups are rather close and, therefore, suggestive. Comments in these publications, which stress the confrontational aspect of Indian–White relations, are accepted as forming the groundwork of a new and broader definition of Indianness.

The perception that threats to the Sekani way of life came from the outside had two results. First, it lifted the constraints on thinking which might otherwise have been engaged in analysing the situation. Once it was accepted that this was a new and in some sense uncontrollable occurrence, the road was paved for the acceptance of new ideas, or at least a new form of discourse. Second, this militant attitude specifically sowed the seed for the rhetoric of modern pan-Indian militancy. Militancy was believed to be an effective counterthrust which could alleviate the recent misfortunes of McLeod Lake residents.[2]

The predisposition to accept militancy is easily understandable in light of recent Sekani history. People's awareness of the inequalities between Indians and Whites has increased as a result of the recent arrival of large numbers of Southern Whites who have had no previous contact with Indians or whose previous exposure to them in the urban South has merely confirmed a sense of prejudice, judging from their casual statements. This situation is exacerbated by the hiring policy of several firms in the region.[3] They have, of course, actively recruited workers from the South instead of passively waiting for workers to arrive on their doorstep. The twenty-fold increase in the local White population is composed of many people who have what might be called, with charity, a narrowly focussed viewpoint on the world; without roots in either the new or their former community, feelings of competitiveness surface easily. These workers also happened to see the McLeod Lake people at one of the worst times in their history, with a high level of violence and a general disorientation in confrontation with the new regime. This either confirmed or inculcated unsympathetic attitudes towards the Sekani.

The Sekani pose an additional discomfiting paradox to the new arrivals. Because they compose in many ways an instant and somewhat artificial community, the White residents of the town of Mackenzie consciously attempt to create and foster new traditions and symbols. One such instant tradition which was adopted is the image of the northern frontiersman. Many Mackenzie residents invariably see themselves as 'roughing it' in the North (many categories of workers get a special 'northern allowance' designed to offset high costs). There is, of course, a realistic basis to this idea in that many of the workers have arrived from the long settled and urbanized South, so the slightest difference in living conditions is amplified to fit the image. None the less, the presence of the Sekani serves as an uncomfortable reminder that this pose is fiction; the Sekani were obviously the first 'frontiersmen', and their standard of living even today makes the workers' affluence obvious. For their part, many of the Sekani were eager to adopt an attitude that outsiders were a threat to them. This was hardly stretching the truth. From the Sekani viewpoint many of these new workers are living and working on land which, until about ten years before, was constantly used by the Sekani.

In sum, many sentiments held by the Sekani are universalist and pan-Indian since they depend on an idyllic interpretation of a past not marked by overt conflict, an idyllic misrepresentation where unity reigned in the absence of an identifiable common enemy, nor do these sentiments refer to the particular qualities of the people involved. They are universalist in the sense of positing a unity – a brotherhood based on social and political solidarity – among the Sekani in the past, the present and a possible future. They are associated with a militant attitude aimed at self-preservation. Ironically, this militancy does not result in united political action.

Pan-Indianism

Used in this context pan-Indianism can be defined as the belief in the unity of all contemporary Indian people, whatever their prior differences. It is associated with a belief that Indians are faced with the threat of cultural extinction at the hands of those elements of the larger society in which Indian society is embedded. "Historically", says Hertzberg in her study of American pan-Indian movements, "American Indians have reacted to alien penetration both in tribal terms and in the assertion of a wider Indian identity."[4] There is some justification for assuming that when faced with possible threats to long-term survival people publicly assert their unity, perhaps in an effort not so much to tell outsiders of their presence as to convince themselves that they have a chance at survival.

Quimby, in his study of the cultural history of the Indians of the upper Great Lakes, uses the term 'pan-Indian' to refer to the increase in uniformity among these tribes as a result of the growing predominance of the fur trade in the region between approximately 1760 and 1820.[5] Since the Chippewa (Ojibwa) were the group most favoured by the conditions of trade, it was their cultural traits which in large part supplanted those of other Great Lakes tribes such as the Ottawa, Menomeni and Winnebago.[6] This early instance of the development of pan-Indianism is largely spontaneous, distinct from the later deliberate attempt to forge a rhetoric and a specific type of political expression aimed at fostering Indian unity and political effectiveness. What this earlier movement had in common with later forms, however, is the fact that unity developed as a response to a crisis initiated by an increase in foreign domination of the economic domain. Modern movements also aim at fostering a common material culture of symbolism, albeit a culture that is very circumscribed in expression and limited to such obvious symbols of Indianness as jewellery, clothing and some religious and quasi-religious rites. The Canadian situation is no different than its United States counterpart in this respect.[7]

In this sense it is incorrect to speak of the recent development of a pan-Indian response. Pan-Indianism has existed since at least the turn of the century in an ideologically coherent form. McNickle places the date of the modern and still extant version in 1961, the year of the University of Chicago conference which dealt with problems of modern Indians.[8] He dates the inception of the Canadian movement at 1969, particularly as a response to the government's policy of the time which disavowed the development of a separate Indian identity.[9] McLeod Lake pan-Indianism, therefore, may be seen as the trend of adopting an already prevalent attitude and political pose. However, it is also an indigenous political response in the sense that it has developed in a particular context and is thus expressed in a manner that is specific to the people of McLeod Lake. This is especially true as regards one of the most important themes of pan-Indianism, the brotherhood of all Indian people.

Pan-Indianism also contains a component of social levelling which is paradoxically associated with a strong sense of identification with the community. Unification with other Indian groups is said to be based on a relationship of identity; hence, there is a widespread sense among McLeod Lakers that all Indians are equal. Yet at the same time McLeod Lake pan-Indianism has accentuated the trends towards division as well as unification that exist within the community. McLeod Lakers are reticent in establishing political ties to non-Sekani Indians, despite strong avowals that they ought to do so, nor are they particularly welcoming towards non-resident Sekani. The stronger the sense of obligatory political unification with non-Sekani, the stronger the statements about unity within the band. Clearly, pan-Indianism cannot be understood as a simple political philosophy in its own terms. One the one hand, the behavioural expression of pan-Indianism is associated with a strong and exclusive sense of the singularity of McLeod Lake as a category unto itself. On the other hand, there is an unequivocal assertion of unity and in a common identity that derive from membership in a single overriding category. This aspect of pan-Indianism can be labelled 'universalism', for want of a better term.

By 'universalism' is meant the a priori denial of discriminatory patterns brought to bear in the formulation of social and political poses. As such, the term is used here in a fashion somewhat reminiscent of the way in which it is used by positivist writers such as Levy and Parsons.[10] Their definitions and usages point to a broadening of the criteria used for membership and recruitment since admission to a group or network is removed from the particular qualities of the individuals involved. As such, universalism tacitly encourages an increase in the internal solidarity of groups since any differentiation within the group must be based on criteria or processes other than those used as a basis by which the group is formed. By definition, all members in a group using objective criteria must be the same. On the other hand, this solidarity is qualified for two reasons. First, unity is proposed by stressing adherence to a rather intangible quality, brotherhood, rather than a more visible and measurable quality; second, the change from highly visible and practically-based work associations to vague categories engages a different way of looking at the world. Solidarity, as such, does not depend on the positive characteristics of the individuals as much as it does on the things they do not do. For example, there is no material expression of pan-Indian solidarity but only an attempt at political unanimity. 'Solidarity' in this context refers to what can be described as a weakened form of group coherence despite the strength of sentiment attached to this political stance. 'Universalism' is not used here to imply that there is a causal relationship between the code or ethic and a particular type of social action or political stance. It simply refers to a lack of discrimination in arriving at particular categories. I use the term descriptively rather than offering it as an explanation for particular thoughts and actions. Universalism, in other words, is a code or ethic which, although not necessarily finding expression in Sekani political action or ideology as such, is used as an underlying principle in formulating particular social structural configurations. As a category that provides a basis for the expression of political solidarity, it is inherently unstable because its strength and applicability depend very much on a situation where people do not do anything, that is, engage by their actions other categories that could acknowledge or strengthen the differences between them.

The Regional Context

Pan-Indian sentiments were not as widely spread among the youth of Fort Ware. This is ironic, since it is precisely in Fort Ware that the McLeod Lake pan-Indianists seek their partners in this new vision. Such partnership is important by definition since the brotherhood of all Indians is a necessary theme in McLeod Lake pan-Indianism. Fort Ware is particularly important since it is the only other Sekani community that maintained its viability after the flooding.

Fort Ware people had been tied to McLeod Lakers by several marriages in the past, though only one such link exists today. Both groups play up the significance of this one instance. Communication between the two was also more intense in the past, for McLeod Lakers often went hunting towards the north while Fort Ware and Ingenika residents came south for supplies. The distance between the two communities, today seen as an important limiting factor in travel, had less significance in an era when villages were merely nodal points in a continuum of residence and travel along the valley of the Parsnip and Finlay Rivers. Differences between the two communities have always existed. Paradoxically, this is still acknowledged by residents of McLeod Lake, who none the less continue to see the residents of Fort Ware as potential allies in their struggles. Unfortunately for McLeod Lake pan-Indianists, the aftershocks of the flooding sharpened the differences between the two communities. These were largely focussed on the 130-mile-long lake which separated them.

Navigation by small boats is now no longer safe due to the size of the lake and to the vast amounts of debris floating on its surface.[11] This debris jams the channel at the northern end of the lake, at the mouth of the Finlay River. The logs are pushed into huge driftpiles by the wind. Transportation is therefore now largely limited to air travel between Fort Ware and either Prince George or Mackenzie. The cost is too high for any but the most serious reasons for travel. Another consequence of this change is the increased cost of shipping food and other supplies to Fort Ware. When navigation by small boats had been possible Fort Grahame and Fort Ware residents obtained their supplies at a trading post near the point where the Finlay and Parsnip Rivers join to form the Peace River (near the site of Fort Grahame). The cost of running a small boat in order to get supplies was in part offset by the other uses to which a boat could be turned. These costs were not regarded as part of the price of goods, since subsidiary but necessary tasks were performed while travelling to get supplies; supplying traplines, communication with neighbours and of course hunting along the shore were all important. Now all transport costs are directly incorporated in the price of food, while boat maintenance is a separate item in the household budget. Boats, of course, are still extensively used for hunting and supplying traplines. McLeod Lake residents, on the other hand, have been unaffected by difficult navigation insofar as the price of food is concerned. They have been supplied by highway since at least 1954. Their food costs, if anything, have decreased as a result of the economies of scale which accompanied the opening up of large markets in Mackenzie. At the very least, the rate of increase in prices was certainly much less than that of Fort Ware.[12]

Perhaps the most important change to emerge recently has been the different rates of violence in the two communities. When violence increased in McLeod Lake residents of Fort Ware added another dimension to their views about McLeod Lakers: they were not to be trusted. Since pan-Indian sentiments in McLeod Lake include a definition of Indian identity which gains its strength and clarity in opposition to Whites, violence almost naturally surfaces as people increase their contact with the White world and frustrations accumulate. This is not the complete story, however.[13]

Many younger McLeod Lakers stereotype Whites as violent. This is not far from the truth, in relative terms, since many of the younger Whites in the vicinity are troublesome and occasionally violent. In fact, the only Whites with whom many of the younger McLeod Lakers come into contact are young men in search of 'drinking buddies', fights and women. If Indianness is in part defined in confrontational terms then violence among Indians inevitably follows when people come into contact with 'tough' Whites. Not surprisingly, many younger Sekani openly state that they are "tougher" than Whites, "wilder" (uncontrolled) and more prone to rash and impetuous acts of violence.[14] The local tradition holds that violence is always caused by the victim, that is, violence is merely a response to a provocation. In the long run this is true even of the tough stance taken by McLeod Lakers *vis-à-vis* Whites but it never translates into direct action; the belief is a more accurate description of Sekani fights. It is however, a good metaphor for the situation in McLeod Lake, since 'toughness' is a response to frustration caused by the White world.

In brief, these points serve to focus attention on the differences between McLeod Lake and Fort Ware. Despite some attempts at unification in order to coordinate a regionally-based response to problems associated with the flooding, reasons are found to explain why such cooperation has not or cannot take place. The basic reason, of course, is that the two communities have different problems and concerns, despite their common source. Practical action invariably focuses on particular problems, and the end result is a further entrenchment of the differences between the two communities. Residents of Fort Ware, for example, are concerned with clearing the lake of the debris which hinders transportation and which, as I have mentioned above, significantly increases their food bills. McLeod Lakers, on the other hand, have no practical concerns with the lake. For them it is a focus of political discourse. They are concerned with the long-term social effects rather than with the mundane. Unlike Fort Ware people, they have mixed feelings about the lake since they could easily get jobs as loggers if they so wished.

Paradoxically, attitudes towards wage labour do not match the relative costs of goods in an expected manner. Wage labour is considered necessary by most McLeod Lakers, despite the relative cheapness of store-bought food. This usually takes the form of part-time work on community projects. In Fort Ware this type of work is considered a supplement, a means of obtaining some cash during the summer months when there is little else to do. Unlike McLeod Lake, Fort Ware hunters are more eager to pursue options involving the bush. Apart from the obvious difference in focus, such activity validates the more traditional values of Fort Ware residents; not only is the land used but social relationships are sustained in terms of bush activities, a theme developed in the previous chapter.

Obtaining the required funding for community projects is handled differently in each case since the size of the cash economy varies tremendously in each community. Since their cash needs are relatively smaller, the Fort Ware Band Council can afford to be more judicious in selecting the projects it desires. There is usually not enough labour available to complete the projects, even those that are deemed necessary (as opposed to 'make-economy' or, to be more accurate, 'cash generators'). Most activity of this type in Fort Ware centres around building government-subsidized houses and maintaining necessities such as the airstrip. McLeod Lake, on the other hand, needs these projects to increase the general level of income. Such activity is decidedly 'make-work' in terms of the stated goal of the project; usefulness is not an enabling criterion here. In 1978 and 1979, for example, McLeod Lakers undertook to build a large hostel for visitors to the Reserve. No one seriously believed that the Reserve needed such a structure since the few visitors who visit stay with their relatives. Another example: one man was paid $10.00 a day to bring five children to the school bus stop one half mile distant. As a source of income, especially for needy families, these activities are in fact necessary.[15] These projects are also considered important in McLeod Lake because the members of the Band Council believe they help foster a sense of unity in the community. Welfare is seen as a destructive force by nearly everyone, and it is thought preferable that people cooperate by working together.[16] It is noteworthy that I never heard anyone argue against welfare in terms of its effect on individual initiative, a familiar enough argument in southern newspapers, for example. It was always the entire group – either "Indians" or "us" – who were said to be negatively affected.

All of these differences point to the fact that each group has different standards in evaluating behaviour. Fort Ware residents tend to emphasize proficiency in the bush as a measure of a man's status. These skills are not well-developed among young McLeod Lakers, however. Fort Ware residents sometimes ironically compared McLeod Lakers to Whites; both were said to be like children in the bush. In reality, quite a few of the older McLeod Lakers have bush skills comparable to those of the Fort Ware residents. When questioned, Fort Ware residents could name only two instances in which a McLeod Laker's bush skills were said to be noticeably deficient. Infrequent contact between the two groups amplifies the belief that all McLeod Lakers are more or less the same in this respect.

The emergent social boundary between the two communities was far from one-sided. Despite the prevalent pan-Indianism at McLeod Lake, many people insisted on creating boundaries between themselves and their Fort Ware "brothers". Many thought that the people of the north were cruder, somewhat akin to our idea of 'hicks'. They were said to live in the bush out of necessity. The lack of modern conveniences such as electricity in Fort Ware was taken as an indicator of a lack of social progress.[17] Ironically, the most vociferous proponents of this derisory view were also the loudest advocates of a revivalistic brand of pan-Indianism. The same type of comments are made of Ingenika people who occasionally reside on the Parsnip Reserve near the town of Mackenzie. Most Fort Ware residents rarely meet McLeod Lakers, so their reservations are more gently expressed.

In sum, the pan-Indian sentiments in McLeod Lake are associated with universalism which, however, is exclusively restricted in its application to the community itself. This limited catholicism, particularly when coupled to the virtual absence of definable and clear patterns of productive activity which might otherwise engage a variety of distinct categories, results in the denial of the existence of divisions – whether political, social or cultural – within the McLeod Lake Band. This solidarity produces a uniqueness which strengthens the sense of isolation McLeod Lakers feel towards other Sekani, and certainly towards non-Sekani. It is obvious that differences between McLeod Lake and Fort Ware are relatively trivial, yet are amplified and elaborated in order to re-establish a boundary already weakened by pan-Indianism. This is as true of the local level as it is of the regional level.

Categories and Boundaries in McLeod Lake

Despite the overt denial of boundaries which is engaged in (or implied in) any discussion of the straightforward expression of pan-Indian sentiments, boundaries of another sort not only emerge in the community they are emphasized in other, non-ideological, contexts. Ironically, these boundaries are often more tangible than the relatively artificial boundaries that McLeod Lakers impose between themselves and the outside world. And despite the notion of brotherhood implicit in pan-Indianism, the most immediate and striking feature of social behaviour in McLeod Lake was violence. The blatant contradiction between the pattern of violence and the ethic of pan-Indianism suggested that the dichotomy served a purpose. A universalist ethic hides boundaries by contradicting them. Indeed, this seemed likely given the strength and the frequency of statements made in a pan-Indian vein. In other words, people said that all men were brothers precisely because they no longer had opportunities for expressing brotherhood or any sort of bond in a very practical or traditional way; people said that no one could restrict hunting precisely because no one hunted, and so on. The most (avowedly) brotherly relationships, in fact, seemed the least amicable. The people most given to ambiguous pan-Indian statements were also those most prone to violence. The pattern does not appear to be unusual. A general comparison of three Athabaskan societies – Kaska, Kutchin and Sekani – suggests a common pattern of hostility and violence when social relationships are plotted on a gradient of closeness and distance.[18] The greatest hostility occurs in the closest relationships between husband and wife or between father and son, for example. The least tension in all three societies occurs at the end of the gradient, between Indians and Whites.

I cannot present much data on violence in McLeod Lake; or rather, I prefer not to. Some of these people became good friends; all would be embarrassed and hurt if details were presented, especially given the small size of the community. In general, there is a general air of tension in the community. At night people are often afraid because of the drinking and its association with acts of violence, some of them completely gratuitous. Gang rapes, incest (father-daughter and brother-sister) and child abuse are not unknown. Drinking is sometimes associated with the neglect of children. The situation is not very different from Shkylnyk's description of a western Ojibwa town.[19] For our purposes, it is enough to note that about one half of all incidents of violence involve spouses;[20] the rest involve other people with different patronyms. An examination of table 5.1 reveals that the greatest proportion of violent acts occurred between members of categories that would, in the past, have been labelled 'close'. Significantly, no violence occurs between Indians and Whites.

Whatever its ultimate cause, the degree of internal violence in Sekani society does not appear to be a reflection of fur trade era values. While early references to the Sekani stressed their bloodthirstiness, as in the *Handbook of Indians of Canada*, this was probably due to a lack of information rather than an accurate description.[21] Even today in Fort Ware the degree of patience and forbearance displayed by many hunters and trappers in frustrating situations is nothing short of amazing. Many instances of difficulty and adversity are attributed to lack of skill or (more commonly) bad luck without a display of anger.[22] People tend to be forgiving and patient; annoyance and impatience are considered bad manners and go against the ethic of individual autonomy. This is not generally true of younger McLeod Lakers,

Table 5.1 Violence at McLeod Lake, 1978

Participants[1]	Category[2]	Remarks
1 BS	Nephew	Fight caused by alleged advances made to daughter of (1).
2 ZHu	B-in-law	
3 Wi	Wife	Three instances observed.
4 ZHuBS		
5 FBSWi		
6 F	Father	
7 none		Continuing feud between two major patronymic groups cited as cause of violence by one of the participants.
8 B, FZHuS, FZHuBS	Brother	Instigated by wife of (1).
9 FBWiBs		Retaliation for the incident above.
10 Wi	Wife	
11 BSWi	Nephew's Wife	
12 none		
13 Wi	Wife	Three instances observed.
14 Wi	Wife	
15 FBS	Cousin	
16 WiFB	Friend	
17 none		Continuing feud between two major patronymic groups cited as cause.
18 Wi	Wife	Five instances observed.
19 Wi	Wife	Two instances observed.

[1] Participants are identified by a number and the genealogical and affinal links they share.
[2] Terminology used by the participants, determined from interviews and observations.

however. Many of them have not been exposed to the discipline required by bush life. Hence, it is not surprising to find that many of the younger men were quick to take offence in tense situations, while younger residents of Fort Ware generally avoided

confrontation. There, extreme provocation always led to a response but never immediately and never without a warning.
A man who is quick to anger is unpredictable. People believe
that life is unpredictable in the sense that the opportunities it
presents are always changing. A man must be predictable by
operating within the bounds of a shared code of ethics that stresses
acceptance of change and the liberty of other people, as they too
must be free to respond to ever–changing conditions. Extreme
unpredictability in the domain of respect for people's rights is
interpreted, literally, as craziness. Yet, given the relative lack of
economic and social opportunities in McLeod Lake, both in the
bush and in the modern sector, the desire to maintain an image
of toughness measured by violence can be interpreted as expressing a desire for control, that is, the imposition of a framework, no matter how detrimental it may appear, within which
actions and their consequences are predictable. Ironically, the
more 'control' of this sort a man seems to have, the less respect
he manifests for others' rights. This is a clear break with past
traditions and it has created a vicious circle: more toughness,
more fighting; more fighting, more toughness.

The high level of violence between spouses may be linked to
the ambiguity that now characterizes close relationships. Ambiguity in this sense means the impossibility of expressing a relationship in visible and traditionally positive terms. The social
ties that had once been tangibly as well as symbolically affirmed
by marriages are now left unclear and unconsummated since
McLeod Lakers rarely, if ever, hunt together using the old patterns of networks,[23] nor do individual nuclear families go out on
to the trapline. Spouses are no longer an economic unit, nor are
ties between families maintained by the older pattern of sharing
risks and results. If the new economic regime has made the
behavioural expression of relationships somewhat ambiguous
and even problematic, then the emotive expression which would
normally accompany the tangible evidence of a relationship is
also ambiguous. Ambiguity allows tensions in other areas to spill
over into close social relationships; conjugal relationships are the
only remaining focus of social interaction and, hence, absorb all
the existing tensions and frustrations. But that is not all. Violence
is now an integral component of the definition of self among
young men in McLeod Lake. It is not the sole component but it
is seen as a legitimate avenue of self expression. How to explain
not only the violence but the pattern which explicitly contradicts
traditional norms and the modern ideology of pan-Indianism?
To a certain extent, the fact that no violence is directed at Whites

suggests that there is an internal dynamic at work. The literature on inversion may be helpful here.

Inversion has usually been recorded as a special instance of social behaviour and not as a norm.[24] Inversion is usually recorded only in contrast to unambiguously defined social behaviour. Furthermore, inversion is usually deemed to contain overwhelmingly clear symbolic elements, in that the normal relationship between symbols and behaviour is transposed. Hence, inversion is often seen as a limited experience, with a beginning and an end. If, in other words, it is clear that actions in the period of inversion are not subject to the normal censures, it is equally clear to participants that such actions do not necessarily spill over into other domains and times. People are therefore free to accept or reject the implications suggested by inversion. They are not bound by their behaviour nor its implications. Inversion thus usually marks some attempt to clarify the normal aspects of life, not to glorify the abnormal.[25] Given this, inversion is a form of play, somewhat akin to Lévi-Strauss's notion of *bricolage*.[26] As structured 'play', it allows existing social elements to be recombined in new ways which may provide an opportunity to solve what are otherwise insoluble problems.[27] If non-violent expressions of close relationships have failed to produce satisfactory results in dealing with the current crisis in McLeod Lake, then may not their opposite form be invoked in an attempt to evolve a new cultural framework? This argument suggests that it is precisely the close and intense relationships in Sekani society that would evoke the greatest intensity and frequency of violence as people seek to disengage themselves from past ties. Hence, it is to be expected that behavioural inversions directly mirror the intensity of relationships in McLeod Lake.

Relationships between men and women, especially those involving marriage, are both the symptom and cause of core problems of Sekani social life. The tensions that are linked to the rise of pan-Indianism have caused these bonds to be intensely scrutinized, largely because the question of the closeness of 'brothers' has been brought to the forefront of social consciousness. The overwhelmingly destructive framework in which this definition of 'brother' is now expressed leads the Sekani to view normally close relations between spouses as fraught with similar dangers and ambiguities. Emotional bonds between husband and wife, once indicative of the ascendancy of conjugal cooperation and support over the divisive tendencies caused by their separate, unequal and opposed contributions to the support of the family and reproduction of important social relationships, have now become ambiguous at best and a focus of violence at worst. This is not to say that family violence necessarily presupposes a weakening of emotional bonds. On the contrary, one might suggest that the dissolution of internal structural criteria ("separate, unequal and opposed contributions") has placed stronger stress on the emotional component of the conjugal bonds, if only because this is the only component left. Consequently, a considerable increase in tension has emerged in conjugal relationships in a search for new patterns or a new contract. Violence in such a context can be seen as resulting from increasing rather than diminishing emotional closeness, all the while allowing new avenues to be explored.

As has been mentioned, none of the violence or tension in the community is directed at Whites. Only a few acts of violence were alleged to have occurred between the McLeod Lake Sekani and the local Whites, including the residents of Mackenzie. There appears to be no correlation between the expenditures for alcohol and crime rate in the regional population (this does not mean that violence is not associated with drinking episodes; it is).[28] Although the number of acts of violence by Indians is high for the entire region, many of the Indians charged and sentenced for such acts in the region were in fact from Prince George or other urban centres. Regional crime statistics show that Mackenzie area Indians composed 17 per cent of the population but were responsible for 22 per cent of all criminal incidents. Not all such incidents were considered crimes, however. Many of these, including cases of assault between adults, were not followed by the laying of charges (table 5.2). Of a total of 796 Offences, 401 (50.4 percent) are charged. Although there are no statistics which compare Indians to Whites in this regard, many of the local police officers believe that the McLeod Lake Sekani are responsible for fewer charges laid, relatively, than the local Whites. More time was spent by the Mackenzie RCMP in dealing with the McLeod Lake Sekani than their numbers warranted simply because the detachment was thirty miles from the Reserve. If the police were required in Fort Ware, they had to fly in, a noteworthy occurrence even for relatively mundane matters. In brief, the relations between the local police and the Sekani were amicable, despite the popular opinion of some Mackenzie residents who preferred to view the Sekani as troublesome.

It would seem logical that the Sekani increase their knowledge of and participation in White society, but their isolation from White society has caused them increasingly to turn to their own cultural tradition. This would not necessarily be negative but for the fact that the outside world is playing a decidedly destructive role in most Sekani activities. The situation is doubly frustrating because it is precisely traditional activities that are impeded. Given their frustration it is no wonder that universalism, with its explicit denial of social and cultural differentiation between people, appears as an attractive alternative. With little

Table 5.2 Crimes by category and disposition, Mackenzie district, 1977

	Total offences	Charged	Warning; caution	Victim–offender separated	Referred to civil prosecution	Referred to provincial prosecution	Reconciliation	Restitution	Victim does not wish to proceed	Detoxication	Offender leaving town	Community service	Seizure
Homicide	1	1											
Sexual offences	2	–	1	1									
Assaults (non-sexual)	27	5	4	5	1	1	2		19	1			
Robbery	–	–											
Offensive weapons	3	1					1			1			
Break and enter	9	5	5				1	1	5				
Theft of motor vehicle	2	2											
Theft over $200.00	–	–											
Theft under $200.00	14	8					1	4	2			1	
Possession of stolen goods	2	1	1										
Fraud	8	3	1				1	1	4				
Arson	–	–											
Disturbing the peace	33	5	14	14			5	1	10	5			
Public morals	1	–											
Obstructing a peace officer	–	–											
Trespass at night	4	–										4	
Wilful damage	6	2	4		1		2	1	4				
Cannabis	7	4	2										
Liquor control act	44	8	1	1						1		5	29
Dangerous driving	2	2											
Not providing breath sample	3	3											
Impaired driving	25	25											
Driving while disqualified	8	8											

Source: K. Jobson, G. Ferguson, M. Fus, B. Ferstman and K. Kaiser, 'Report on Northern Justice', unpublished paper, Victoria: University of Victoria, 1978.

or no chance to develop social relationships with Whites and with no chance to develop positively expressed social relationships with Sekani outside the immediate community, expressions of solidarity have evolved in such a way that they cannot be tested against the realities of the outside world. In a word, pan-Indianism is clearly attached to a credo of universalism. As such, it is a retreat from the acknowledgement of well-defined ties between people, especially those ties once associated with the performance of practical tasks. Violence disengages people from the limitations imposed by mutual expectations of a tangible sort. Pan-Indianism provides a new content – a new bond – but on a more abstract level. Ironically, pan-Indianism opposes Indians to Whites and thus may contribute to the idea that Indians must measure themselves, albeit negatively, on the same scale of values that the Sekani believe are in use in White society, namely, toughness in the face of competition. It is a clichéd view of White society and like all clichés it has limited descriptive power, but it is the only side of White society that many McLeod Lake people see.

This suggests that an inversion is engaged when newly emerging relationships with the outside world become problematical. Difficulties in defining the problem of intrusion have caused negative consequences for affective display within relationships since there is little opportunity for their expression. The definition of closeness which surfaces from pan-Indianism suggests impersonality and hence social distance. Socially isolated from the outside world, first by chance and then by choice, the nature of social bonding is now being questioned. Violence is a clear indication that the general rules are under revision.

The Politics of Pan-Indianism

It could be expected that local politics in McLeod Lake is an arena in which solidarity is developed and reinforced. Pan-Indianism, after all, is a type of political discourse. Instead, one finds fragmentation and factionalism of the same intensity and kind that occurs in personal relationships. Pan-Indianism is not an ideological inversion because it contains a definition of solidarity which is opposed to the European world view which prevails in the rest of Canada; it is contradictory because it is untestable against the matrix provided by the Sekani themselves. This particular model of political action is used as a means of relieving tensions within the community by moving the arena for action to an idealized realm with somewhat limiting and limited content. Some of its apparent radicalism is due to the prior knowledge that the guidelines for pragmatic action contained within pan-Indian ideology can never be effectively put into practice. There are several reasons for this, some of them spontaneous, while others are deliberately engaged.

Elders at McLeod Lake, for example, are not adherents to this system of political thought because for them – like most of the northern Sekani – the older system of social categorization still means something. They still think of non-McLeod Lakers as outsiders, and yet many had kinship and work ties with people living outside the community. On the local level these people still operate in a world of already-formed networks that divide the population into categories of marriageable and non-marriageable people and senior and junior partners. Although their views and networks do not necessarily take account of the new dimensions to life which are rapidly emerging, there is no opportunity or, indeed, need to test these older views since the elders are, to all extents and purposes, 'retired'. Past their prime as hunters and trappers, the older men would not in any case be reforming working relationships at this stage of their lives, especially now that no younger men are emerging as potential junior partners. In a word, older people are generally indifferent to pan-Indianism.

There is another dimension to this that further widens the gap between young and old. Older men in particular are the ones who have had the most experience of the outside, albeit non-White, world. Some of their experiences with outsiders do not fit into the positive mould proposed by the younger adherents of pan-Indianism. However, for the young, the strongest proponents of this new regime, the older system of social categories remains imprecise in critically important ways. Even though they are the advocates of a moral order of brotherhood among all Indians, they are in some ways the most mistrustful of outsiders. There are several reasons for this.

Although the younger generation has the most exposure to modern White education, many young people have, ironically, the least practical exposure to the rules and guidelines for action in the outside world. If hunting and trapping are memories from the past for men of the younger set, work in the modern sector of the local economy is almost completely unknown. Only one person worked in Mackenzie during the period of research and he did not consider himself part of the pan-Indian 'crowd', either in belief or action. Many young McLeod Lakers are not considered suitable candidates for employment by the local Whites who are in a position to offer them jobs. Their relatively high profile makes such discrimination easy.[29] Their elders are remote and resigned to the changes. In short, younger residents of McLeod Lake are remote from the outside society and are strangers within their own. Unlike their elders they are not resigned; instead, they are bitter, since all paths to practical action are blocked.

From this perspective pan-Indianism is the ideological response that correlates with the isolation of the young. The violence in which they engage is generally directed at other young people. Although they have, relative to their elders, a wide circle of superficial contacts outside their own society, this has not moved them any closer to developing a workable political formula based on pan-Indianism nor has it allowed them to develop amicable relations with non-Sekani. To put it briefly, universalism violates traditional boundaries and contradicts the experiences of elders in their contact with non-Sekani. And, as we shall see, difficult relations with outsiders are the norm rather than the exception for the Sekani. It is therefore unlikely that any close relationship can develop from casual associations, despite avowals of brotherhood. It is also unlikely that McLeod Lakers are unaware of the implications of their actions and thoughts *vis-à-vis* outsiders, especially those outsiders who are potential converts to the new pan-Indian confraternity.

One such area in which Sekani intentions are clear is in the domain of political leadership. The situation in McLeod Lake is unlikely to allow for the emergence of strong leaders who are pan-Indianists. On one very practical level, for example, there is a split in the Band Council itself. The youngest member of the council, an avowed proponent of pan-Indianism and a natural candidate for a leadership post, was a member of a patronymic category that was not only different from that of the other members of the council – including the Chief – but members of his patronymic network were also usually politically opposed to the people of the other major patronymic present in the community. A large number of violent actions were ascribed as resulting from this long-standing emnity.[30] More important, the Chief did not like many of the ideas of the young Councillor. In this he had the support of much of the community, except for the Councillor's large immediate family.

Some of the Chief's support arose no doubt because of shared patronymic affiliation, but at least one prominent member of the opposite patronymic supported him. The Chief was regarded as a traditionalist by most of the community. He was a man with a certain vision of the future and generally worked within existing channels, which, as is usual in many small Indian bands, involves close contact with the White bureaucracy. For example, the Chief certainly favoured the idea of submitting a land claims proposal to the federal government but he was equally interested in obtaining good quality housing for Band members. For the Chief, good housing meant that the community could once again attract Band members who had left the Reserve. More people meant a stronger claim as well as a chance to curb the violence among the young by having, in his words, "a real community". The younger idealists were not concerned with this, however. For them, the eventual acceptance of a land claims proposal by the government would resolve all other problems because, according to the credo of pan-Indianism, all problems stemmed from a White-enforced alienation from the land.

The reluctance to engage in activity that would test pan-Indianism is linked to the lack of a solid political base from which any one faction can draw support. Fragmentation, in other words, must stop at some point if unity is to emerge. Some authors have argued that revitalization movements are a nascent form of nationalism.[31] The success or failure of this aspect of revitalization seems to depend on the prior existence of some real basis for group unity. This is clearly not the case for the Sekani. The divisions and unifying tendencies of McLeod Lake pan-Indianism are reflected in the structure of political action in Fort Ware as well as in McLeod Lake. Selection of people to fill political office within the Council or to fill non-Council positions reflects and reinforces existing boundaries. The position of Chief, the most important political role in both communities, is in effect a position of political compromise between patronymic factions. This, however, does not lessen the Chief's power since he can and does threaten one or another faction with the loss of Band jobs. In fact, given the very real divisive forces at work, he must take effective control if he is to accomplish anything. Ironically, the same situation that gives him power also leads to a dilution of his effectiveness because of the need for constant compromise between the factions.

The position of Chief in both communities is filled 'according to custom' (a term used by the DIA, which monitors elections, to acknowledge that Indian political processes rarely correspond to Western ideas of democracy). Not much information was available about the electoral process at McLeod Lake, but an election did take place during my stay in Fort Ware. The election was uncontested and the incumbent was re-elected by acclamation. The election had been forced on the community by the DIA when an administrative officer noticed that an election had not been held for five years. People were annoyed and embarrassed by this intervention; embarrassed that they did not 'measure up' to White standards by seeming lackadaisical in a stereotypical Indian way to the White bureaucrats and annoyed that they were forced to do so. People's apparently lax attitude towards formal elections points to the importance of non-political forms of social control. The power of the Chief depends very much on community consensus.

As much as elections are considered unnecessary in Fort Ware, they are sometimes the subject of warm discussion in McLeod Lake. The situation is best described as pluralistic factionalism, in which groups compete for power within a framework that allows some accommodation. Although no election was held during my stay, people talked freely of the changes they wanted and how these changes would have to be implemented by "someone new". This reflected the very difficult position the Chief was in, since the community was much more politically divided that Fort Ware; young and old, traditionalists and pan-Indianists, various patronymic networks, all had to be accommodated but each faction saw any concession to the other as a reason in itself for continued opposition. Appointments to Band jobs reflect the social context since these are based more on a person's patronymic affiliation than skills. Ironically, the lesser-paying jobs such as secretary tend to be given on the basis of skills while the more remunerative appointments (e.g. Band Manager) are more obviously political. The Band Secretary, for example, has few responsibilities, so getting the job done is easily measured; either the secretary can or cannot type. Band Managers, on the other hand, have greater responsibilities and their performance can only be evaluated in the long run: has he (no women had ever held the job) brought funds into the community, administered them wisely and honestly, and so forth? This double standard is both a boon and a bane for employees, however, since a person appointed on the basis of one criterion can always be removed on the basis of the other.

Part of the Chief's continued power comes from the efficient fulfilment of his duties, namely, acting as an intermediary between the Band and the outside world. If he cannot accomplish this to the satisfaction of the majority of Band members, there will be grumbling and eventually he will be removed from office. The system of pluralistic factionalism that is engaged in the selection of Band employees confirms the Chief's power while simultaneously undermining it. Politically motivated appointments may come back to haunt the Chief especially if these prove to be, literally, inexpedient. The Chief must then 'double up' and perform the tasks that he had delegated to others. This system has its own internal coherency, and a person whose skills are to be improved by training received outside – for example, Band Health Officer or Band Manager – can turn the tables on the Chief. These people soon test the belief that their position is due to a particular social identity and not to their capabilities. The few people who follow these training courses rarely return with improved skills, yet they are now doubly difficult for the Chief to remove. First, by meeting other people in similar positions people soon become aware, if they did not already suspect, that their positions are not vital to the continued survival of the community. Second, they now have 'official' technical 'qualifications' as well as their social position. Third, they learn that if jobs are not done, relatively little in the way of bad consequences follows. With a few exceptions (for example, the Band Health Officer – a sort of public health nurse) the duties involved in most positions are relatively light. At least part of this diffident attitude emerges when the White bureaucracy, especially the Department of Indian Affairs, blatantly relaxes standards as part of their policy of developing skills by encouraging active 'hands-on' participation in the job market. Theoretically, this means that a few people are sent on various training programmes so that they can improve the efficiency of the Band administration. The selected candidates go because of the prestige, the money and the fear of being judged not up to the task. These people may be honestly disposed to learn something, but most are not used to living away from the Reserve among strangers. As a result, they often do badly since they withdraw from active interaction with their temporary employers, teachers or colleagues. The result is the adoption of a patronizing defensiveness about a job in which they feel insecure at best. When they return, they hide their insecurities, lack of skills and fear of ridicule by doing as little as possible; a badly done job is obvious, whereas a job left undone cannot be immediately measured. The administrative inefficiency is aggravated by the small size of McLeod Lake and Fort Ware, which have only a small pool of substitutes who are not otherwise busy. In addition, people who are disposed to fill Band jobs are often marginal within the community at least as regards the more traditional values, rendering their effectiveness problematic at the best of times. There are accordingly few candidates for the more difficult jobs like Health Officer when other plums, like Band Manager, are available.[32]

The role of local politics in job appointments does not favour the Chief's family at the expense of others. Given its importance, political considerations eventually evolve a structure in which representatives from each of the major patronymic groups are equally involved. Nor are skills as such lacking in both communities, relative to the actual technical requirements involved, but sometimes skilled people will be passed over because of political considerations. The Chief can appoint somebody to a position which is not too onerous knowing full well that the person is unskilled for the role but also knowing that he himself can occasionally perform the light duties (typing a letter, writing several Band cheques, etc.) if need be. Finally, not all appointments are made cynically. Political considerations might be something as mundane as trying to get some money to a person who genuinely needs it to raise their family or to increase their economic independence; a crucial consideration, as we have seen, for inclusion into the community.

As if to confirm the importance of political considerations in job appointments, the occasional case of a person with technical skills being unable to perform his job sometimes arises. One Band Manager was appointed because of his technical aptitudes but he lacked the social skills to adapt to the community. He had been raised outside in the big city and felt just as isolated as the local people do when they go to the city. His business skills were somewhat advanced for the community; after several weeks on the job he chartered a plane by using the name of the Chief, went to Prince George and cut a wise swathe with the town merchants by taking the Band chequebook along for the ride.[33] Needless to say, this Band Manager's business skills did nothing to further the ideals of bureaucratic efficiency in the community.[34]

In sum, the power of the Chief exists within a specific arena defined by local 'kin'-connectedness and efficacy as a political mediator with the outside. Chiefs issue no orders, nor do they merely lead by example. Politics, especially in McLeod Lake, is rather like the expression of community will at work. The extent to which the community is both riven and united by certain tensions is reflected in the politics of the Band Office. The almost complete politicization of local and small-scale events because of the narrow focus of pan-Indianism and the almost complete absence of meaningful activity in other domains is a telling indicator that inversion maintains the status quo of traditional factions as much as it represents a drastic change.

Universalism in Comparative Perspective

Much has been made of the definitional aspects of revitalization movements and crisis cults such as pan-Indianism.[35] Such examinations focus on two general issues: (1) problems of definition according to the organizational basis of the movement, and (2) problems of definition according to the professed or implicit aims of the movement. The first question is not very important in this context, however, because McLeod Lake pan-Indianism is a system of thought with only limited practical expression. It does provide the McLeod Lakers with some sense of unity, although the final result is no more than a reaffirmation of the traditional limits of the band. The nature of the divisions within the community, including their immediate causes, are such that this unity never overcomes the tangible problems and tensions in McLeod Lake. Furthermore, pan-Indianists do not subject their beliefs to rigorous testing. It is not used to regulate their political or social lives, so there is little by way of feedback. The emergence of leadership and the development of cult-like rituals are also precluded, although the exigencies of practical politics in McLeod Lake may account for this as much as the content of pan-Indianism itself.

If McLeod Lake pan-Indianism does not meet the minimum requirements of the definition of a revitalization movement, then can its inclusion in the more general category be significant? There are several factors which suggest that this is a fruitful line of enquiry. First, pan-Indianism has a definite anti-colonial theme with its appeal to the unity of all Indian people, opposed as they are by Whites. Second, the idea of hearkening back to the 'good old days' before the arrival of the Whites contains an allusion of the revitalization of traditional culture. Third, the appeal to unity as a means of obtaining some unspecified goal in the future – a future where Whites are absent or not in a dominant position – contains more than a hint of millenarianism.

There is thus an implicit dichotomy in the Indian response to White domination. On the one hand is the modern and strictly political expression of Indian groups; on the other lies a revival of interest in characteristics which are defined as uniquely Indian. Pan-Indianism as part of the modern political response builds on this revitalized culture. Indeed, most of the characteristics of modern pan-Indianism listed by Lurie in her review of the American situation consist of older cultural traits applied as solutions to problems of modern political organization.[36]

It is possible, however, that revitalization movements are

misnamed or at the very least are a model of reality that does not adequately describe the situation in McLeod Lake. Although messianic revitalization movements or crisis cults have been reported for Athabaskans like the Bear Lakers and the Kutchin, there is some evidence that an earlier messianic movement in which the Sekani participated was not due to a crisis.[37]

The Ghost Dance of the various Plains Indian groups described by Mooney has generally been considered an example of the effects of cultural disintegration due to contact with White society.[38] Spier, however, argued effectively that this movement, popular in the 1890s, could be traced back to at least the 1870s when a similar movement swept through the people of the Great Plains. Hence, there is more than a hint of cultural continuity involved in the expression of what could otherwise be described as two examples of political, social and cultural dissent. Although Mooney had acknowledged this particular historical connection, Spier believed that the messianic Plains complex could be traced back to the even earlier Prophet Dance of the Northwest Plateau region in the early 1800s.[39] The Prophet Dance was a pre-contact phenomenon to which were added Christian elements when these were congruent with Indian practices.[40] The issue of the aboriginality of these messianic and revitalization movements is not only complex; it is an important step towards understanding the implications of Sekani pan-Indianism. The Sekani, after all, were adherents of the Prophet Dance cult, and a tradition of prophesying was not unknown to them.[41]

There are two factors in dating the movement which relate to these issues. The first is the time when the original prophet flourished, and the second is the content of his prophecies. Peni was a resident of New Caledonia and apparently a Gitksan Indian, although he may have been a western Carrier.[42] Morice dates his emergence around the time of the christianization of the Carrier, which would be circa 1842.[43] Morice implies that the movement was pre-missionary, although it followed the arrival of two mission-educated Oregon Indians to the New Caledonia district.[44] The Carrier, Morice reported, believed that Peni had no prior knowledge of Christianity at the time of the inception of his movement.[45] Spier, on the other hand, cites a personal communication from Barbeau that suggests that Peni flourished during the 1820s.[46] Barbeau, however, had given no such impression in his earlier work.[47] According to him, Peni antedates the arrival of missionaries into the district and even the appearance of the first White man in the northern uplands.[48]

Peni had a dramatic vision in which he "died" and disappeared during the month of February. He later re-appeared in the month of May, claiming to have returned from the dead.[49] Barbeau believed that Peni could not have travelled to a trading post in his two– or three-month absence, although it was likely that he encountered some Cree or Iroquois Indians (hired by the Northwest Company, some of these eastern Indians are reputed to have settled near Jasper, Alberta, at this early date) or some French Canadian *coureurs de bois* in his travels.[50] Peni was old before the Whites arrived in New Caledonia (the name assigned to the area by the fur traders). This supports the argument for the aboriginality of the Prophet Dance in this district. Peni died disappointed because his prophecy regarding the generosity of the Whites proved to be false; Morice states that Peni died as a common shaman.[51] So ends the story of Peni.

There are many similarities between Peni's vision and Christian doctrine and rituals. Peni no longer spoke his native tongue when he returned from the land of the dead but instead spoke the language of the Sky People. These were ruled by two head chiefs, the Father and the Son.[52] The son was named Zazeekry, which is suspiciously similar in sound to the French pronunciation of 'Jesus Christ'. Peni's followers had to be baptized, abandon the potlatch and observe Deemawse, which is again reminiscent of the French *dimanche*. Barbeau himself pointed out this latter similarity to the French but not the former resemblance.[53]

It is clear that this movement is neither entirely aboriginal nor is it entirely based on contact with Europeans. Elements of Christianity are present despite later Carrier avowals to the contrary, and yet it is clear that it is not direct contact which precipitated a crisis from which emerged the Prophet movement. In fact, the delay in timing between the prophesied contact with the Whites and actual contact led the movement to become temporarily moribund.[54] The question remains: what caused this reaction to the Whites before any significant threat to their local traditions was perceived by the Carrier, the Gitksan and the Sekani? It is likely that we shall never know the exact motives. What is striking, however, is the fact that little or no threat of contact was necessary for its adoption by members of all three groups and Peni continually stressed adherence to an idea of conformity to an idealized definition of Indianness.

Accepted theories of crisis cults lead the researcher into a particular methodological stance, namely, the seeking of crises.[55]

The evidence suggests, however, that 'crisis' may be too strong a term to describe the circumstances surrounding Peni's movement. It is possible that the Prophet Dance of the late 1700s and/or early 1800s was a reaction against the introduction of European technology among the peoples of the Cordillera. Yet the evidence is simply too weak to allow even this moderate conclusion. Although the acceptance of a foreign technology implies that a clash exists between contrasting or at least different forms of social organization, it is unlikely that this could have developed so soon after the introduction of European technology by a third party. As we shall see, in some ways the Sekani made a very successful adaptation to the fur trade, even though most of this trade was marked by very difficult conditions. There is no evidence to suggest that a similar reaction was typical of this later and even more stressful period. The question remains: why the Prophet Dance and why pan-Indianism?

It seems reasonable to suspect that this earlier Prophet Dance, like pan-Indianism today, was a continuation of an already long-established tradition of cultural expression. This is indeed the position taken by Ridington in his examination of the modern Beaver Prophet Dance.[56] Here, the movement is linked to cycles of adjustment to the natural world by means of instructions and advice from the supernatural domain. In other words, the Beaver and other Athabaskan groups who possess a Prophet Dance tradition do not react to difficult dilemmas with irrational and escapist cults. These Athabaskans appear to have one trait in common, however; they anticipate certain kinds of problems before a final paradox is presented. It may be that Athabaskan cult activity, including pan-Indianism, is a means of producing a heightened awareness of potential problems and sustaining that awareness until some sort of resolution is reached. Promulgation and popularization of the problem gives everyone a chance to engage in a new discourse. As Burridge argues, prophets and other leaders of this sort are those people whose solutions are more appealing by virtue of their congruence with an already developed discourse;[57] their views and visions are thus adopted, even if temporarily. Whether or not the discourse moves from the ideological to the political domain probably depends on the particular situation, whether there is a classic colonial situation of settlement, forced labour and the like. Cultic movements, in other words, are not so much reactions to a crisis as a form of anticipation which allows an examination of the situation from perspectives which are not normally accepted within the culture. The end of the movement signifies success in a people's search for a solution, not necessarily the failure to find a solution. Regardless of what we believe about the nature of revitalization movements, it is obvious that the idea of forming wide networks of people organized around shared notions that transcend tangible differences between categories of people was certainly not new to Athabaskans and to the Sekani in particular.

Conclusion

There is a high degree of strife and tension in McLeod Lake. Social solidarity, manifested in common action, is weak. Individual autonomy, always traditionally valued, has assumed even greater importance. The almost non-existent sense of social solidarity is associated with a reduced field of action in the new social, political and economic regime. The older system of work is made difficult if not impossible by logging, and employment opportunities are few. On the other hand, unity as such in McLeod Lake is now expressed on a more abstract level through the notion of pan-Indian brotherhood, which is also manifested in identification with the community as a whole. There are, in other words, no unambiguous intermediate levels of association between the individual and the community. Pan-Indianism fills the void created by the disintegration of normal avenues by which solidarity could be achieved. Pan-Indianism is a body of thought which strongly supports the idea of a lack of social differentiation. It thus allows a reversal and even an inversion of the categories that traditionally distinguished people in their everyday activities.

As a solution to social disintegration, however, pan-Indian brotherhood is not without serious limitations. It unites people in a manner which is almost entirely removed from the realities of contemporary life in McLeod Lake. Nor does unbounded and universalistic brotherhood have any precedent in the traditional culture of the Sekani, although, as we shall see, there were antecedent forms of brotherhood that also implied a limit on the networks that were created. The adherents of a pan-Indian philosophy appear unable or unwilling to subject such spurious, fragile and obviously postulated unity to the demands of an active and effective political organization.

However, McLeod Lake pan-Indianism is not merely a view of idealized political action. In the sense that political acts that accord with pan-Indian philosophy are immediately subverted by appeals to different ideas and ideals, pan-Indianism is a clearly considered system of thought that must remain untested. More precisely, actions and practices associated with pan-Indianism are placed in a category so abstract that it cannot possibly survive empirical verification and validation without serious collapse. This will not be risked because pan-Indianism is seen by many as the only viable response to an otherwise totally frustrating situation. It is a system of thought, a system that exists not as an adjunct to the world of real and material experience – as a system of signs, in other words – but as something that is separate and yet opposed to the sad realities of contemporary life in McLeod Lake. For example, pan-Indianism in McLeod Lake is associated with violence. Pan-Indian ideology postulates a sense of unity among people who are experiencing great stress and divisiveness due to the disruption which has followed the appropriation of their land. Violence is in part a reversal of traditional values, especially as an avenue which expresses close relationships. Violence disengages people from the emotional closeness that normally accompanies intense relationships. A cycle develops in which pan-Indian unity is regarded as a solution to the divisiveness associated with violence, but at the same time it is viewed as a substitute for other, more concrete, forms of solidarity and closeness. The presence of violence is tolerated because McLeod Lakers see it as a culturally viable response to the fluidity of socio-political patterns associated with the new regime; in other words, violence is tolerated because of its indirect association with pan-Indian brotherhood.

In sum, I have argued that McLeod Lake pan-Indianism contains its own negation. People profess a belief in pan-Indian sentiments, but the implied brotherhood is very limited in its application. It is a bounded universalism. This circumscription is not only the product of the divisive economic and social forces that characterize the modern regime. As we shall see, it is also the product of a Sekani tradition with roots firmly entrenched in history. One of the difficulties which the Sekani are facing is their apparent inability to transform the new system of political thought into viable forms of action. This problem is primarily due to the lack of cohesion and of a practical means of reconciliation between this new world view and the traditional bounded categories.

Notes

1. An analysis of the literature was undertaken by Price. He concludes that the North American Indian literature can be divided into two domains: the rural-based newsletters, which tend to be "newsy" and limited to presenting the facts, and the larger urban-based periodicals of national scope which tend towards explicit pan-Indianism in their outlook. The latter have more resources, a wider circulation, and a greater appeal to the theme of pan-Indian unity as a viable response to cultural encroachment by White society. Price notes that in general the Canadian literature tends to be more extreme and emphatic than the American literature. See J. Price, 'U.S. and Canadian Indian Periodicals', *Canadian Review of Sociology and Anthropology* 9: 150–62, 1972, p. 158. Such literature is indeed distributed to both the Fort Ware and McLeod Lake Band councils, as well as to individuals within each band. The more prominent periodicals are *Akwesasne Notes, Tawow* (a DIA publication), *The Native Voice* and *Unity: Bulletin of the Union of B.C. Indian Chiefs* (which sometimes reprints material from other sources with national interest). The first is an American periodical with a very international flavour. The others are Canadian. In addition, both Band councils receive regional newsletters that sometimes adapt articles from the major publications to local conditions. One incident at McLeod Lake reinforced the supporting role played by these publications. *Akwesasne Notes* had once paid a great deal of attention to the Navajo of the southwestern United States. This appears to have been due to the successful renaissance of the Navajo during the last few years, who are also discovering effective forms of political expression. The Navajo are seen by some Sekani as a model for development. Some politically active advocates of pan-Indianism at McLeod Lake have encountered Navajo while visiting the United States for a religious-political meeting. They were impressed by the linguistic similarities between Sekani and Navajo. In fact, their weak knowledge of Sekani hid the extent of the differences between the two languages. In brief, they were delighted to have found people elsewhere who were "like us" and, moreover, who were relatively successful in fighting for their rights. This had as an effect a reinforcement of the themes of pan-Indianism. Ironically, the local epithet for Indians among some Whites is "Navajo", presumably obtained from Hollywood westerns.

2. The Sekani reinforced these sentiments – if, indeed, they needed reinforcing – by reinterpreting the facts to suit their political needs. For example, many Sekani know that logging helps increase some species (under almost ideal conditions: if the logging companies move out after they are finished and burn their garbage). As the forest regenerates new shoots attract moose, who are generally scarce in mature timber stands. Some militants use this knowledge in order to justify a virulent pan-Indianism: people could go and live in the bush like they "used to" and shoot anyone who comes after them. The increased moose population would feed the new society, they say.

3. The two major companies are British Columbia Forest Products Ltd and Finlay Forest Industries Ltd. I interviewed an Industrial Relations Supervisor who worked for one of these industries, who maintained that his company had an "open door" policy for an Indian wanting to work.

4. H.W. Hertzberg, *Search for American Identity: Modern Pan-Indian Movements*, Syracuse: Syracuse University Press, 1971, p. viii.

5. G.I. Quimby, *Indian Life in the Upper Great Lakes, 11,000 B.C. – 1,000 A.D.*, Chicago: University of Chicago Press, 1960, p. 147.

6. Ibid., p. 148. Sometimes the Winnibago are included with the Ojibwa by some scholars. See J.V. Wright, 'A Regional Examination of Ojibwa Culture History', *Anthropologica* 7: 189–277, 1965.

7. F.G. Patterson, *The Canadian Indian: A History Since 1500*, Don Mills, Ont.: Collier–Macmillan Canada, 1972, p. 20.

8. D. McNickle, *Native American Tribalism: Indian Survivals and Renewals*, New York: Oxford University Press for the Institute for Race Relations, 1973, pp. 115–18.

9. Ibid., p. 147. See S.M. Weaver, *Making Canadian Indian Policy: The Hidden Agenda 1968–70*, Toronto: University of Toronto Press, 1981, for an analysis of confusion in government policy towards Indians in this era.

10. Parsons suggests that universalism is an 'objective' basis of social classification, that it is independent of the particular social relationship which links people. In Parsons's scheme universalism is associated with a rational bureaucracy acting in the interests of the capitalist enterprise, particularly in the United States. In other words, he regards universalism as an ethic or code which he sees as providing a particular value orientation for a predominant set orientation towards social action. Levy adds that universalism is an ethic to which people subscribe when they seek to pose as modern, by which he evidently means 'westernized'. In such situations universalism appears a more 'rational' and 'scientific' because it is a supposedly objective basis for action and thought. Its counterpart, particularism, is attributed to a more traditional form of association. Levy, like Parsons, sees universalism as a form of group and network recruitment which has as its basis an impartial criterion of discrimination. See T. Parsons, 'Democracy and Social Structure in Pre-Nazi Germany', in *Essays in Sociological Theory*, New York: The Free Press, 1954, pp. 40, 41, 112, 113; idem, *Structure and Process in Modern Society*, Glencoe, Ill.: The Free Press, 1960, p. 115; idem, *The Social System*, Glencoe, Ill.: The Free Press, 1951, pp. 101–12; M. Levy, Jr., *Modernization and the Structure of Societies: A Setting for International Affairs*, Princeton, NJ: Princeton University Press, 1966, pp. 52–5, 140–2.

11. 'Deadheads' are also feared. These are trees left in place before the waters rose to cover them. Over the years the water loosens their roots, and they come flying up to the surface like wooden Trident missiles. They are certainly dangerous for small boats. It is difficult to get any information on this and other related matters from British Columbia Hydro officials, who are reluctant to talk about the debris problem. A channel is occasionally cleared for river barges.

12. Goods are shipped to Fort Ware after being trucked from Prince George, transshipped at Mackenzie to a large lake barge and finally transferred by river boat to their destination. These last two stages (from Mackenzie to Fort Ware) were estimated in 1979 to cost $0.16 per pound, according to the local trader.

13. A more detailed exposition of the literature on violence and drinking can be found in my article, 'La Désunion Fait La Force: Survie et tensions chez les Sekani de la Colombie-Britannique', *Anthropologie et Sociétés* 14(2): 117–41, 1990.

14. I was occasionally used as an informant about the outside world. I was asked to confirm the image of Indian-as-violent. It upset people ("you mean there are people tougher than us?") when I pointed out that, in my view, they were not as violent as many of the local Whites (whom they knew in any case).

15. It is ironic that labour was recruited with difficulty for the project. At least one worker lived in Mackenzie and commuted the thirty-mile distance daily. Several women were employed because, according to the Chief, it was difficult to find men to work on the project. See the section on Band level politics for a discussion of why people are often reluctant to commit themselves to "White jobs".

16. It is also believed by some Council members that welfare (in one form or another) encourages people to stay in the community and to cease hunting. The view that land use is a core issue in their lives is typical for the Sekani as well as other Athabaskan groups.

17. A noteworthy market of 'roughness' between the residents of Fort Ware and McLeod Lake was the chewing of tobacco. Many residents of Fort Ware chewed; the practice was unknown in McLeod Lake. Although derided by some McLeod Lakers, they are aware that the chewing of tobacco is traditionally associated with Indianness. They therefore show disdain to a strong symbol of Indianness, all the while affirming their Indian identity through pan-Indianism. The irony was known and clearly emphasized when McLeod Lakers called Fort Ware residents "real Indians" in the context of the tobacco-chewing habit of the latter. The contradiction between being "tough" but not "rough" is never mentioned, but it exemplified the contradictory attitudes that typify McLeod Lake pan-Indianism.

18. There is some similarity between this situation and the Vunta Kutchin of Old Crow studied by Balikci. He was struck by the bad behaviour and hypocrisy that characterized a great deal of social life. This he attributed to social atomism, the weakening of organic social bonds. This in turn was caused by acculturative pressures to which the Kutchin had been subjected. These, especially the presence of Anglican missionaries and the fur trade, resulted in several specific pressure points on traditional social organization. New items introduced by the fur trade had to be paid for in currency. This led to a redistribution of population as the old patterns of collaboration became obsolete. Cooperation also declined as a result of the introduction of new items in the economy which allowed for greater individual self-sufficiency. This argument, states Balikci, corroborates the findings of Leacock and of Murphy and

Steward for eastern Algonkians. There is another parallel with the Sekani: an apparent breakdown of the older system of social categories. Balikci specifically mentions the Anglican church as playing a role in the disappearance of the Kutchin moiety system. Balikci suggests that the intensity of relationships does not change along with social structure. Both good and bad feelings characterize relationships, a conclusion similar to Honigmann's studies of the Kaska. Balikci suggests that in close relationships, "Ambivalence develops and leads to hostility. In this perspective the hostility pattern corresponds to an intense interest in the other, constituting a negative binding element'. In other words, the weakness of the formal integrative mechanisms in society leads to ambivalence in social relationships. The result is conflict, and social cohesion comes to depend on this conflict. See A. Balikci, 'Perspectives on the Atomistic Type Society: Bad Friends', *Human Organization* 27(3): 191–9, 1968, pp. 191, 192, 194, 198, 199. E.B. Leacock, *The Montagnais 'Hunting Territory' and the Fur Trade*, American Anthropological Association Memoir No. 78, 1954. R.F. Murphy and J.H. Steward, 'Tappers and Trappers: Parallel Process in Acculturation', *Economic Development and Social Change* 4, reprinted in R.A. Manners and D. Kaplan, eds, *Theory in Anthropology*, New York: Aldine, 1956. J.J. Honigmann, *The Kaska Indians An Ethnographic Reconstruction*, Yale University Publications in Anthropology No. 51, New Haven: Yale University Press, 1954, and idem, 'Interpersonal Relations in Atomistic Communities', *Human Organization* 27(3): 220–9, 1968.

19. A. Shkilnyk, *A Poison Stronger Than Love: The Destruction of an Ojibwa Community*, New Haven: Yale University Press, 1985.

20. Without singling out any one particular argument for undue criticism, there are a number of weaknesses which are shared by many arguments about male and female relationship in Athabaskan societies. Sharp, for instance, contends that beatings are a normal expression of affection within Chipewyan marriage. Beatings are sometimes provoked by women as a measure of their husbands' interest in them. While a valid observation in the Chipewyan context, it seems to me that violence must have multiple dimensions to the Chipewyan if such hostility can mark an equation between violence and affection. Perry notes that the low status assigned to women in many Athabaskan societies is associated with the supernatural power with which women are imbued, especially during childbirth and menstruation. These qualities are inimical to male hunting in many societies, as Lévi-Strauss has pointed out; certainly this was true of the Sekani. Perry seems to be presenting an argument that is derived from Douglas's emphasis on the necessity of keeping categories clear – female blood is a pollutant because it breaks down categorical distinctions between female (blood), hunting (blood) and male (hunting). Perry admits that the association between femaleness and insecure affinal links may play a role in creating the negative associations between femaleness and general insecurity. Perry's arguments seem to lie on the level of a gender-based division of labour. Sekani division of labour does not automatically engage a contradiction.

Instead, the important role of women as markers of social boundaries in the past and present encourages the use of what is after all a gender-based division of labour as a forum in which certain idealized statements about their society can be valorized. In sum, arguments about tension between men and women in Athabaskan society are generally insufficiently powerful because they seek one cause as explanation. This in turn can be attributed to the feebleness of the models which describe the manner in which structure is constituted in Athabaskan societies. See H.S. Sharp, *Chipewyan Marriage*, Ottawa: National Museum of Man, Mercury Series, Canadian Ethonology Service Paper No. 58, 1979, p. 64. R.J. Perry, 'Variations on the Female Referent in Athabaskan Cultures', *Journal of Anthropological Research* 33(1), 1977, pp. 105, 112. C. Lévi-Strauss, *The Savage Mind*, London: Weiderfeld and Nicolson, 1966, p. 51. D. Jenness, *The Sekani Indians of British Columbia*, Ottawa: National Museum of Canada, Canadian Ethonology Service Paper No. 67, 1980, Routledge and Kegan Paul, pp. 55, 56. M. Douglas, *Purity and Danger*, London: 1966.

21. J. White, ed., *Handbook of Indians of Canada*, Ottawa: Appendix to the Tenth Report of the Geographic Board of Canada. Reprinted Toronto: Coles, 1971, pp. 413, 414.

22. One man, for example, had a mechanical breakdown in his snow-mobile several miles from Fort Ware. Although it was late and very cold he calmly repaired the motor, greasing his hands so that they would not stick to the bare metal. Unfortunately, he dropped a piece of string into the cylinder of the motor. A complete strip-down was necessary, by the light of a campfire and bare-handed; all this was accomplished without anger. It may be that some setbacks are always expected while in the bush and that anger leads to poor judgement when dealing with problems. The Chipewyans of Patuanak, for example, know from long experience that patience means a better chance of survival in the bush. See R. Jarvenpa, *The Trappers of Patuanak: Towards a Spatial Ecology of Modern Hunters*, Ottawa: National Museum of Canada, Canadian Ethnology Service Paper No. 67, 1980, p. 123.

23. A point examined at length in the next chapter.

24. B. Babcock, ed., *The Reversible World: Symbolic Inversion in Art and Society*, Ithaca: Cornell University Press, 1979. E. Norbeck, 'Rites of Reversal of North American Indians as Forms of Play', in E. Norbeck and C.R. Farrar, eds, *Forms of Play of Native North Americans*, 1977 Proceedings of the American Ethnological Society, Washington, 1979.

25. Inversions are traditional sources of humour and to a certain extent are still frequent in Sekani joking. For example, a man may address his sister's six-month-old son as "uncle", inverting the genealogical and classificatory relationship between them. This was seen as a joke by the baby's father, due to the age difference of nearly forty years. The McLeod Lake Sekani, like many people, see some humour in violence. Violence at parties is often the subject of joking among men the morning after. It is generally well accepted by scholars (Bergson, for example) that dichotomous contrasts are a source of humour. While not suggesting that

violence is a joke, the violence I have described as an inversion may be seen as just that by the Sekani. At first I suspected that people were merely taking sides in disputes when they laughed at someone involved in a violent episode. A few suggestions quickly suggested otherwise, however. For example, one of two brothers (who had a close relationship) joked about the severe beating his brother received while drinking. The aggressor in this case was someone not well liked by either brother. Even while threatening reprisals, both men laughed and joked and in general made light of the situation. In the end, no reprisals were taken. One caveat: women do not laugh at the same things as men do. They may laugh at stories of violence between men, but never did I observe humour when the subject was domestic violence. This is hardly surprising, since women are often the losers rather than the victors in such disputes. See Norbeck, 'Rites of Reversal', pp. 60, 61. H. Bergson, *Le Rire: essai sur la signification du comique*, 399th edn, Paris: Quadrige/PUF, 1981, pp. 99–100.

26. Lévi-Strauss, *The Savage Mind*.

27. Jackson's study of particular kinds of social deviance, for example, concluded that much in the way of deviance makes tolerable or acceptable what is otherwise unacceptable to a person. See B. Jackson, 'Deviance as Success', in Babcock, ed., *Reversible World*, p. 265.

28. K. Jobson, G. Ferguson, M. Fus, B. Ferstman and K. Kaiser, 'Report on Northern Justice', unpublished paper, Victoria: University of Victoria, 1978, p. 56.

29. Again, young McLeod Lakers by and large define themselves on the same scale of values as Whites. Many local Whites are not, according to their standards, racist since they like "good" Indians. By this they mean the older McLeod Lakers who are competent in non-White areas such as guiding and hunting and young people who like to drink and fight like they do.

30. This is another example of the inversion of sentiment. Patronymic affiliation is usually used as a marker in the formation of important social and economic partnerships. Even violence between spouses would sometimes be justified by pointing to the spouse's link to his or her domestic group of origin.

31. P. Worsley, *The Trumpet Shall Sound*, London: Paladin, 1970. W. LaBarre, 'Materials for a History of the Studies of Crisis Cults: A Bibliographic Essay', *Current Anthropology* 12(1): 3–44, 1971.

32. Another candidate for potential leadership in the Band Office is the Chief's nephew. His uncle is reluctant to appoint him because this might be construed as an overt attempt to "pack" the council and Band administration. With the exception of one office – one of the Councillors – the local administration would then have been entirely composed of people with the same patronymic identity.

33. Some Prince George merchants are used to people acting on behalf of the Chief, given the relative difficulty of transport, but they are not used to people ordering seven or eight stereo sets "for the Band". The Band Manage was soon caught; Jackson's study on 'Deviance as Suc-

cess' (note 27, this chapter) may be relevant here. It is as if the poor
fellow desperately wanted to do something that was uniquely his: a
case of exaggerating technical accounting skills that he had painfully
acquired beyond all limits in a local context that not only did not recognize but even denied such skills as a barometer of inclusion into the
community.

34. Band Office jobs are not the only rewards available. The Fort
Ware Chief was the largest employer in the region in his capacity as a
guide-outfitter. He regularly hired from ten to twenty men in the fall
hunting season. The Chief certainly could, and did, use his economic
clout to get things done in the community. Band members, for their
part, have recourse to the same pool of power. Their skills as guides en-
ables them to 'bargain' with the Chief. The Chief needs these men, after
all, and there are other guide-outfitters in the region who are eager to
hire Fort Ware men; at least two men in 1979 mentioned that the Chief
was "too hard" on them and that they preferred to work for someone
else. The McLeod Lake Chief had even more power. He was employed
as a foreman in a logging camp a few dozen miles south of McLeod
Lake and well respected by the local White community. Logging fore-
men have considerable power, since in the logging industry there are
few middle-management positions; foreman is one. His power was
limited by the fact that no one in McLeod Lake wanted to work for
wages, no matter how high (and they were high at the time). A few
McLeod Lakers were explicit. They felt uncomfortable being dependent
on the Chief and preferred to work elsewhere or not to work at all.

35. See, for example, LaBarre, 'Materials for a History'.

36. N.O. Lurie, 'The Contemporary American Scene', in N.O. Lurie
and E.B. Leacock, eds. *North American Indians in Historical Perspective*,
New York: Random House, 1971, pp. 444–48.

37. C. Osgood, *The Distribution of the Northern Athapaskan Indians*, Yale
University Publications in Anthropology, 7:1–23, New Haven: Yale
University Press, 1936. R.A. McKennan, *The Chandelar Kutchin*, Arctic
Institute of North America, Technical Paper No. 17, 1965.

38. J. Mooney, *The Ghost Dance Religion and the Sioux Outbreak of 1890*,
Chicago: University of Chicago Press, 1965. For an example of this view,
see M. Harris, *Culture, People, Nature*, New York: Harper and Row, 1980,
pp. 422–43.

39. L. Spier, *The Prophet Dance of the Northwest and its Derivatives: The
Source of the Ghost Dance*, Menasha, Wisc.: George Banta Publishing
Company, 1935, p. 8. For an insightful analysis of the Plateau Prophet
Dance, see C. Miller, *Prophetic Worlds: Indians and Whites on the Columbia
Plateau*, New Brunswick: Rutgers University Press, 1985.

40. Spier, *The Prophet Dance*, pp. 36, 37.

41. Ibid., p. 62; A.G. Morice, *Au Pays de l'Ours Noir: Chez les sauvages
de la Columbie Britanique*, Paris: Delhomme et Briguet, 1897, p. 116.

42. M. Barbeau, *Indian Days in the Canadian Rockies*, Toronto: Macmillan Co., 1923, pp. 19, 207.

43. Morice cited in Spier, *The Prophet Dance*, p. 36, Morice, *The History*

of the Interior of British Columbia (formerly New Caledonia) from 1660–1880,
London: John Lane, 1906.
44. Morice, *The History*, p. 225.
45. Ibid., p. 239, footnote.
46. Spier, *The Prophet Dance*, p. 63.
47. Barbeau, *Indian Days*.
48. Ibid., p. 33.
49. Ibid., pp. 54, 55; Morice, *The History*, p. 240.
50. Barbeau, *Indian Days*, pp. 19–25.
51. Ibid., p. 33.
52. Ibid., p. 26.
53. Ibid., p. 29.
54. Ibid., p. 34.
55. The debate on the aboriginality of the movement has been addressed by several writers. It is an important debate because of the
issues it raises; namely, the nature of revitalization, social disintegration
and responses to crises. Aberle argues that the Prophet Dance cult could
have been caused by cultural deprivation associated with indirect contact with Whites. Spier, Suttles and Herskovits disagree and maintain
that although the Prophet Dance later added elements intended to deal
with cultural distress the cult was not itself caused by contact-induced
stress. Walker suggests that indirect contact played a role in Plateau
culture, as shown in late pre-contact era changes in burial customs.
Even if the Prophet Dance is aboriginal as Spier claims, Walker suggests
that it is linked to the disruptive effect of Indian-White contact. Disruption is in part caused by the desire to acquire White goods; hence, it
contains some cargo cult elements. Miller, on the other hand, argues
that the Plateau Prophet cult arose from a concatenation of several
centuries of cooler weather (which played additional pressures on scarcer
resources) and waves of social dislocation due to the eastern fur trade
(which introduced the horse, guns and disease and pushed eastern
peoples on to the Plains, who in turn placed military pressure on the
Plateau). In his view, the Prophet Dance is a re-alignment of the ideological world in light of the newly emerged militarism and political
alliances which eroded traditional village autonomy. Elsewhere, I have
argued that the Plateau Prophet Dance was tied to the village and political
organization of Plateau peoples. See D.F. Aberle, 'The Prophet Dance
and Reactions to White Contact', *Southwestern Journal of Anthropology*
15:74–83, 1959. L. Spier, W. Suttles and M. Herskovits, 'Comments on
Aberle's Thesis of Deprivation', *Southwestern Journal of Anthropology*
15:84–8, 1959. D.F. Walker, 'New Light on the Prophet Dance Controversy', *Ethnohistory* 16: 245–55, 1969. Miller, *Prophetic Worlds*. G. Lanoue,
'Orpheus in the Netherworld in The Plateau of Western North America:
The Voyage of Peni', *Proceedings, Orpheus Seminar Series*, ed. G. Masara-
chia, Rome: Dipartimento di Studi Classici, Universita' di Roma 'La
Sapienza', 1991.
56. R. Ridington, *Swan People: A Study of the Dunne-Za Prophet Dance*,
Ottawa: National Museum of Man, Mercury Series No. 38, 1978, pp. 2–4.

See also A.C. Mills, 'The Beaver Indian Prophet Dance and Related Movements Among North American Indians', Ph.D. dissertation, Harvard University, 1981, esp. pp. 168–73.

57. K.O.L. Burridge, *New Heaven, New Earth: A Study of Millenarian Activities*, Oxford: Basil Blackwell, 1969, pp. 11–14.

Chapter 6

Band Organization in the Early Historic Era

I have suggested in the previous chapters that Sekani actions are the outcome of the interplay between external economic and political pressures on the one hand and a local tradition on the other. The most striking impressions about life in McLeod Lake are the tension, violence and disillusionment, especially as it affects relations between men and women. In Fort Ware the picture is calmer, but it is none the less clear that men and women play very different roles in the social structure and that these roles have little to do with the economy as such. There, the patronymic system of classification acts as a base from which pragmatically-oriented relationships evolve. In McLeod Lake few people follow this older system in order to develop work associations, but the tension and violence follow lines that are surprisingly close to the traditional categories. Furthermore, the McLeod Lake people are disposed to a pan-Indian form of political discourse; they seek to construct a political identity that is far removed from the negative aspects of their everyday lives. Any associations that develop from a universalizing philosophy of pan-Indianism, however, soon fail as factionalism and regionalism are allowed to usurp universalism. This too suggests that the base of their system of political and social classification lies in categories that do not directly depend on pragmatic considerations. In a word, the Sekani seem to be caught between opposing tendencies on every level. Patronymics are an abstract, inflexible means of classifying people, yet the resulting networks are so loose that pragmatic considerations are generally uppermost when selecting a partner. Everyone has definite personal freedom, but the system of partnerships is restrictive enough that some people become marginal to the point of emigrating. There appears to be a considerable degree of sexual freedom, but there is also a considerable amount of tension and violence between men and women.

If this tension is linked to an earlier tradition, it may be that aspect of the local tradition in which women marked important boundaries between the networks of hunters. Hunting is primarily a male activity, and it comes as no surprise that the Sekani see themselves as a male dominated society. And yet, in more general terms, I believe that this tension is linked to the crucial role which women play in defining – though not participating in – those social relations which the Sekani traditionally think of as their core. In terms of contemporary political culture, the indigenous cultural tradition interprets pan-Indianism in such a way that regional boundaries divide the theoretical unity of all Indian people and even (and especially, it might be said) of all Sekani. In brief, the tendency to unite large numbers of people by means of membership in an abstract category is today so uniquely expressed that it appears to be linked to an older notion of unity.

In the following chapters I will examine the source of this cultural tradition. First, I will examine the available documented evidence regarding prehistoric occupation of the Trench by the Sekani. Then I will speculate on the pre-contact arrangement of people in the area by examining the post-contact evidence. The Sekani were particularly influenced by the fur trade; hence, this too will be the subject of a chapter. Finally, I will evaluate the evidence of contact between the Sekani and their neighbours in order to shed light on the origin of the Sekani as a self-defined people, including the constraints that are part of the Sekani notion of unity.

The Evidence of the Prehistoric Era

The available records dealing with Sekani life in the pre-contact era (prior to 1805) are sparse indeed.[1] The archaeological evidence, little as it is, suggests that there were no village sites in the Trench. Whoever occupied the area left very little evidence of their passing. Cassidy reviewed the available evidence and concluded that the terrain and resources encouraged a transient population.[2] The bone and stone tools found in the area cannot be effectively evaluated against the descriptions we have of early Sekani technology contained in travellers' accounts. Those that are likely to be part of Sekani material culture show no great time depth.[3] The Trench area was so harsh and unreliable as a source of game compared to adjacent areas to the west and east that full-time occupation was likely to be the exception rather than the rule.[4]

Nevertheless, there are several riddles in the archaeological record. Obsidian tools found at one site suggest trade with western groups since the closest source of this material is near Telegraph Creek to the northwest.[5] The lack of associated historic era artifacts suggests a pre-contact date for their deposition. The lack of any evidence of occupation below the 2,200 foot contour level is also puzzling. This is the height of the former river terrace, and it therefore provides a relatively clear zone for travel compared to the scrub forests below. This implies that the Sekani were foot travellers rather than rivermen, and, indeed, historic evidence suggests that the Sekani only used relatively inefficient spruce bark canoes or moosehide craft and, later, a very few dugout canoes. Again, this accords with the analysis of faunal remains which suggests that intermittent rather than full-time occupation was the rule; the Trench was primarily a travel corridor rather than a homeland.[6] Mackenzie's observations of iron implements during his historic 1793 voyage to the Pacific Ocean also indicates rather wide pre-contact networks of trade and travel.[7] I could find no other evidence for pre-contact trade in the region, although in the historic era on the coast (still prehistoric in the interior) there might be mention made by the coastal Indians of the hinterland customers, among whom the Sekani were undoubtedly numbered.[8] Local tradition at McLeod Lake suggests that this trade was extensive, although from the point of view of the coastal Indians it probably formed only a small portion of the total.

The Historic Era: Some Definitions

The historic records are, in their own way, unfortunately not much more illuminating than the archaeological data. In general, the Sekani were so few, so relatively unimportant to the fur trade and so unimpressive in material culture to the western Europeans who ventured there that only the most impressionistic of records survive. None the less, at least something survives of the first contact situation, enough so that we know that the Sekani were probably poorer and more afflicted by their environment than their neighbours.

Early references to Sekani social organization are ambiguous. It is clear that each account recognizes two levels of organization. This, however, is not made explicit even after a close reading of the evidence. Each writer speaks of 'bands'. Sometimes these are clearly nothing more than hunting groups – one or two families or domestic groups. At other times they are referring to something larger, something akin to Helm's notion of regional band.[9]

Helm suggests that the local band is composed of one or more domestic groups or nuclear families and that it is structurally equivalent to the hunting group. The Sekani evidence, however, suggests that the two are not necessarily coterminous. The former persists as an identifiable socio-spatial unit for one or two years; the latter is more enduring. The local band is a somewhat more abstract category than the hunting group. It is primarily a network rather than a group.[10] Helm describes the regional band as differing from the local band in degree, not in kind. It is slightly larger and longer-lived. It tends towards the tribal end of the socio-spatial gradient. 'Tribe', in the Sekani case, is a somewhat abstract category. Neither shared linguistic competence, nor common origin and descent system, nor shared cultural heritage taken in isolation from each other represent sufficiently precise criteria for tribal membership. Only when all of these are combined and claimed as a set of necessary conditions do they serve as the indicator of tribal identity. For the Sekani it is not at all clear that a sense of tribal identity and autonomy existed or was claimed, even in its modern diluted form, before the creation of Williston Lake. Nor does such classification tell us much about the processes of group formation and recruitment which are contained in, emerge from and transcend these units. In the early contact period, for example, the place of the patronymic networks (which did not even exist as such) might have been more or less taken by the structurally equivalent local band, but the set of possible connections within these networks is so large that little is gained from using the classification as a means of understanding the social processes that were at work. The evidence is confusing and so have been past attempts to clarify it in the Athabaskan context.

We can see from the evidence that groups, however they are defined, were generally quite small. Early records state, for example, that the 'bands' attached to McLeod Lake post at the time of early contact were: Tabata's 'band' consisting of four men; the Montenge de Boute with five men; the Marie Dents de Biche with two hunters and two boys;[11] the Powder's 'band' with five men;[12] and a fifth unnamed group with five men.[13] The "party" of Indians encountered by Mackenzie on the Parsnip in 1793 consisted of three men, three women and seven or eight children.[14] These people told Mackenzie that they "did not amount to" more than ten families,[15] which implies that McLeod Lake was populated by about 140 people, if the Parsnip River party was indeed one family. Stuart had listed the population of McLeod Lake post at thirty-five in 1823 although there is no record of the number of women and children.[16] The list of 'bands' accounts for twenty-one of thirty-five hunters. Five other hunters are listed by name in the accounts, although they are not listed as belonging to any particular 'band'. Other configurations were sometimes encountered. Samuel Black mentions an encounter, probably in 1824, with a Sekani family hunting alone. They consisted of a man, wife, daughter and son-in-law, plus a few young children.[17]

On the other hand, there is a second level of organization which emerges from the evidence, particularly when the same writers refer to it in special terms. Black mentions a leader named Methodiates and his band, encountered at the northern bend of the Finlay River, which consisted of seven married men, "about as many young men", and two other families who were living at Bear Lake to the west.[18] This suggests a size of twenty-five people at the very least. The presence of people whose specific identity was clearly linked to another territory indicates that this was at least a local band. Regardless of the confusion between hunting band, local band and regional band, however, the circumstances of contact with Europeans and with neighbouring tribes contrived to produce a level of organization somewhat larger in scope and size than a group whose existence depends on accomplishing immediate tasks. In brief, the result was a system of regional band organization and, later, phratries.

The Historic Era: The Evidence

Alexander Mackenzie was the first European to record his impressions of the Sekani. He passed through the upper Peace River valley (sometimes called the Peace River portage) in 1793 on his way to the Pacific. He mentioned two groups of Indians, one in the Parsnip River valley itself and one living on the shores of McLeod Lake.[19] A distance of fifteen miles separates the two locales. The presence of iron implements among these previously unknown people augured well for Mackenzie, since it suggested the likelihood of a link between his present location and his destination. It is not clear where the iron was obtained, however, but the Sekani traded moose and beaver skins for it at a "carrying place" (a portage) eleven days' march from McLeod Lake.[20] The only portage at this distance from this location is the Giscome Portage between the Arctic and Pacific drainage basins, just north of the present-day town of Prince George and about seventy-five miles south of Mackenzie's location; other passes into the Pacific drainage basin are too far north to be reached in only eleven days. Mackenzie's description matches the characteristics of the Fraser River. A ex-trader who had lived in McLeod Lake from 1913 to 1916 told me that McLeod Lakers had then said that they had once traded with the Carrier for iron in return for moosehides. The route of that trade was a trail, still used today, between McLeod Lake and Fort Saint James; there is no "carrying place", however, on this trail. The presence of dentalia shell ornaments among the women also spoke of trade with the coast. When Mackenzie crossed the divide the Indians of the upper Fraser appeared to him to be clothed in mooseskins obtained from the Rocky Mountain Indians. This points to a second trade route towards the south in addition to the overland western connection with the Carrier. Although not significant in themselves, Mackenzie's comments on the appearance of the Sekani suggest that living conditions were difficult at best.[21]

Several years later, Simon Fraser described a group of "Meadow Indians" who lived in the upper watershed of the Beaver and Sinew (Pine) rivers.[22] They are reported to have lived in a location three days' journey from McLeod Lake, which is somewhere in the upper reaches of the Parsnip River near the location of one of Fraser's camps.[23] Another group of Meadow Indians, allies of the first, lived in the same vicinity. They traded furs for iron around the Skeena River to the northwest. No further details are offered, but this group might correspond to the second group Mackenzie saw, the one observed near McLeod Lake. The Meadow Indians traded with the "Nahanes", who to judge from their location are Liard River Kaska. The name 'Kaska' is so loosely used in the literature, however, that this is far from certain.[24] Another group of Big Men were reported to live near the upper reaches of the Nation River, northwest of McLeod Lake (the Nation joins the Parsnip about thirty miles north of the mouth of McLeod Lake). These Big Men, said Fraser, were of a "different family" than the McLeod Lake Big Men.[25] Fraser is implying that two more or less politically (if not culturally) distinct groups lived in the Trench at the time. The Meadow Indians lived to the east and northwest, while directly south of them were the McLeod lake and Nation River Big Men. In our terminology, perhaps two tribes and four regional bands lived in the Trench.

Daniel Harmon lived at Stuart's Lake Post, founded by Simon Fraser in 1806. He had first encountered the Sekani while stationed on the eastern side of the Rockies at Rocky Mountain Portage. Harmon's evidence is significant, for he is definite in assigning an original location to the Sekani east at the Rocky Mountains. According to Harmon, the Sekani wintered on the Plains and spent the summers in the mountains of the Trench.[26] The annual east-west migration, he believed, pointed to the eastern origins of the Sekani, and hence he deduced that the Sekani were originally members of the Beaver tribe who had been forced into their present abode by some sort of dispute. He also notes Sekani susceptibility to adopting Carrier customs when they were in Carrier country and their lack of manufacturing skills, which he took to be more evidence of their unfamiliarity with the country.

At least one other contemporary observer independently arrived at the same conclusion as Harmon. Archibald McDonald, who accompanied the Hudson's Bay Company's newly appointed governor, George Simpson, on his famous voyage through the Northwest in 1828, met "Chicanee" Indians just above the Peace River Portage; that is, on the west side of the first range of the Rocky Mountains.[27] They were from Trout (McLeod) Lake and had come to trade their beaver skins at the Peace River posts, despite their dispute with the local Beaver people.[28] McDonald also identifies a band of permanent residents of the Finlay and Peace junctions who were not Sekani.[29] A few days later he writes that the residents of McLeod Lake numbered twenty-six "exclusive of the Chicanees, and not counting those about Finlay's Branch".[30] Were there three different groups encountered by Simpson and his party between the Portage and McLeod Lake, or are we looking at a lexical error ('exclusive' instead of 'inclusive') by McDonald or his printers? "Chicanee", in this account, seems to be restricted to those Indians who live at the Portage itself. Whatever the situation, the general picture which emerges is that the people west of the first range of the Rockies were constrained for some reason in their contacts with people east of the Rockies. This hints at an emergent self-identity within the Trench, as does the use of the name itself, 'People of the Rocks'.

Interlude: Sekani Relations with Their Neighbours

Given the evidence that they were newcomers to the Trench, that they had not arrived voluntarily but had been displaced as a result of conflict and that access to European goods had to be negotiated through posts in unfriendly territory, some jostling and friction between the Sekani and their neighbours must have been inevitable. The Sekani seem to have been caught in a web of hostility and closeness, both probably originating with their need to obtain European goods and yet survive in a hostile political environment. Their relations with the Beaver, the Carrier, the Cree, the Tsimshian and the Kaska appear to have been ambiguous, both friendly and fearful. With the Shuswap, however, there was a period in which no quarter was given or expected. Harmon also specifically mentioned the conflict between the Sekani and the "Tacullies and Atenas" (Carrier and Shuswap) in the Trench, and between the Sekani and the Beaver and the Cree on the Plains.[31] Teit recorded statements by Shuswap informants who remembered some very bloody battles with the Sekani.[32] In 1785 a considerable band of Sekani appeared at the headwaters of the Fraser River (over 110 miles south-southeast of McLeod Lake) and drove out the resident Shuswap.[33] This was apparently the first Sekani venture this far to the south; this too is indirect evidence for the late arrival of the Sekani into the Trench. After intermittent raiding by both groups the Shuswap were evicted after a decisive raid into the North Thompson River country in which some of their number were taken prisoner.[34] The Sekani had made this bid in order to seize the headwaters of the Fraser, said by Teit's informants to be a poor salmon fishery but a very good hunting ground.[35] The intrusion went unchallenged for several years. The North Thompson Shuswap and the Fraser River Shuswap joined for the first and last time to drive the Shuswap out in a massive retaliatory raid.[36] One half of the entire Shuswap tribe was said by Teit's informants to be camped near the "big bend" of the Fraser River (near the modern location of Prince George). All the men save two or three were killed, and twenty or thirty women were made prisoners.[37] Some of the women were given to the North Thompson Shuswap in compensation for their losses suffered at the hands of the Sekani a few years prior. Since that time, say Teit's informants, the Sekani have been a small tribe and kept within their boundaries.[38] The general situation stabilized, since the Shuswap showed little inclination to move northwards into areas with no salmon. The Shuswap describe themselves as poor hunters compared to the Sekani.[39] This hints at the motive the Sekani may have held for the southwards drive. Since they are hunters, they may have hoped that a move into an area which was poor in salmon would go unpunished by the Shuswap, who are good fisherman but poor hunters. No doubt the ferocity of the encounters and their results were somewhat exaggerated by Teit's informants, but there undoubtedly was hostility.

Jenness believed that peace reigned in the Trench from about 1850 onwards. Althought not commenting directly on the situation, he certainly implies that relations with neighbouring groups were not friendly before this time.[40] But even later relations were not as idyllic as Jenness suggested. During the 1890s economic conditions at Fort Grahame were exceptional by regional standards, as we shall see in the next chapter. The Hudson's Bay Company journals report that outsiders were trapping and trading in and around Fort Grahame.[41] They were drawn there by the unique possibility of summer trapping. Whatever the facts of the previous bad relations between the Sekani and their neighbours, this time the problem was on their own doorstep. All previous encounters had been in a sort of no-man's-land on the fringes; now foreigners were in the Trench. Even if people were only trading at the post, some extra pressure must have been exerted on local food resources. Small comfort as it was, the Sekani could at least retire to the Trench proper after the Shuswap fiasco; less than 100 years later this peace was denied to them. Cree raiding on Sekani settlements and ambushes of hunting parties continued well past the mid-century mark, according to the people of McLeod Lake and to the Hudson's Bay Company journals.[42] It seems clear from the weight of the evidence that tension existed precisely because there were conflicting claims to land between the Sekani and their neighbours. This was to play a not inconsiderable role in defining the Sekani idea of brotherhood.

The Historic Era Once Again

Knowledge of the Sekani's northern landholdings and boundaries comes to us from another explorer/trader, Samuel Black. In 1823 he was ordered by Governor George Simpson of the newly re-structured Hudson's Bay Company to explore the upper reaches of the Finlay River.[43] Black noted that the Beaver and Sekani differed little in language.[44] He presents us with an interesting problem when he notes that a McLeod Lake Sekani knew nothing of the area around the upper Finlay River.[45] If this were true of all McLeod Lakers then the degree of contact and even of common origins of the various Sekani groups must be called into question. Unfortunately Black made no further notes on this matter. However, we can be reasonably certain that before setting out on a northern voyage of exploration he would have actively sought out and recorded all information about the upper Finlay that was known in McLeod Lake. Hence, it seems reasonable to guess that the northern and southern Sekani had little contact at that time. Black travelled up the Finlay, then abandoned canoes and walked northwards along the Trench after the Finlay turned west (and later south, but he had no way of knowing this). He stated at one point that, "none of the [Sekanis] ever go further than these rapids", apparently a point in the canyon of the Liard River between Hell Gate and the future site of Fort Halkett.[46] This is a point a little farther north than most

later descriptions of the northern boundary of Sekani landholdings.

Black's evidence complicates the question of Sekani origins
and self-identity. After reading Harmon's, Fraser's and Mackenzie's journals, Jenness had concluded that the Sekani had come
from the east through the Rocky Mountain Portage and settled
into a loose cultural amalgamation of several groups with southern and western trade orientations. There is no doubt that the
southern and western boundaries of the Sekani were defined by
the presence of the Carrier, Shuswap and Gitksan. Trade with
the Kaska to the north had been mentioned by Harmon and was
therefore known to Jenness. But Black's evidence, which was not
published until nearly twenty years after Jenness's work, suggests that the Sekani ventured farther north than either Harmon
or Fraser believed. Since only Black visited the north (and encountered northern Sekani), we may be reasonably certain that
the Sekani were occupying a larger range than Jenness believed
to be the case and that Jenness was accurately reporting *southern*
Sekani traditions. Certainly by 1924, nearly one hundred years
after Black's visit, Jenness was viewing a situation in which the
presence of the trading post at Fort Grahame had pulled the
northern Sekani somewhat southwards. As we shall see in Chapter 7, this played a part in the adoption of phratries. Black also
provided some evidence about the connections between the
Sekani and their northern neighbours. He noted the existence of
a trail between the northern Finlay and the Fishing Lakes to the
west (the ultimate source of the Finlay after the river turns west
and south).[47] This suggests rather intensive contact in that direction, especially with or by the so-called Caribou Hide Indians,
who abandoned the area in the 1940s, according to Fort Ware
residents. These may have been the people to whom Black applied
the name "Thloadenni", 'The Grass People';[48] they may also be
Jenness's "T'lotona", 'The Long Grass People'.[49] Although Jenness considers them distinct from the Sekani proper, the people
of Fort Ware believe that these people are the ancestors of a great
many Fort Ware families. Furthermore, the eastern terminus of
the trail may have been Fort Ware (there still exists a western
trail which is used to hunt the interior plateau towards the
Caribou Hide area), although the information presented in Black's
writings is not unequivocally convincing.

Black also confirmed Harmon's observations that in 1824 the
Sekani scarcely ever spent winters in the mountains but instead
moved to the eastern plains through the various mountains passes.
At the same time, the evidence in Appendix II shows that the

moose population was apparently increasing in the southern Trench. Hence, it seems reasonable that all but the easternmost and northern groups of Sekani (on whom we have little information) were by this time staying in the Trench year-round. Black calls these the Peace River Portage Sekani, thus, further emphasizing their separateness and, by implication, the greater homogeneity of the southern Trench Sekani.

We are fortunate that the close of the last century saw the emergence of another important observer of the Sekani, A.G. Morice, whose main contribution is a detailed report of the location of various local groups.[50] Morice spent a great deal of time among the Carrier and developed an interest in Sekani-Carrier contact. Unlike Harmon, he argued that the differences between the two people were so great that contact was not likely. This indicates that a separate sense of Sekani identity had gelled in the fifty years or so since Harmon's time. Morice also mentions – somewhat puzzlingly, given his observations on the isolation of each group – the Carrier practice of obtaining Sekani brides to ensure access to Sekani hunting territory.[51] This was not a new development; Harmon had also mentioned this trait.[52] Trade was undoubtedly the circumstance which brought these unions about, notes Morice, especially as the Carrier were the initial source of iron for the Sekani in pre-contact times. These unions must have taken place in an atmosphere of tension and distrust, given the inequality in the terms of trade. As the fur trade progressed, the Sekani clearly resisted these Carrier advances. In the fall of 1805 (when the Sekani got their own post at McLeod Lake), the McLeod Lake Big Men killed a Carrier and even as late as 1911 two Carrier males were expelled when they came to McLeod Lake looking for brides.[53]

Father Morice had been impressed by Harmon's account but did not live to see Black's journal. He agreed with the notion of the eastern origin of the Sekani but followed a different line of reasoning, namely, by analysing the Sekani language. His belief was merely confirmed by reading Harmon after he had committed himself to print.[54] He was unsure of the degree of closeness between the Carrier and the Sekani and would not guess how long they had been distinct. Morice confirms that the Sekani of that time regarded the Arctic-Pacific divide about twenty miles north of the modern city of Prince George as the southern boundary of their territory.[55] The western boundary was the continuation of the divide, which swings northwards just west of a line between the bend of the Fraser River and McLeod Lake. Connolly Lake, on the western side of the divide, is both easily accessible from McLeod lake and is stocked with salmon. None the less, the Sekani shunned it.[56]

Morice identified various sub-groupings of the Trench Sekani based on information he had gathered in the 1890s.[57] Because I want to examine the emergence of self-identify, it is worth considering the evidence in some detail. The groups mentioned by Morice are (following his spelling):

(1) The Yu-tsu-t'qenne, who inhabit the region of McLeod Lake to the Salmon River, roughly at the Arctic-Pacific divide. "From time immemorial", states Morice, "[they have] bartered out to the Carriers . . . axes and other primitive implement."[58]

(2) The Tse-Keh-ne-az, the "little people of the rocks", who lived between McLeod Lake and the eastern chain of the Rocky Mountains. This would place them immediately south of the areas inhabited by the Meadow Indians, in the middle of the Parsnip River watershed.

(3) The To-ta-t'qenne, a group located on the eastern slopes of the Rockies and the adjacent plains in eastern British Columbia.

(4) The Tsa-t'qenne, the Beaver people, who inhabit the large prairies contiguous to the Peace River.[59] These, like the To-ta-t'qenne, lived in contemporary Beaver country.

(5) The Tse-'ta-ut'qenne, people of the base of the Rocky Mountains on the north side of the Peace. These may be the Finlay River Sekani.

(6) The Sarcees, part of the historic Blackfoot Confederation, located east of the Rockies much south of the Trench area. This group is obviously only included on linguistic grounds.

The last three groups listed by Morice all occupy the Finlay River basin:

(7) The Saschut'qenne, people who traded at Fort Connolly and later at Fort Grahame.

(8) The Otzanne, "people who claim . . . the land which intervenes between the territory of the Saschut'qenne and that of the Tselohne on the west side of the Rocky Mountains".[60]

(9) The Tselohne, who are north of the Otzanne and who traded at Fort Grahame.

Instead of adopting this latter triadic scheme to describe the people of the Finlay River basin proper, Jenness rejected it on the basis that the term 'Sekani' should refer only to people of the Trench proper.[61] Three of Morice's nine groups lived east of the Rockies and are definitely classified separately today; two Beaver groups (the To-ta-t'qenne and the Tsa-t'qenne) and the Sarcee. Jenness, however, believed that at the time of earliest contact and most intensive European exploration (1793 to 1824) there were six Sekani groups in the region, although no one explorer cited by Jenness (and here) ever mentioned more than four distinct groups.[62] These are as follows.

(1)   The Beaver, noted by Mackenzie, who lived at the junction of the Smokey (Pine) and Peace Rivers at the falls below Vermillion. Jenness believed that this group had already adopted Cree culture at the time of Mackenzie's visit.[63] Apart from the linguistic similarity, there is no apparent reason why these are called "Eastern Sekani" by Jenness.

(2)   The Beaver, as described by Harmon and Fraser. They lived at the junction of the Peace and Smokey Rivers westward to the foot of the Rockies in the area of Rocky Mountain Portage. These are today the Hudson Hope Beaver. Again, it is not clear why two groups outside of the Trench proper are included in the category of Sekani. Unknown to Jenness, however, Black had noted the existence of a band of Sekani around the Rocky Mountain Portage.[64] They had hunted there for a session in order to supply a trading post with food.

(3)   The Bawcanne, thus named by Fraser and whose name strongly resembles the French word for 'smoke'.[65] Hence, they might be associated with the river of that name and, indeed, are reputed to have lived near the headwaters of the Smokey River east of the Rocky Mountain Portage. They traded at McLeod Lake post. Since there are no later accounts of this group Jenness believes that they were exterminated, although it is more likely that they were one of several Sekani groups who migrated annually. They were thus either absorbed by the Beaver or the McLeod Lake Sekani. Fraser, on the other hand, placed their homeland somewhat south of the area designated by Jenness after local Indians at the Arctic-Pacific divide informed him that the Bawcanne lived at the "upper end" of the Fraser River, or, in other words, at least seventy miles southeast of Fraser's position.[66] He would have assumed that "upper end" was almost due east of his position, but the Indians undoubtedly knew that the Fraser turns southwards after its south-north route is

blocked by the Arctic-Pacific divide. This makes it considerably less likely that the Bawcanne were indeed Sekani; perhaps they were Shuswap. They were enemies of the Carrier, a description which could be applied to either the Sekani or the Shuswap at the time but which obviously eliminates the Carrier themselves as potential candidates for the name.[67]

(4) A group who lived at the headwaters of the South Pine River and the Parsnip River. Fraser calls them Meadow Indians, and by 1924 Jenness believe that halfbreeds around the Peace River country towns of Pouce Coupé and Grand Prairie were their descendants. This conclusion was based on the use of the term 'T'lakotenne' by the McLeod Lake Sekani to refer to one of their own divisions in the past. This is translated as 'Meadow Indians', although there are several 'Meadow' and 'Grass' groups who could claim the designation. The McLeod Lakers, however, used to meet Fraser's Meadow Indians on the Pine River.[68] Fraser had overtaken 'his' Meadow Indians on their way to the "Beaver Country", i.e. southwest of Fraser's position, beyond "Finlay's Branch".[69] These may be the people who inspired Harmon's descriptions about the migrant Sekani groups who wintered on the plains east of the Rockies, since Fraser overtook these Meadow Indians on 26 May; hence, they were perhaps returning from a winter on the plains.

(5) People of the junction of the Nation and Parsnip Rivers. These would therefore be due west of the Meadow Indians. Jenness implies that some members of this group had ties to the Carrier to the south and west, the people just north of Stuart Lake. The same village, said by Jenness to have been founded by the Sekani on the shores of this lake, was described by Morice before the publication of Jenness's book (although after his visit) as merely reflecting some Sekani influences that came about by means of trade. After visiting the village, Morice asserted that it was Carrier, despite the past presence of a few Sekani men who had married Carrier women.[70] Hence, the "Nation River Indians" were more than likely Sekani of the Trench and not errant Carrier. Jenness apparently ignored a point mentioned by Fraser, who described these Indians as related to the McLeod Lakers.[71]

(6) The Finlay River Sekani, called Sicaunie by Harmon. They traded with the Gitksan to the west, the Kaska to the north and the Carrier to the southwest. They lived immediately north of the Nation River Big Men, around Bear Lake country. Black had cited a report from an Indian who said that these Indians did not winter on the plains,[72] although he later spoke to the chief of the

band, who did indeed admit to doing so on occasion.[73] There was little connection between these northern Sekani and the southern Sekani centred around McLeod Lake, a point which had also been implied by Black.[74] They were said by Fraser to be relatives of the Meadow Chief, which suggests that they were indeed tied to the eastern "Sekani"/Beaver who lived east of the Rockies rather than to the McLeod Lakers.[75] Fraser urged them to trade at McLeod Lake, but they evidently did not keep a promise made to that effect.[76]

It is remarkable that while Jenness listed two groups of Finlay River Sekani – and this is true only if we include the residents of the Nation-Parsnip junction, whose Sekani pedigree is not without suspicious taint – Morice had listed three such groups. Nor did Jenness refer to or quote Morice's introductory statement made before the latter's description of group number seven: "to the north of all of the above subdivisions".[77] It certainly seems clear enough that Morice is implying the existence of a division between these three northern groups and the other six Sekani groups whom he listed. Three of Morice's tally of six 'southern' groups are not even adjacent to the other three, who form a contiguous and uniform southern block. Morice is implying that there was more cultural homogeneity in the Trench than existed externally, despite cultural and linguistic affinities between the Sekani of the Trench and other Athabaskan-speakers outside of it. Of the two writers Morice seems more credible than Jenness and his scheme agrees more closely with the bulk of the literature; there do not appear to be any of the irregularities which mark Jenness's treatment.[78] Furthermore, Jenness's list was a review of the literature and apparently intended as background to his own enquiries, though this is not explicitly stated as such. In any case, Jenness must have had doubts about its usefulness since he substituted another one, this list based on information given to him by McLeod Lakers in 1924.

Four groups were said to have existed at the turn of the last century. Two of these four are clearly the same as those noted by Harmon and Fraser; these are the Finlay River Sekani.[79] Two of the four were said to be already amalgamated as a result of the founding of Fort Grahame in 1890.[80] The result was a group called the Otzanne. They occupied the territory around the Fox and Kechika River basins; the territory of the Tseloni, in other words. The Sasuchan belong to the vicinity of Fort Grahame.[81] The re-arrangement of names which Jenness is proposing sounds like a defection of the Sasuchan to the Tseloni or, more likely, the collapse of these distinctions as people began focussing ever increasing amounts of their time in the areas around the trading post. Fort Grahame was indeed located in the middle of Sasuchan territory.

Jenness mentions a fifth group called the T'lotona, the "Long Grass Indians", who lived west of Sasuchan territory on the upper reaches of the Stikine River on the western slope of the central range of the Rockies.[82] They may be a temporary alliance of Gitksan and Sasuchan Sekani.[83] Certainly, the location does not lead us to believe that they were an integral part of the Trench scene, nor is their territory precisely defined on Jenness's map. Indeed, the minimal contact they had with the Sekani allowed Tahltan and Gitksan traits to surface among them. It is not known when they arrived into the area, but by 1923 they were composed of only eight families.[84] It is likely that these were the Caribou Hide people of Metsantan, who in 1948 were moved to Telegraph Creek by the government and who are claimed as ancestors by some in Fort Ware.

From an examination of the data it can be concluded that a southern group was centred around McLeod Lake and that this group may have represented a union of the two southernmost local bands, the Tsekani and the Yutuwichan. There was another regional band centred around Fort Grahame, possibly divided again into two local bands, the Sasuchan/Tseloni/Otzanne group in the north and the Sasuchan to the south.[85] I suspect that these groups existed as self-defined groups at some time around the third quarter of the last century, certainly no earlier than 1870 and probably no later than 1885 or 1890. Some general and pressing problems must be disposed of if we are to believe that the four-fold classification proposed by Jenness disappeared around 1850, as he implies. It is difficult to see how the few people who arrived helter-skelter in a huge area after 1750 or so could arrange themselves into a relatively fixed pattern with clear boundaries in so little time, or that four distinct groups of Sekani arrived more or less simultaneously into the Trench only to disappear one hundred years later. Jenness is not clear on the time depth of his informants, nor is he clear on the nature of the groupings he is describing; the terms 'regional band' and 'local band' are modern interpretations of the data. The problem is in part not solely attributable to Jenness, since the earlier data are clearly speaking of a system of local and regional bands, while the later data – the information Jenness was given – is probably describing units of a different stripe altogether. As we shall see, phratries were emerging at the close of the last century, and, with them, a new definition of brotherhood was in the air. Although there are some doubts about Jenness's disposition of the data, the fact that he is describing a four-fold system remains compelling. After all, he did not invent the scheme but was reporting what people were telling him. I will return to the significance of this quadripartite scheme when I examine the tripartite phratric organization of the Sekani.

There is one further significant piece of evidence regarding Sekani possessions and distribution of people. In November 1823 a Trader and four employees of the Hudson's Bay Company were murdered in Fort Saint John on the western side of the Rockies because of the actual or threatened relocation of the post; the records are unclear on this latter point.[86] In a letter to John Stuart, William McIntosh indicated that he believed that the Beaver were responsible. Chief Trader Stuart replied that they were not Beaver but Rocky Mountain Indians.[87] Another letter to Francis Heron followed, in which Stuart again sought to lay the blame (and the object of HBC retribution) on the correct party.[88] Stuart worried whether or not the similarities between the Beaver and the Sekani were not so great as to render distinguishing them difficult.[89] The last word belonged to Samuel Black, who neither had trouble telling a Beaver from a Sekani nor did he believe that either group were responsible for the deaths.[90] The Rocky Mountain Indians were a distinct group, implied Black, and it was they who had dealt this blow to the Company. Stuart replied that the Rocky Mountain Indians were so similar to the Beaver as to blend in with them unnoticed, although they were also "similar" to those in McLeod Lake.[91] It was later determined that the Beaver indeed had been responsible for the murders. The Fort Saint John post was abandoned in favour of the one at Rocky Mountain Portage to accord with Sekani wishes. They would not trade at the former post on account of their enmity with the Beaver.[92] The Beaver had been upset by the removal of the post since it removed the basis of their power over the Sekani and, as they well knew, invited reprisals. By 1849, the easternmost Sekani – the Rocky Mountain Portage Indians – were labelled Sekani. By 1849 the fur trade had created significant rifts and alliances in the Northwest, and the Sekani were largely created as a self-defined people as a result of these shifts. Cultural similarity is no guarantee of political closeness; if anything, political differentiation and distancing are more likely.

Summary and Conclusion

The information on the origins of the Sekani and their disposition in the Trench into northern and southern amalgamations of various local bands is complicated but can be summarized as follows. (1) Morice implies that a distinction between north and south was important when he uses a dual scheme to organize his classification. (2) There were two major trade routes in use, one heading west and north to the Gitksan and Kaska and one heading southwest to the Kaska. These routes were important as sources of iron for the Sekani and skins for their neighbours, and were frequently used. This suggests that the northern and southern Sekani groups had to respond to different political exigencies. (3) Black's evidence from a McLeod Laker who knew nothing of the upper Finlay suggests little contact between northerners and southerners. (4) Jenness's suggestion is that two of the four groups merged into one. The northern groups were very similar, it is implied. (5) Jenness also suggested that the two southern groups merged into one, centred around McLeod Lake Post. (6) Harmon and Fraser both suggested that the northern Sekani groups (two in Fraser's account, one in Harmon's) alternated their summer and winter residence, while the southern Sekani around McLeod Lake were more settled and limited in their travels. There are, in addition, five sources of information which suggest that a close link once existed between the Beaver and the Sekani. These are as follows. (1) Harmon's journal, in which this conclusion is explicitly stated, as are statements attributed to the Sekani themselves. (2) Mackenzie's declaration, also explicit, that some Trench Indians were Beaver in origin, although he does not explicitly call these people Sekani. (3) Morice's linguistic analysis, which, however, contains no data with which to substantiate the claim. (4) Stuart and Harmon's contentions, recorded in correspondence written around 1823 and in a journal written in the 1830s but only published in 1849 (and hence not available to Harmon, thus independently confirming his assertions). (5) Dyen and Aberle's linguistic reconstruction (examined in the next chapter), which also supports the Beaver-Sekani link.

The Sekani witnessed the emergence of at least two levels of political integration shortly after contact. The landscape was dotted by small and relatively autonomous hunting groups, each with about eight to fifteen people. The nature of the links between these groups is unknown but at the minimum must have been expressed by intermarriage. The Sekani also seem to have possessed something akin to Helm's notion of regional band.

They had two such groups. Each came to be associated with one of the major trading posts established by the Northwest Company and later taken over by the Hudson's Bay Company. Whether such a regional organization preceded or followed the establishment of the posts is unclear, but the bulk of the evidence favours the former proposition. Between these two extreme levels of organization were the local bands, which seem to have been as ephemeral as the hunting bands.

The question remains: what was the nature of the bonds which linked all of these various networks together? The evidence suggests that there was a different basis for bonding which emerged in the latter half of the last century. This category was somewhat smaller in scope than the regional band but was certainly larger than the local bands or the modern patronymics. It was particularly active in regulating marriages, especially marriages between Sekani and non-Sekani. More important, this category had a different origin and different implications for social organization than the band network. This category is the phratry. Its emergence is strongly linked to the circumstances which marked Sekani involvement in the fur trade. The trade had a very strong impact in defining Sekani traditional culture, but as we shall see, not entirely in the ways which the anthropological literature assumes. The next chapter, therefore, is as precise an examination of that impact as the available records allow. As such, it can be treated as an interlude which establishes how the Sekani occupied land during the last century.

Notes

1. There are several reasons for the scarcity of historical data: (1) much of the archaeological evidence which could have supplanted the historical data was destroyed by the flooding of the Finlay and Parsnip River valleys; (2) after the fur trade was established in the New Caledonia region further exploration and settlement were discouraged due to the difficult nature of the terrain and the poor returns which were foreseen; (3) once it was established that the Fraser River was virtually impassable as a transport route, travellers were few in the region; (4) all of Jenness's field notes have since disappeared; according to National Museum staff. I have already mentioned the fact (Chapter 3, note 17) that most church records were destroyed (they were burned in the late 1960s).

2. S. Cassidy *et al.*, 'Preliminary Report on the Archaeological Potential of Those Areas Affected by the McGregor Diversion Project', Victoria: Archaeological Sites Advisory Board, 1976, p. 11.

3. R. McGhee, 'An Archaeological Survey in the Area of the Portage Mountain Dam Reservoir', Victoria: Archaeological Sites Advisory Board, 1963, p. 20.

4. Ibid., p. 23.

5. Ibid., p. 21.

6. The tradition of making and using spruce bark canoes is not remembered today. Sekani do remember using dugouts and moose hide craft; the latter were used to float downriver after the hunter had walked north, carrying the hunter and his kill to Fort Ware. Such craft were dismantled after one use. Dugouts seem to have been associated with the Hudson's Bay Company's resupplying of its posts in the period between 1880 and 1915; the Sekani were often hired as canoe men or drovers when horses were used by the Company to link Fort Saint James and McLeod Lake.

7. A. Mackenzie, *The Journals and Letters of Sir Alexander Mackenzie*, ed. W.K. Lamb, Toronto: Macmillan, 1970, pp. 287, 319.

8. I think that such a discovery in the appropriate archives is unlikely since the Sekani would have only been indirect and unimportant clients of the coastal Indians. See A. Krause, *The Tlingit Indians: Results of a Trip to the Northwest Coast of North America and the Bering Straits*, Vancouver: Douglas and McIntyre, 1979, pp. 126–37, for a description of Tlingit trade with the interior, including a reference to their possession of iron as early as 1741.

9. J. Helm, 'Bilaterality in the Socio-Territorial Organization of the Arctic Drainage Dene', *Ethnology* 4: 361–85, 1965, p. 380.

10. See, for example, HBC Arch. B119/a/4, fo. 4d.

11. HBC Arch. B119/a/4, fo. 5.

12. HBC Arch. B119/a/I, fo. 5.

13. Mackenzie, *The Journals*, p. 287.

14. Ibid., p. 287.

15. HBC Arch. B119/e/1, fo. 6.

16. HBC Arch. B119/e/1, fo. 6.

17. S. Black, *Black's Rocky Mountain Journal, 1824*, ed. E.E. Rich, London: Hudson's Bay Record Society, 1955, p. 197.

18. Ibid., p. 51.

19. Mackenzie, *The Journals*, p. 286.

20. Ibid., p. 287.

21. Ibid., pp. 286, 287.

22. S. Fraser, *Simon Fraser, Letters and Journals 1806–1808*, ed. W.K. Lamb, Toronto: Macmillan, 1960, p. 164.

23. Ibid., p. 169.

24. Another 200 Meadow Indians were located at the Hudson Hope encampment on the Peace, east of the Rockies. These were distinct from the "Big men" of McLeod Lake, who traded extensively with the Carrier Indians. This confusion in names is typical of the times. See ibid., p. 191.

25. Ibid., p. 195.
26. D.W. Harmon, *Sixteen Years in the Indian Country: The Journal of Daniel Williams Harmon 1800–1816*, ed. W.K. Lamb, Toronto: Macmillan, 1957, p. 130; Fraser, *Simon Fraser*, pp. 130, 131. Harmon respected the Indians. After completing his service in the Northwest, he returned east with his Indian wife and married her in the church. This was a rare event in the Northwest, particularly as Harmon's wife was full-blooded. Another famous case involved Chief Factor Douglas of Fort Saint James, who also married a woman who was half-Carrier, half-White. He was later to become Premier of the province. However, abandoning the 'country wife' was the more usual practice for the men of the Hudson's Bay Company. Harmon's sympathy with the Indians lends weight to his assertions that conditions in the Trench were difficult indeed. Morice points out that many of Harmon's observations should be treated gingerly since we cannot be sure if they flowed from Harmon's own pen or from the pen of his feverishly romantic editor, Rev. D. Haskel. Haskel admits in one edition of Harmon's diary that Harmon was such a poor writer that the account had to be totally re-written. The real problem was probably not Harmon's rudimentary education but the boredom that was typical of the Northwest fur trade; the result was probably an unexciting document. Haskel added spice to the account for readers who wanted vicarious thrills and not the tedious business of the fur trade. Morice corrects several such aggrandizements, especially as regards Harmon's (or Haskel's) geography. It is clear in the text, however, that all such errors were areas which Harmon admitted he had never visited personally. Hence, even Harmon's provisos and caveats should be taken as tokens of good faith and of the value of his direct accounts. On the other hand, Morice's reservations about Harmon's account of scalping among the Sekani are probably justified, but this titbit is undoubtedly a Haskelism. Morice, too, can come under the same criticism when he refers to the Indian as a "grown up child". On the whole, there is no pressing reason why Harmon's account should be dismissed. See Harmon, *Sixteen Years*, p. ix. See A. G. Morice, 'The Fur Trader in Anthropology', *American Anthropologist* 30(1): 60–84, 1928, pp. 62, 62, 65. See J.S.H. Brown, *Strangers in Blood: Fur Trade Company Families in Indian Country*, Vancouver: University of British Columbia Press, 1980, for a comprehensive description of marriage in the fur trade.
27. A McDonald, *Peace River: A Canoe Voyage from Hudson's Bay to the Pacific*, Ottawa: J. Durie and Sons, 1872. Reprinted Toronto: Coles, 1970, p. 20.
28. Ibid., p. 20.
29. Ibid., p. 21.
30. Ibid., p. 21.
31. Relations with the Beaver, however, were not all bad in Harmon's time. Some Sekani lived on the eastern side of the Rockies at Fort Dunvegan. Mackenzie had also noted the east-west migration of the Sekani but had not commented upon their Beaver origins. Two Dunvegan Rocky Mountain Indians had told him that his use of their name

for the inhabitants of the upper Peace was incorrect. These people, said Mackenzie's informants, were recent migrants into the area and were still ignorant of the lands and rivers in the vicinity. Mackenzie, however, does not identify the Rocky Mountain Indians of the Parsnip with those of the same name in the upper Peace. Although some similarity is implied by the use of the same name for the two groups, the credit for linking the McLeod Lake Sekani with those of the upper Peace (Mackenzie's Rocky Mountain Indians) goes to Harmon. See Harmon, *Sixteen Years*, p. 132; Mackenzie, *The Journals*, pp. 249, 250, 287–8.

32. J. Teit, *The Shuswap*, Memoirs of the American Museum of Natural History 4(7) of the Jesup Expedition, New York: AMS., 1909.

33. Ibid., p. 542.

34. Ibid., p. 546.

35. Ibid.

36. Ibid., p. 541.

37. Ibid., p. 548.

38. Ibid.

39. Ibid., p. 472.

40. D. Jenness, *The Sekani Indians of British Columbia*, Ottawa: National Museum of Canada, Bulletin No. 84, 1937, p. 26.

41. HBC Arch. B119/a/2, fo. 8.

42. HBC Arch. B249/a/6, pp. 1, 2.

43. This he accomplished so thoroughly that Simpson subsequently complained about the wordiness of the report. Its length, however, was probably due to Black's realization that the Trench was one of the last unexplored frontiers in North America at the time. Black was probably chosen precisely because of this fact. He was an old and somewhat unrepentant Northwest Company man, and some backwater or other was viewed by Simpson as a suitable locale where such a person could exercise his not inconsiderable talents as leader and explorer. The resulting journal was lost until found and published in 1955, 131 years after Black's difficult journey. It was therefore not available to Morice or Jenness, the two most important observers of the Sekani to date.

44. Black, *Black's Rocky Mountain Journal*, pp. 5, 6.

45. Ibid., p. 15.

46. Ibid., p. 25.

47. Ibid., p. 44.

48. Ibid., p. 127.

49. Jenness, *The Sekani Indians*, p. 13.

50. Morice was personally acquainted with the Sekani from 1885 onwards, so we can reasonably assume that his reports cover a period dating at least thirty years before; that is, from the 1850s. See Morice, 'The Fur Trader in Anthropology', p. 70, fn. 30.

51. Ibid., p. 81.

52. Fraser, *Simon Fraser*, p. 256.

53. Ibid., p. 165.

54. A.G. Morice, *The History of the Interior of British Columbia (formerly New Caledonia) from 1660–1880*, London: John Lane, 1906, p. 29, fn. 2.

55. Idem, 'The Fur Trader in Anthropology', p. 30.

56. Ibid., p. 79.

57. Idem, *Notes on the Western Dene*, Toronto: Transactions of the Canadian Institute, 1892/3, pp. 28, 29.

58. Ibid., p. 28.

59. Ibid., p. 29.

60. Ibid.

61. Jenness, *The Sekani Indians*, p. 10.

62. Jenness's more restricted meaning was probably based on his agreement with the definition contained in the standard reference at the time, the *Handbook of Indians of Canada*. J. White, ed., *Handbook of Indians of Canada*, Ottawa: Appendix to the Tenth Report of the Geographic Board of Canada, 1913. Reprinted Toronto: Coles, 1971, pp. 413, 414.

63. Jenness, *The Sekani Indians*, p. 7.

64. Black, *Black's Rocky Mountain Journal*, p. 41.

65. Fraser, *Simon Fraser*, p. 220.

66. Ibid.

67. Ibid.

68. Jenness, *The Sekani Indians*, p. 7.

69. Fraser, *Simon Fraser*, p. 188.

70. Morice, 'The Fur Trader in Anthropology', p. 80.

71. Fraser, *Simon Fraser*, p. 195.

72. Black, *Black's Rocky Mountain Journal*, p. 43.

73. Ibid., p. 53.

74. Fraser, *Simon Fraser*, p. 191.

75. Ibid., p. 190.

76. Ibid., pp. 191, 192; Black, *Black's Rocky Mountain Journal*, p. 51.

77. Morice, *Notes*, p. 29.

78. In defence of Jenness, the vagueness of the record, the overlapping of names and his mistaken impression that Morice had never visited the Sekani north of the divide may have combined to discredit Morice's list in his eyes. Morice in fact frequently travelled to McLeod Lake. See A.G. Morice, *Au Pays de l'Ours Noir: Chez les sauvages de la Columbie Britanique*, Paris: Delhomme et Briguet, 1897, p. 115.

79. Jenness, *The Sekani Indians*, p. 11.

80. Ibid., p. 14. The post was actually founded in 1870, although Jenness did not know this. See note Chapter 7, note 28.

81. Jenness, *The Sekani Indians*, p. 14.

82. Although this is the sixth group mentioned, in fact it is only the fifth since two other groups had amalgamated by that time. See ibid., pp. 13, 14.

83. Ibid., p. 13.

84. Ibid.

85. Compare this conclusion with G. Denniston, 'Sekani', *Handbook of North American Indians, vol. 6: The Subarctic*, ed. J. Helm, Washington: The Smithsonian Institution, 1981, pp. 432–5. She accepts Jenness's quadripartite scheme as the base from which other developments emerged.

86. HBC Arch. B119/b/1, p. 8.
87. HBC Arch. B119/b/1, p. 99.
88. HBC Arch. B119/b/1, p. 101.
89. And a crucial issue it was. To allow an incident of this gravity to go unpunished was to jeopardize all future trade prospects. Hudson's Bay Company traders often thought that 'respect' involved some sort of force, actual or potential.
90. Perhaps Black was referring to another group of Rocky Mountain Indians north of his winter encampment. Michea suggests that a group now claiming the headwaters of the Keele River as their own and who live in Fort Norman, NWT, are also called Rocky Mountain Indians. Their history is uncertain, however. Alexander Mackenzie's Rocky Mountain Indians were called Sekani, but he also reported that the westernmost Beaver Indians claimed this name for themselves. The Beaver described the "other" Rocky Mountain Indians as latecomers to the upper Peace. This supports Harmon's assertions and Dyen and Aberle's reconstruction of Sekani history. Additional arguments are contained in Karamanski, who states that "Thekannies" visited Fort Liard in the summer of 1828 (quoted from HBC Arch. D5/3, fo. 274d). This group claimed to reside on the west branch of the Liard River "below the Falls" and "in the Mountains". Karamanski calls them Sekani but gives as his reference Petitot, who, in fact, makes reference to the Mountain Indians who live "below latitude 66⁰ N". On Petitot, p. 37, however, the Sekani are listed as belonging to the Montagnard Indians, of whom "only very few venture as far as the upper Peace and Liard Rivers". See HBC Arch. B119/b/1, pp. 103, 104. J. Michae, 'Les Chitra-Gottineke: essai de monographie d'un groupe Athapascan des Montagnes Rocheuses', Ottawa: *National Museum Bulletin* 190: 69–93, 1963, p. 50. T.J. Karamanski, *Fur Trade and Exploration*, Vancouver: University of British Columbia Press, 1983, p. 88. I. Dyen and D.F. Aberle, *Lexical Reconstruction: The Case of the Proto-Athapaskan Kinship System*, London: Cambridge University Press, 1974. Mackenzie, *The Journals*, pp. 249, 250. E. Petitot, *The Amerindians of the Canadian Northwest in the 19th Century, as seen by Emile Petitot: vol. II, The Loucheux Indians*, ed. Donat Savoie, Ottawa: Northern Science Research Group, 1970, p. 33. See J.C. Yerbury, 'The Social Organization of Subarctic Athapaskan Indians: An Ethno-historical Reconstruction', Ph.D. dissertation, Simon Fraser University, 1980, for a detailed evaluation of Athabaskan movements and the fur trade.
91. HBC Arch. B119/b/1, p. 104.
92. J. McLean, *Notes on Twenty-Five Years Service in the Hudson's Bay Company*, London: Richard Bentley, 1849, p. 235.

Chapter 7

The Influence of the Fur Trade

In the previous chapters I have suggested that several distinct categories of Sekani social organization could be identified. Even though I have used these designations for the sake of convenience, Sekani categories do not necessarily correspond to what is usually defined as the local band, the regional band and the tribe; more importantly, we gain very little by deciding that a group is a regional or local band since all the evidence suggests that whatever the level of organization, there was something other than a straightforward common interest in hunting that brought people together. The evidence points to a process of an emerging common identity as separate groups moved in and out of the Trench and adjusted to continually changing political and economic conditions. The interaction of the Sekani with their neighbours helped strengthen the notion of belonging to a regional band. In brief, a sense of membership in a larger unit, combined paradoxically with the sense that local 'bands' were economically and even politically autonomous, was strengthened by the circumstances surrounding the arrival of the Sekani into the Trench and by subsequent developments of the fur trade. These circumstances seem to have aggravated the important problem of unity; the fur trade was involved in structuring at least two levels of social organization, the regional band and the tribe.[1] More importantly, the fur trade created the circumstances which eventually led to the adoption of phratries by the Sekani. Phratries represent a very special definition of unity with implications for the modern era. But even the notion of phratry must be understood from within the context of the fur trade, since the northern and southern regional bands expressed a different degree of interest in the idea and each interpreted 'phratry' in its own way.

The Fur Trade: General Background

Jenness believed that the presence of two major trading posts on Sekani territory intensified the north-south division, although we have seen that its basis was established before the arrival of the Europeans.[2] Even before this time, the Sekani had been pushed from the Prairies into the Trench because of fur trade rivalries. Their traditional political culture, therefore, is defined by the fur trade as much as by hunting. In general, we can even oppose the two, since the fur trade tended to homogenize responses which were otherwise local and expressive of a sense of local autonomy.

At least two general responses have been documented for the fur trade era Athabaskans. First, when prices were too low to allow continued participation in the trade, people withdrew from the money economy and increased their participation in the traditional country-food economy.[3] Second, people could take advantage of the long shipment times needed to bring goods from Europe by offering food to the sometimes starving and always hungry traders. European traders were eager for such foodstuffs and traded goods in order to obtain them.[4] The result was little disruption to the traditional economy of the Indians. The relatively inelastic demand for European goods by Indians also favoured this strategy, since it meshed with an interest in pursuing traditional occupations. The Sekani, however, used a third strategy. This was the continual movement from post to post or to various Indian intermediaries in order to continue traditional pursuits while avoiding repayment. Repayment could be avoided because of the locally autonomous bureaucracy of the fur trade and the poor communications between posts, even when such practices were attacked by the Hudson's Bay Company.

The North-South Split and the Fur Trade

Fort McLeod was the southernmost of two posts, founded in 1805 by Simon Fraser.[5] Although located in the Arctic drainage basin, for purposes of administrative record-keeping it was grouped with other posts in New Caledonia in the Pacific drainage basin. This area was a source of prime furs and it fuelled the expansion of the rival Northwest Company. Hence, quite a few documents survive from this period, although most of them treat those groups on the Pacific side of the region rather than McLeod

Lake. Descriptions of the more settled groups in New Caledonia, who could depend on seasonal salmon runs, are therefore not representative of conditions north of the Arctic-Pacific divide. In general, the records for McLeod Lake and Fort Grahame are relatively sparse.

McLeod Lake, 1805–1891

There were a number of small bands who traded at this post in the early period of the fur trade, as we have seen. The evidence suggests that bands were not necessarily families, since at least one record mentions a pair of brothers who belonged to different bands.[6] This accords with local tradition at McLeod Lake, which holds that hunting was not organized around families. Samuel Black noted that each of the larger bands was divided into discrete smaller groups, each with a headman and a second-in-command.[7] Although other explorers fail to mention anything on the matter of leadership, later evidence from the Hudson's Bay Company archives suggests that Black was indeed accurate. Bands, as we have seen in the previous chapter, were often referred to by the name of the presumed leader. The Hudson's Bay Company employees did not jot down this information out of idle curiosity; there was a specific reason for familiarizing themselves with the movements and habits of each band. There were always problems supplying these bands for the coming hunts due to the irregularity of their movements. The general evidence from the archives makes it clear that these groups did not confine themselves to particular territories.[8] The Hudson's Bay Company tried very hard to break this pattern of free movement, especially because it needed accurate information in order to estimate how many items to ship to particular posts. This was a considerable problem given the rough terrain and the length of time necessary to move goods about. Poor communication between posts in the early years of the fur trade also exacerbated the situation. Each trader at the post received some credit from the Company if his post was doing well, thus helping his chances for promotion.[9] Hence, each had a personal incentive to make sure that the Indians returned to their posts year after year. Unfortunately for the traders, there was little they could do at this early date to stop the Indians from moving about. A McLeod Lake Post trader named Fleming tried to deal with the problem by sending out two men with each of the several bands that are mentioned in the journals he kept during his tenure at the post. The men were to tell the others the date by which they should return to the post, although there is no mention of how this was to be accomplished.[10] Given that the trading post only had two or three employees, two men per band could only mean that these men were Indians and not Whites. They were probably given a small advance to accomplish their task. We can probably only guess where their sympathies probably lay, but chances are that they were not with the Hudson's Bay Company.

William Connolly's report of activities in New Caledonia for 1826 mentions the problem of balancing the amount of goods against the number of people. He states that only thirty-two men were attached to McLeod Lake Post since the Rocky Mountain Portage Indians, despite an occasional visit, generally refused to trade at McLeod Lake because of the unreliable supply of local food.[11] These conditions made smaller posts somewhat more desirable for both parties, as there was little point in having a large trading post which was unable to attract customers for fear of starvation. Smaller post meant less of a drain upon local resources during the period of trade. On the other hand, they meant a decrease in efficiency since the Company would be sacrificing the obvious economies of scale which came from consolidation of transport and personnel. From the Sekani viewpoint, the presence of smaller – and perforce isolated – posts potted over the landscape was also desirable because it increased their chances of trading at favourable rates and it fitted in with their desire to move frequently from area to area. To a certain extent, these pressures resulted in at least one other post being established, Fort Grahame. The advantages were not all on the Sekani side, however, since the traders knew that the Sekani wanted some European goods and that they would eventually have to come to them in order to obtain them.[12]

The situation was worsened by the lack of large game animals in the Trench at the time. The problem of supply was not all on the shoulders of the Hudson's Bay Company. Black himself had noted the relatively few moose in the Trench during his journey. There were plenty in the north, in the Liard River area, but the Sekani never ventured that far.[13] Moose, these northern Sekani said, were never found in "their Mounts", by which they meant the Trench area between Fort Ware and the Nation River.[14] Dried fish, usually whitefish, formed the bulk of the Hudson's Bay Company employees' rations during the winter, but even the relatively modest needs of two to four men were sometimes too great a burden on the meager resources around the post. Dried salmon from Fort Saint James were regularly shipped to McLeod Lake to make up for the chronic shortages.[15] Ironically, if Sekani reluctance to trade at the posts was strongest in spring and in summer, then the reverse was true in winter. The post became the only assured supply of food in the region; hence, the hunters were reluctant to leave. Tod again wrote to Connolly, this time complaining that, as of 28 December 1829, the Sekani would not leave the post because he had not been able to "assist" them with provisions from his own meager supplies. Without this inducement they would not leave and risk hunger while hunting. This characteristic action was typical of the early 1800s in McLeod Lake. It was not an inconsiderable problem for the Hudson's Bay Company, since the winter hunts (stretching into early spring) were by far the most productive in quantity and quality of furs. In sum, the arrival of the Europeans initially affected Sekani patterns of movement by influencing the numbers which aggregated around the posts. This influenced decisions regarding movement by placing greater pressures on local resources. Not surprisingly given the diffuse Indian idea that trade was exchange negotiated through personal bonds, the Sekani expected the Hudson's Bay Company to share its food with them, no doubt since the bulk of it was locally obtained country food in any case.

The Hudson's Bay Company tried to alleviate some of this pressure by taking a small outfit of trade goods from McLeod Lake to a point about eighty miles north, near Finlay Forks and the future site of Fort Grahame. The northern Sekani were to trade there and hence ease the pressure on McLeod Lake. This compromise was started in 1829 and was still practised in 1845, according to the only fragmentary record which survives from this period.[16] Each of the five traders who kept the post journal during this period mention that the rendezvous was "usual".

Yet even then the Sekani had a strong bargaining position; they could withdraw from the trade altogether. In 1824, for example, Samuel Black recorded that somewhere north of the forks of the Finlay and Peace Rivers old Methodiates, a northern Chief, wanted him to establish a post around Thutade Lake, near the source of the Finlay. Methodiates argued that if Black did so, the Sekani would stop wintering in the plains and remain in the mountains to hunt beaver.[17] Even as late as 1845 the Sekani had not arrived at Finlay Forks as expected but had gone straight to their winter hunts without trading. This suggested that the Sekani were still not totally dependent on European trade goods even after nearly forty years of trading and that they still ranged quite freely and widely over the northern Trench. Continued references to the Sekani making "no hunts" (for furbearers, obviously) year after year hints that they had alternative sources of European supplies. This bothered the Hudson's Bay company traders considerably.[18]

The Sekani also increased their leverage *vis-à-vis* the Hudson's Bay Company by refusing to acknowledge their debts when they could do so with relative impunity. After all, it was the Europeans who wanted the furs and who had come to them. "[The Indians] are deeply indebted at this post", state the records, but the traders were eager to continue trading nevertheless.[19] In fact, they resorted to using liquour as an inducement, but this soon backfired as the supply had to be stopped to induce them to hunt at all.[20] This negative reinforcement had become necessary because the traders had, ironically, given the Sekani "gifts" of staple European trade goods (knives, axes, kettles, etc.); hence, the Sekani needed fewer items through legitimate trade. The Sekani did not operate under the same assumptions about debt as did the Europeans. Although it is hard to guess motives from such scarce data, advances by the traders might also have been seen as gifts rather than as a sign of a bond of obligation. Not only did the Sekani ignore their debts and trade with other Indian groups whenever they could, they also moved from post to post. They threatened to trade at Fort George, about ninety miles south of McLeod Lake. Without a burden of debt to repay at that post, they could obtain fresh supplies virtually for free.[21] The traders, as employees of the Hudson's Bay Company, worked to centralize the trade, especially after the 1821 amalgamation of the Hudson's Bay Company and the Northwest Company. Yet some traders, as individuals, were willing to allow such practices to continue in order to gain more personal profit. Between 1845 and 1848, for example, two bands (we are not told how many people these included) were believed attached to McLeod Lake and both of these were believed to trade elsewhere.[22] The East Band was believed to trade at Fort George, while the Mountain Band was believed to venture as far as Dunvegan on the east side of the Rockies.

It was inevitable that a cat and mouse attitude developed between both parties in these circumstances. Food was sometimes given, for example, but the donated salmon was of the poorest quality.[23] The Sekani sometimes traded with the Beaver,[24] but this may have been under duress as much as it may been strategic. Because of the uncertain comings and goings of the Sekani the company found itself, at least on one occasion, with insufficient goods on hand. We can imagine that the Sekani, who traded with the Beaver when goods were in any case available at McLeod lake, must have been somewhat more reluctant to approach the Beaver when they had no leverage in their bargaining position. As late as 1876, one commentator observed that the Sekani were still in almost constant movement throughout the year.[25] By 1891, the last year for which regular records are available, the Sekani had reduced but not eliminated their movement from post to post. This almost certainly reflects the increasing success the Hudson's Bay Company had experienced in "attaching" Indians to particular posts. Yet it took them seventy years of effort.

One important tool in stabilizing the movement of the Indians was the control of prices. Prices on trade goods of course reflected the initial cost of manufacturing and transport costs. The near monopoly position of the Hudson's Bay Company allowed high rates of profit to be included in the price as well, however. This left a large margin with which prices could be adjusted. In the past prices had been set centrally, but there was always some flexibility left to the individual traders. Variations in prices were accentuated, if not caused, by the year or two it took for the goods and pricing instructions to reach the posts. Local conditions varied dramatically in that span of time, so prices sometimes had to move downwards. As late as 1891 one inspection report mentions that the prices on two staples, flour and bacon, were much too low in McLeod Lake Post.[26] The fact that these were food items and not durable goods suggests that low prices were linked to the poor economic climate then current rather than to a desire to increase the volume of sales. As time went on, however, downwards price adjustment increasingly became the exception rather than the rule.

The Founding of Fort Grahame

Besides trading at McLeod Lake, the northern Sekani also traded at Bear Lake (Fort Connolly) to the west or at Fort Saint John on the eastern side of the Rockies. In all likelihood they also traded with Beaver or Kaska intermediaries, since there is no mention of Sekani in the journals of Hudson's Bay Company posts surrounding the Trench.[27] Fort Grahame was established in 1870 just north of the old rendezvous point used by the McLeod Lake traders during the period between 1820 and 1840. The decision finally to establish a post at that location was not entirely a concession on the part of the Hudson's Bay Company to Sekani demands,[28] as an 1891 report makes clear, but was made to take advantage of the large number of moose in the area. The report also states that prices were a little lower in the area, as were the prices set on furs, compared to other posts in the district.[29]

The importance of the moose harvest and the possibility that prices were lowered as an inducement to attract hunters to the post is suggested in the records. Whereas only fifteen people used the post in 1889, in 1891 and 1892 there were numerous people in the region. Besides four Rocky Mountain Indians "belonging" to rocky Mountain Portage Post,[30] others who traded at Fort Grahame included "the Priest's band",[31] "Davie and his family",[32] a man named Maheegah and "five families of Stickeen Indians",[33] "Matchay and family",[34] and "Worthlay [or Woolthley, in other records] band",[35] which had eight hunters.[36] There are three other groups of names listed, although none are called a family or a band,[37] but the internal evidence suggests that they were local bands on the order of the Woolthley group. Even if we omit the Rocky Mountain Portage group (since they were "attached" to another post), a total of seven hunting groups traded at Fort Grahame.

There was a limit to the concessions the Hudson's Bay Company could or would offer to attract the Sekani, despite the Company's eagerness to acquire moose hides. Prices were attractive but they were not as low as at McLeod Lake. Perhaps this reflected the increased cost of transportation to the northern post. The average value of Made Beaver (MB) at McLeod Lake[38] was about 47 cents for furs traded compared to 90–5/8 cents for good purchased, and even this large difference was computed on goods which had been sold "far too cheap".[39] While flour sold for $18.50 per hundredweight in Fort Grahame,[40] the same quantity sold for $14.40 in McLeod Lake.[41] But the Sekani of McLeod Lake were "said to be very poor",[42] an admittedly chronic condition.[43]

If the Hudson's Bay Company was starting to be tougher on the Fort Grahame Sekani during this period, the Sekani for their part were still hedging their bets. They maintained contact with people of Telegraph Creek and the Liard River area and they still travelled far and wide in their hunts. They were obviously not as attached to Fort Grahame as the Company desired. The contacts with other groups helped the Sekani maintain their independent stance, but the paucity of food around Fort Grahame no doubt helped encourage this independence.[44] While debt

continued to accumulate, Sekani independence made repayment somewhat negotiable. At the heart of the Sekani attitude
was the intimate relationship between food and furs which had
marked the fur trade since its inception. By 1890 food around
Fort Grahame had grown scarcer: "[The Indians] did not make a
very satisfactory fall trade. Indians report Beaver very scarce
although they worked they could not get as many as formerly
but hope to do better in the Spring. They intend going farther
away."[45]

By 1894 the Sekani of Fort Grahame were still trapping farther
than usual in order to obtain "a pretty fair hunt".[46] Another
reference is even more explicit:

> The Band of Indians belonging to this place left today, [I] was forced
> to give them a little jawbone [debt] to start with. They appear to have
> been rather out of luck on their hunt through sickness in their fami-
> lies, and scarcity of furbearing animals within 4 days journey of the
> Fort so that they were unable to pay up all their old debts.[47]

Although not stated explicitly, it is difficult to conceive of a
situation in which the Sekani had to go farther afield to trap if
food had been plentiful around the post. Most trade goods the
Sekani desired at this time were of the durable variety like guns,
axes and kettles; these rarely required annual replacement. In
any case, non-durables were in short supply. If the Sekani went
farther than usual, it could have been motivated by the need to
hunt for food and not to trap furs. Nor did travelling farther than
usual mean that more supplies were taken along for the trip.
With people travelling northwards, as they normally did from
Fort Grahame, supplies were limited to what could be carried on
foot. Only if people were to travel south could they take advantage of the southwards-flowing and rapid Finlay current. The
longer distance and relatively fixed amount of supplies meant, in
real terms, more difficulties and dangers for the hunters and
their families.

Why were the Sekani travelling farther than before? There is
one obvious possibility: to obtain food. The increase in distance
must indicate that the Sekani were used to hunting around the
post before 1890. If that is the case, then food supplies must have
been relatively plentiful before that time. There is no direct
evidence for this, yet it remains compelling that the post had
been established to take advantage of the large numbers of moose
in the vicinity (the hides were exported by the Company) in
1870. Since no records exist before 1891 certainty is impossible,

yet it is hard to imagine a scenario in which the Hudson's Bay Company establishes a post and the Sekani are secure enough to "attach" themselves to it if the economic conditions had been anything other than favourable. It is also hard to imagine that the ever-increasing Fort Grahame credit load carried by the Hudson's Bay Company was a problem in the period 1870 to 1885. The Company was not usually so slow to close posts which were unprofitable in other areas. Hence, credit must have been relatively manageable for both parties at this time.

Conditions changed, however, and the people of Fort Grahame had to go farther than usual. The winters of 1893 and 1894 were sufficiently hard to have caused some instances of starvation.[48] Difficulties of this sort notwithstanding, the drop in prices which accompanied the worsened conditions attracted people from outside the Trench. Unlike other areas, Fort Grahame was exempted from trapping and trading restrictions that had been passed in order to offer some relief from starvation. The 1893 journal, for example, mentions forty-six hunters, of whom twelve were "attached" to other posts. Of these twelve, one was from Bear Lake to the west, five were from the Portage to the east, two were "Stickeen" Indians (Tahltan) to the northwest, four were from Delyare, reference unknown.[49] Although it seems surprising that low prices attracted people rather than drove them away, it indicates that normal controls on trapping were in part suspended. The irony of the situation could not have been lost on the Sekani. After all, the increase in foreign hunters must have placed additional pressure on already thinly spread resources.

Several conclusions about the fur trade economy emerge from these considerations. First, when game was plentiful, the trade went well for both the Sekani and the Hudson's Bay Company. When food supplies were low, fur returns were fewer because the Sekani were less willing to gamble on trapping. Second, in the rugged environment of the Trench the good years must have been few compared to the years of struggle. Life must have appeared as a series of crises to the Sekani, especially to the northerners.[50] Third, in times of relative abundance, such as the period 1870 to 1885 in the north, the range of movement of the hunting groups decreased; the reverse was also (paradoxically) true: food shortages led to more aggregation around the posts. The aggregation of people around Fort Grahame between 1870 and 1885 is an exception that is probably explainable by the co-incidental increase in the number of moose in the region that occurred at the same time as the founding of the post. When taken together these points imply that the Sekani were not yet entirely dependent upon the fur trade for their survival but they were obviously familiar with the stratagems and circumstances of the new economic regime of the marketplace.

McLeod Lake in the 1890s

Conditions in McLeod Lake in the 1890s were only slightly better than those at Fort Grahame. Fur prices were lower than those in surrounding areas, though apparently not as low as those in Fort Grahame.[51] Not surprisingly, McLeod Lakers lessened their participation in the fur trade, as some frustrated comments by the local trader makes clear: the Sekani refused to hunt "while they have a belly full".[52] No doubt the irony of the Sekani being too lazy to trap yet motivated enough to make sure their bellies were full was lost on the trader. The situation is not strictly comparable to conditions in Fort Grahame, however. The main point of difference seems to be in the options McLeod Lakers could take in devising trade strategies. Their refusal to trap furbearers notwithstanding, more goods were available to McLeod Lakers than were available to their northern cousins. Table 3.11 (p. 58 above) shows a typical fall outfit for a McLeod lake trapper. His purchases included 125 pounds of flour, 25 pounds of dried salmon, 23 pounds of lard, tallow and bacon and 12 pounds of beans. The higher cost of transportation made these prohibitively expensive in Fort Grahame, while they appear to be run of the mill purchases in McLeod Lake.

By 1900 game increased, moose returned to this part of the Trench from the north[53] and conditions improved.[54] With a healthier economy the Hudson's Bay Company could afford to be more rigorous in its accounting of debt. It departed from the barter system and decided to operate on a cash basis. One obvious reason why the Hudson's Bay Company wanted to move from a credit to a cash basis of operation can be seen through the analysis of accounts at McLeod Lake. In 1902, a time when conditions were showing a slight improvement for the southern Sekani, twenty-one men and fourteen women came in to trade after the spring hunt (see Appendix III). Total goods with a value of 1,461 Made Beaver were purchased by the men, while the women bought 322 worth of goods. In October of that year the men paid in furs to the value of 564 MB to cover their debts; the women 191.5. The balance owing was 748.5 for the men, including the 61.5 MB of debts cancelled outright and a credit of 2 MB.

The net balance of furs owing was 825 MB. The women owed 140.5 MB; 2.5 MB were cancelled. The total debt owing was 889 MB for approximately one half of the trading season. Three men and three women paid their debt in full. One person managed to trade sufficient furs to obtain 10 MB worth of credit on his account. In sum, debts could outweigh income by a factor of two to one. This was a risky business, and a problem which the Hudson's Bay Company used to rationalize its price differential between MB paid out and MB income (this price differential was, in McLeod Lake, slightly greater than two to one).[55] Regardless of the amount of trapping and trading they did, the Sekani were never able to pay their debt in full. Rather than creating a condition of monopoly control for the Hudson's Bay Company, this situation required the Company to cancel debt occasionally if trading was to occur at all. The viability of the Hudson's Bay Company was of course never threatened by such actions, but the total risk involved was much higher than if business were conducted on a cash basis. The local trader was afraid to "cut everybody off for fear they will go to Quesnel or Hudson's Hope [where independent traders could be found]".[56] The implications for Sekani trading are not entirely clear from the records since the Hudson's Bay Company made few references to its competition, but there are hints that the Sekani bargaining position was improved.[57] Woolthley, a Sekani chief, was given an outfit by a rival company to induce him and his band to trade with them. The Hudson's Bay Company replied in kind, so Woolthley had two outfits that season. Furthermore, the representative of the Quesnel firm paid "big prices for furs" at Finlay Forks.[58]

Fort Grahame after the 1890s

Economic conditions also improved for the northern Sekani around the turn of the century. On 2 June 1900, "all Indians paid their debts in full";[59] a remarkable enough occurrence to be noted in the post journal. This exceptional improvement (for the Hudson's Bay Company) was perhaps due to the fact that for the first time the "upper" Indians from Akie, about sixty miles north of Fort Grahame, came to trade.[60] This affluence was indeed temporary, as the winters of 1902–3 were very hard. Several deaths from illness were reported.[61]

The year 1905 was also significant for the Sekani, since it marked the first year in which the federal government played a direct role in their internal affairs:

Some of [the Indians] went to see Corporal McLeod [of the North West Mounted Police] this morning telling him that they had absolutely nothing to start out with and that they expected to starve before they could obtain food for themselves. He came to see [the trader] this morning about it. I told him my instructions from the H.B.Co. was [sic] very clear that the Indians were to get to more debt and also that I could not give them anything as Relief to sick and destitute Indians as they were not sick and from all accounts I had heard there was no scarcity of furbearing animals but that they were destitute through their own faults staying here doing nothing for 3 weeks although I had urged them to go out. . . . [They said] there was a danger of going a distance away leaving their wives and children. The N.W.M.P. [North West Mounted Police] rationed all Indians for 3 days, amts. to $100.03.[62]

Later, the trader relented and issued additional credit to the Sekani. It appears that the Canadian federal government stepped in just as the Hudson's Bay Company was moving from a credit to a cash system. The Hudson's Bay Company's tighter control which would follow from such a move was to a certain extent alleviated.

Conditions seem to have improved only to be followed by another depression. The boom seems to have started in 1915 or 1916 (see note 66). Unfortunately, prices fell dramatically during the First World War: the 38 beaver, 5 fisher, 2 black bear, 1 red fox, 48 lynx and 1 mink traded in one trading session were valued at $150.00, "miserable prices", since they would have been worth $1,200.00 the previous year.[63] With scarce food resources and low prices, the Sekani once again were reluctant to leave the vicinity of the post, living under the uncertain and meager protection afforded by the charity of the Hudson's Bay Company and the federal government.

McLeod Lake in the 1900s

Although 1900 was a good year for game, it was to be a high point followed by a long decline in economic conditions. By 1907 cases of death by malnutrition were recorded:[64] "The population of this tribe numbers 97, comprising 19 men, 25 women and 53 children. This year there were six births and six deaths. The mortality is increasing every succeeding year, consumption and scrofula being the cause."[65] Conditions improved in 1916, at which point a boom in fur prices gave rise to a better standard of living, at least until 1929.[66] Possibly the difference between conditions at

McLeod Lake and Fort Grahame immediately following the turn of the century can be attributed to the actions of the Hudson's Bay Company. In 1905 they had repealed an earlier ban which forbade trapping beaver, possibly in an effort at conservation. This repeal did not apply to McLeod Lake, hence conditions there were slower to improve than in the north. Possibly these difficult times can account for the McLeod Lakes evicting, on 11 June 1911, a Stuart Lake Carrier who had married a Sekani woman.[67] This single event marks the beginning of true dependence on the fur trade for the Sekani. Allowing such marriages (and contracting their own) had always been part of the strategy of maintaining ties with outsiders which the Sekani seem to have practised, the resultant tension notwithstanding, since the time when the first records have survived. The reality of the fur trade had always been one of independence gained during periods of relative abundance of food supplies, when the Sekani did not mind hunting for furbearers instead of primarily hunting for food. Each good period was inevitably followed by a period of difficulty, and it is during these difficult periods that the Sekani were forced to face the consequences of becoming attached to and even dependent upon European goods.

Summary of the Historical Data and Conclusions

Relatively small and discrete bands roamed the Trench at the beginning of the historic era. The nature of the ties between these bands is not known with certainty, but it can be reasonably supposed that each was semi-autonomous and was linked to others by means of marriages. The division into northern and southern branches of the Sekani was apparent at the time of initial contact, but it was in any case intensified by the establishment of two major trading posts. The various bands were attached to one of these two posts, largely at the instigation of the Hudson's Bay Company but at least on one occasion, in 1870, cessation of movement was voluntary.

In order to maintain some degree of independence, at least in terms of prices for furs and goods, the Sekani adopted several strategies. One of these, moving from post to post to forestall the payment of credit extended by the Company, was particularly effective. The success of these strategies, however, was ultimately dependent on a relatively plentiful supply of food in the area around a post. In general, when food was scarce the Sekani tended to stay near the posts. In 1870 the Fort Grahame

Sekani took advantage of an apparent increase in the local moose population to stay near the newly founded post. Food resources were not as abundant in McLeod Lake at this time. After 1890 the Fort Grahame Sekani resumed movement over a wider range of territory for reasons that will be explored in more detail in the following chapter. Conditions continued to worsen at least until the second decade of this century, with a slight amelioration between 1900 and 1902 or 1903. There was another short-lived boom between 1915 or 1916 and 1918 for the northerners, although this began and finished later in McLeod Lake. These latter booms and busts are not important here, however, except to illustrate the cyclical pattern of the economy and the fact that the cycles always appear to have moved from north to south. This also suggests that moose were moving from north to south in cycles; 1870 seems to have been a peak for the northerners while the evidence in the previous chapter suggested that moose arrived in McLeod lake only around 1913. The arrival of the federal government added another dimension to the trade and in one sense prolonged some of the features of the older relationship between the Sekani and the Hudson's Bay Company, even as the economic regime was changing dramatically.

In sum, Sekani responses to the fur trade were made within their traditional culture. Even the most dramatic impact imaginable – establishing two posts instead of one – was consonant with an earlier division which, as I have argued in the previous chapter, was largely the result of different circumstances of contact between the immigrating Sekani and their neighbours. The initial Sekani response to the fur trade was a guarded participation which depended on the Sekani being able to manipulate certain factors to their advantage. Even their later response, at a time when there can be little doubt that some sort of dependency was present, demonstrated the Sekani concern with integrating changes in mobility with an already long-established political context. With the aid of the information presented here, it is possible to offer a model of Sekani development, especially in the area of political responses to economic change.

Notes

1. Insofar as the fur trade accelerated the process of coming together at particular nodes, it caused people to react by creating the phratric system of identification, thus emphasizing wide-ranging ties. Insofar as the fur trade also increased the sense of isolation of the hunting groups from each other it caused people to strengthen their identification with the regional band. Both responses are similar, in that they are attempts to broaden and strengthen networks. They are different in their particulars, in the basis of the widened network. I divided the evidence into several chapters for convenience, not because these are different issues.

2. D. Jenness, *The Sekani Indians of British Columbia*, Ottawa: National Museum of Canada, Bulletin No. 84, 1937, p. 16.

3. M. Asch, 'The Impact of Changing Fur Trade Practices on the Economy of the Slavey Indians: Some Preliminary Conclusions Regarding the Period 1870–1900', Winnipeg: Paper delivered at the Canadian Ethnology Society Symposium on early mercantile enterprises, 1976, p. 2.

4. Idem, 'The Dene Economy', M. Watkins, ed., in *Dene Nation: The Colony Within*, Toronto: University of Toronto Press, 1977, p. 49.

5. At least one Hudson's Bay Company document, however, mentions 1802 as the founding date. See HBC Arch.

6. HBC Arch. B119/a/1, fo. 22d.

7. S. Black, *Black's Rocky Mountain Journal, 1824*, ed. E.E. Rich, London: Hudson's Bay Record Society, 1955, p. 50.

8. HBC Arch. B119/a/1, fo. 25d.

9. The diaries and journals of these early traders are full of rumblings about their fellow traders' efforts to make extra money from the Indians. Few are motivated by outraged honour; most seem angry that they were not in the position to do what others were practising. Such practices must have been common in an era of poor accounting methods, but are obviously hard to verify.

10. HBC Arch. B119/a/4, fo. 5

11. HBC Arch. B188/a/5, fo. 146

12. This set of counterpoised pressures is reflected in a journal entry from the period: "I regret to say that on my arrival [22 September 1829], at the place of the rendez-vous [Finlay Forks, at the junction of the Finlay and Parsnip Rivers], I found that but a small of the Indians there encamped – a scarcity of provisions had previously compelled part of the Band to a more distant part of the country and thereby rendered it impracticable to [undecipherable] with their [undecipherable] for the winter." Even if the number were only thirty hunters and their families, this small a number must have seemed ample in an area with an always notoriously low supply of game. The pressures on local resources were aggravated by bringing people together, a fact which the traders knew accounted for some of the reluctance of the Sekani in the trading process. HBC, Arch. B188/b/8, fo. 5, 6d.

13. Black, *Black's Rocky Mountain Journal*, p. 26

14. Ibid., p. 62.

15. A letter from John Tod at McLeod Lake to William Connolly in Fort Saint James indicates that the problem was a chronic one. See HBC Arch. B188/b/8, fo. 9. The letter states: "a place from whence we have these many years past acquired a stock of fish sufficient for the maintenance of the post for no inconsiderable portion of the winter" (HBC Arch. B188/b/8, fo. 9). In this case the writer is referring to the failure of the fishery at the southern end of McLeod Lake. This fishing station provided insufficient amounts of food for the winter.

16. Glenbow Archives BB12.M165, p. 1.

17. Black, *Black's Rocky Mountain Journal*, p. 188.

18. This is not an isolated case. Ray's survey of the Algonkian data suggests that the fur trade was generally geared to Indian demand for goods and not to the European demand for furs. The demand for trade goods was relatively inflexible. See A.J. Ray, 'History and Archaeology of the Fur Trade', *American Antiquity* 43(1): 26–34, 1974, p. 30; for a general overview of the early fur trade, see A.J. Ray and D. Freeman, *'Give Us Good Measure': An Economic Analysis of Relations Between the Indians and the Hudson's Bay Company before 1763*, Toronto: University of Toronto Press, 1978, esp. pp. 53–62.

19. Glenbow Archives BB12.M165, p. 6.

20. Ibid., p. 6.

21. The manipulation of debt by the Indians was typical of the entire Athabaska District, including the Peace River area. Yerbury, in his study of the effects of the fur trade on Athabaskan social organization, notes that Indians often accumulated debt at one post in the fall and returned to a rival post in the spring. In the early years of the fur trade the Sekani were favourably located to take advantage of trade rivalries between the already established Northwest Company (McLeod Lake and Rocky Mountain House) and the expanding Hudson's Bay Company (Fort Saint Mary in the Peace River area). The trader at Fort Saint Mary received reports that the Portage Sekani were eager for trade and that they wanted the Hudson's Bay Company to establish a post in their country. The Sekani went so far as to conceal provisions for the trader's men at various points along a route they often travelled. HBC Arch. B190/a/2, fo. 35, cited in J.C. Yerbury, 'The Social Organization of Subarctic Athapaskan Indians: An Ethno-Historical Reconstruction', Ph.D. dissertation, Simon Fraser University, 1980, pp. 225, 229.

22. Glenbow Archives BB12.M165, p. 7.

23. Ibid., p. 9.

24. Ibid., p. 22.

25. See Fr. Lejacq, 'District de N.-D. de Bonne Esperance, Lettre du R.P. Lejacq a Mgr. Herbourg', *Missions de la Congregation des Missionaires Oblats de Marie-Immacule* xii: 346, 1874. This statement was probably made about the southern Sekani who lived around McLeod Lake, since they would be the people of whom Father Lejacq had the most knowledge. It therefore seems even more likely that the northern Sekani were less restricted, being less attached to a particular trading post than their

southern cousins since the post was recent and apparently ill-supplied.
26. HBC Arch. B119/a/2, fo. 4
27. HBC Arch. B56/a/3; B56/a/2; B299/a/1; B299/a/2.
28. Explanations for the locations of posts in this general area have
stressed other factors. Harris and Ingram state that small posts were
established throughout the New Caledonia area in the 1870s in order to
thwart competition from independent traders. No data are presented
which would substantiate this, however. According to records and to
local tradition, independent traders did not reach the Sekani until the
late 1890s or early 1900s. Three criteria are mentioned by Janes in his
discussion of the location of posts in the Mackenzie Valley: (1) accessibility to interior lakes for fishing and contact with dispersed hunters
and trappers; (2) accessibility to the Mackenzie River for reasons of
transport; and (3) access to well-drained sites with plenty of wood for
fuel and construction. In New Caledonia practical considerations made
transport a matter of some importance to the Northwest Company and
to the Hudson's Bay Company, but this had been overridden owing to
the necessity of inducing higher levels of trade with the Sekani. See
HBC Arch. B119/a/2, fo. 8; B249/a/6, fo. 28; C.G. Ingram and D.A.
Harris, 'New Caledonia and the Fur Trade', *Western Canadian Journal of
Anthropology* 3(1): 179–94, 1972, p. 183; R. Janes, 'The Athapaskan and
the Fur Trade: Observations from Archaeology and Ethnohistory', *Western
Canadian Journal of Anthropology* 4(3,4): 159, 1975.
29. See HBC Arch. B249/e/2, fo. 11. The 1891 report also mentions
the continued movement of Sekani over large tracts of land. Mooseskins
became a valuable trading commodity for the Hudson's Bay Company,
and the lower prices on food may have been a way of luring the Sekani
back into the Trench in order that they harvest the skins. The information on fur prices is corroborated by an inspection report from 1900. See
notes 50 and 59, this chapter.
30. HBC Arch. B249/a/1, fo. 4
31. Ibid., fo. 12.
32. HBC Arch. B249/a/2, fo. 13.
33. HBC Arch. B249/a/4, fo. 4d.
34. HBC Arch. B249/a/2, fo. 20.
35. Ibid., fo. 3d.
36. HBC Arch. B249/a/8, p. 82.
37. Ibid., fo. 2d., 20d., 21.
38. One Made Beaver was equal to approximately seven prime
beaver pelts.
39. HBC Arch. B249/e/2, fo. 4.
40. Ibid., fo. 8.
41. Ibid., fo. 4.
42. HBC Arch. B119/a/2, fo 9
43. HBC Arch. B119/e/4, fo. 10.
44. By the 1890s supplies of game animals around Fort Grahame were
no higher than at McLeod Lake. The trader had to give out more credit
than was usual on account of starvation. There is no mention as to what

is meant by "debt" in the records, but given difficulties in transporting goods it could not have been a large amount of food. The trader, it is obvious from this record, was caught between his sympathies for the starving Sekani and his unwillingness to keep them too near the post and dependent on his food supplies. See HBC Arch. B249/a/4, fo. 13.

45. HBC Arch. B249/a/2, fo. 4.

46. Ibid., fo. 9.

47. HBC Arch. B249/a/1, fo. 20.

48. Ibid., fo. 6d.

49. HBC Arch. B249/d/8, fo. 1, 1d.

50. The poor prices paid for furs at Fort Grahame are also suggestive of the newly emergent relationship between the Sekani and the Europeans. The record states: "The Indians attached to this fort live principally on game, having little fish, and hunt all year round, this to a great extent accounts for the proportion of inferior skins called attention to a year or two since [this report is unavailable]. It will be observed, however, that the prices paid are extremely low" (HBC Arch. B249/e/2, fo. 5). The poor conditions of the furs was due to continuous overtrapping and to trapping out of season. Though not an immediate concern to the Hudson's Bay Company, it was later to become a major problem.

51. HBC Arch. B119/a/2, fo. 8.

52. HBC Arch. B119/a/6, fo. 9.

53. The level of moosehide exports (the only record of moose kills which is available) indicates a wide range of fluctuation. The accounts show that in 1891 none were exported, 129.5 were shipped in 1893, 151 in 1894, 225 in 1896 and 123.5 in 1897 (see Appendix II). It is clear that exports had dropped at the beginning of the decade and only increased when the Sekani resumed their visits to areas farther from the post.

54. HBC Arch. B119/e/4, fo. 10.

55. The evidence suggests that the avoidance of repayment of debt was a problem for the Hudson's Bay Company from the inception of the fur trade. Since an anticipated rate of default on repayment was in one sense built into Hudson's Bay Company accounting and price structure, it is clear that the Indians were merely displacing the costs over time and postponing the position of dependency which inevitably emerges in all trade relationships of this kind. The evidence for this is clear. A 1900 inspection report from Fort Grahame states that the average cost of a Made Beaver (MB) was $0.43, while the average cost of goods sold was $1.11 per MB. This difference of $0.68 equalled 158 per cent "advance" (as the inspector called 'profit') on the capital stock of the post. The equivalent rates at McLeod Lake were $0.42 per MB in furs bought and $0.75 per MB on goods sold, which gave a profit of 78.5 per cent. These figures seem entirely unremarkable to the inspector. See HBC Arch. B119/e/4, fo. 5; HBC Arch. B249/e/2.

56. HBC Arch. B119/a/6, fo. 1.

57. Although the people of Fort Ware told me that independent traders arrived in the area a few years before 1900, there is no documented evidence of this. The Hudson's Bay Company records – and it

is to be expected that rivals would be mentioned here – indicate that the first independent trader was a man named Tommy Barlow, acting as a representative of a firm called Marion of Quesnel (a town south of Prince George). See HBC Arch. B249/a/6, fo. 28.

58. Ibid.

59. Ibid., fo. 15.

60. Ibid., fo. 6, 10d., 23, 24d.

61. One complication that arose was the product of year-round trapping that had apparently been the norm a decade before. Furbearers declined. Hence, an act was passed in 1904 prohibiting the trapping of beaver altogether. Morice had also noted that the beaver were "near extinction". Economic conditions at the post were evidently so bad that in November, 1905, "through Mr. Thomson's efforts an Order in Council has passed exempting the northern part of B.C. from the act passed last Spring prohibiting the killing and selling [of] the Beaver. So that the Indians can still have the Beaver to help them eke out a more miserable existence". See HBC Arch. B249/a/8, p. 13; A. Morice, *The Western Denes, their Manners and Customs*, The Canadian Institute, Proceedings for 1888–1889, vol. 7, 1890, p. 131.

62. HBC Arch. B249/a/8, pp. 18, 19.

63. Ibid., p. 265.

64. Little hope was held for the survival of the band under these conditions: "No one around here but three old hags; [undecipherable] with the deaths and other causes such as the scarcity that there is and will be no furbearing animals . . . . The place is gradually decaying away to nothing and in the near future will probably not pay expenses in the absence [of] some trade with White men who may be prospecting around." In more personal and poignant terms, the local trader expressed his assessment of the Sekani: "My god what a band of useless, wretched, brainless Indians. They are heartless, mean, ungrateful and cantankerous . . . . Gratitude is an unborn virtue in this band. When done a kindness, first opportunity they have they revenge it, makes a man sorry for trying to help them. Still a man cannot help but pity the poor devils. The only way they can possibly have sufficient food summer and winter is for the government to supply them with nets & herd them like cattle on some good lake and compel them to fish, the old men and the widows, & the younger men can hunt moose or go look for work. They are dying off faster than they can make babies. A few more years there will be none for the government to bother with." See HBC Arch. B249/a/9, pp. 307, 308; B119/a/12, p. 117.

65. HBC Arch. B119/a/12, p. 72.

66. A. Sherwood, "Some Remarks About the Athapaskan Indians", *Anthropologica* 6–8: 51–6, 1958/9, p. 55.

67. HBC Arch. B119/a/12, p. 197.

Chapter 8

The Politics of Land Ownership

In the previous chapter I have argued that the fur trade was responsible for strengthening a particular arrangement of people over the landscape. The aggregation of people around a trading post, the gradual yet inevitable inculcation of dependency on European trade goods and the subsequent re-alignment of social networks and attitudes to conform closer to the exigencies of the fur trade – all of these more or less standard responses were not unique to the Sekani. Much of the general effects of the fur trade on the Sekani are similar to those which have been noted in the general literature on the Canadian fur trade and its impact on Indian societies. One unique feature, at least from the perspective of the anthropological literature, is the adoption of phratries in the 1870s. Phratries arose in conjunction with the developing fur trade, especially the increasingly common trend of the aggregation of people around a post where food supplies were relatively assured in times of general scarcity. The circumstances of the fur trade created a crisis in political autonomy which resulted in a new definition of exogamy and unity. Phratries form the basis of the modern version of universalistic brotherhood and were its most potent expression from the past.

Phratries and Clans: The Historical Evidence

Jenness stated that matrilineality was a tendency of the Sekani. Like the workings of African clan systems described in anthropological classics, lineality greatly depends on organizing people into categories that are abstractly defined and that do not depend on mundane or practical conditions. Its presence among people who were hunter-gatherers is somewhat unusual. Lineality, for the Sekani, is manifested in a tendency towards exclusivity at all levels: community, patronymic category and family. In the past matrilineality was limited to regulating membership in one of three phratries (see table 8.1). People were assigned to these categories regardless of their location and the type of practical associations which they formed. It is worth quoting Jenness at length:

Table 8.1 Phratries and clans: Sekani, Carrier and Gitksan

Group		Name			Unit
Gitksan	Raven	Wolf	Fireweed	Eagle	Phratry
Fort	Frog	Wolf	Beaver		Phratry
Graham	Frog	Wolf	Beaver		Clan
Sekani	Toad	Grizzly	Owl		Clan
	Marten	Black Bear			Clan
	Beads				Clan
Stuart					
Lake			Beaver		Phratry
Carrier	(four untranslatable)				Phratries
T'Lotona	Raven	Wolf	Fireweed		Phratry
Sekani	Raven	Wolf	Fireweed		Clan
	Eagle	Black Bear	Sun/Moon		Clan
	Frog	Small Owl	Grouse		Clan
	Toad		Big Horned Owl		Clan

Source: From information in D. Jenness, *The Sekani Indians of British Columbia*, Ottawa: National Museum of Canada, Bulletin No. 86, 1937.

Children belong to the phratries of their mothers, marriage within the phratry is discountenanced and a phratry of a man (or woman) who dies at Fort Grahame arranges and pays for his burial by one of the other two phratries. During the greater part of the year, however, the families are scattered over a wide range of territory and the phratric system lapses completely. It really functions, in fact, only during the months of June and July when people gather at Fort Grahame, though it can be revived at any season of the year by individuals visiting the Carrier and the Gitksan. Some of the older people who do not roam outside the Sekani territory hardly know to what phratries they belong, and depend for guidance on their kindred.[1]

Phratries, in other words, only functioned when there was a question of regulating or adjusting membership in specific categories: at birth, marriage and death. Only the Finlay River Sekani centred around Fort Grahame fully adopted this custom.

Jenness clearly implies that phratries where an expediency adopted by the Sekani in order to placate their Carrier, Tahltan and Gitksan neighbours, all of whom possessed phratries and all of whom were sources of iron for the Sekani in pre-contact times. Before posts were established in their country, the Sekani, based on the evidence that they had been pushed into the Trench because of their late access to European goods such as firearms, were undoubtedly in an inferior bargaining position in any trading with their powerful and well-organized Coastal neighbours. Hence, it is not unreasonable to believe that phratries were adopted at the insistence of their Coastal trading partners in order to regulate trade. The motives of these neighbouring groups can only be guessed at, but it can be supposed that phratries lessened internal competition by creating specific lines along which goods could circulate.

By 1924 the system of phratric identification[2] had weakened or disappeared:

> The McLeod Lake Sekani entered the road [of phratric organization] sixty or seventy years ago, but turned back. The Long Grass Band [the people centred northwest of Fort Grahame in the early 1900s] completed the process apparently, but the history of this band is obscure and it is fast disintegrating, if it has not already disappeared. The Finlay River Sekani have travelled half of the distance. They had set up a phratric system in which descent rigidly follows the female line. But their system now functions for a few weeks only, and the advancing tide of Europeans will surely prevent it from rooting, even if the band maintains its place for another century.[3]

According to the people of Fort Ware the system had completely disappeared by 1979. Nor are the names of the categories mentioned by Jenness meaningful to them. They said that they had never heard of them.[4]

Phratries and Clans: Theories of Diffusion

There is no doubt that some of the formal characteristics of interior Athabaskan phratric systems were the result of Northwest Coast influence. Most recent arguments about the impact of the people of the Northwest Coast on the groups of the interior stress the distinction between the adoption of a crest system, which refers to ranked categories and the adoption of a principle, often lineal, of group recruitment. Goldman, for example, suggests that the westernmost Carrier adopted crests from the

Bella Coola in order to regulate Bella Coola pressure on Carrier resources.[5]

Trade between the coast and the interior is not usually deemed to be a sufficient reason for the adoption of a crest complex. Political and economic competition also play an important role in the decision to adopt phratries and crests since, many writers agree, the crest system is a uniformly respected marker of ownership. De Laguna, for example, suggests that although sibs and septs[6] are probably of indigenous origin among the Carrier, crests were the major impact of the Tsimshian on the Carrier.[7] The association of these crests with sibs in the north or with septs in the south depends on the identity of the influential group, whether Tsimshian or Bella Coola, respectively. It is clearly implied that crests regulate access to resources. Ownership of resources is also stressed in Kobrinsky's explanation of Tsimshian influence on Carrier social organization.[8] He argues that the phratry/clan system is linked to Carrier participation in the fur trade economy in the early post-contact era. The phratric system overlays another set of socio-spatial categories, which in turn is an elaboration of the pre-contact system of regional bands.[9] Kobrinsky argues that Carrier phratries and associated titles and crests, despite their Tsimshian origin, are uniquely Carrier. The inversions between the two systems point to the new uses to which the Carrier have put the system. One such use is the peaceful regulation of access to furbearers. Unlike the Gitksan, the Carrier distinguish fine-fur animals from food animals. Furbearers belong to the phratry while food animals can be claimed by all members of the sept/regional band.[10]

The Sekani also possess a two-tiered idea of ownership. Furbearers belong to the owners of specific traplines while game animals belong to the band. The antiquity of the distinction is not clear, although it likely arose with participation in the fur trade. Hence, Kobrinsky's argument is plausible. Nevertheless, I think it unreasonable that the Carrier or Sekani would adopt a complicated clan and phratric system merely to distinguish two types of animals. Most other northern hunters manage to make the distinction clear and accordingly regulate access to resources without a phratric system. As De Laguna argues, the distinction between crest and group may explain the mechanics by which a system of social categories is adopted but it does not illuminate the origin of the underlying phratries, sibs and septs. De Laguna hypothesizes that sibs among western Athabaskans may serve to facilitate the movement of individual families.[11] De Laguna proposes that a system of sibs permits wider networks and hence allows a wider range of resources to be exploited than does mere bilaterality, depending as it does (at least in anthropological definitions) on tracing 'actual' kinship links. The wider networks are made possible through the more abstract criteria by which people are linked to one another, since sibs bypass the often-used delimiting criteria of proximity and interaction upon which the regional band is based.

The basic issue is the alleged function of matrilineal phratric systems. Dyen and Aberle address this thorny point in their study of proto-Athabaskan and its concomitant forms of social organization. Two pieces of evidence, they argue, suggest that early northern Canadian social organization – which, in their scheme, includes early Athabaskan variants – featured matrilineal descent. First, the reconstructed proto-Athabaskan kinship terminology emphasizes lineal features. Second, the only form known of lineal descent in historic times among Athabaskan speakers is matrilineal.[12] They are aware of and point out the problems of this interpretation: (1) some of the historic eastern Athabaskan groups were not lineal but bilateral; (2) the proximity of matrilineal Pacific Coast groups to interior Athabaskans implies recent adoption rather than retention of an earlier feature; (3) some groups, including the Sekani, southern Tutchone, Ross River Tutchone, western Kaska and Tahltan, were of eastern origin. They were displaced westwards as a result of the fur trade. It seems clear that these particular groups borrowed their matrilineal features from their new neighbours. This undermines the hypothesis that matrilineality is a proto-Athabaskan survival. Despite these possible exceptions Dyen and Aberle hold to their original suggestion that all early Athabaskan groups were matrilineal because they believe that it is easier to lose a characteristic trait of social organization than it is to acquire one.[13] Since the evidence for diffusion of matrilineality is strong in only two cases, the Sekani and the Kaska, it is reasonable to conclude that a few groups lost matrilineality rather than many developed it. Thus, the principle of parsimony of explanation and the strong evidence of the lineal features of early Athabaskan suggest that matrilineality was the norm. This trait was dropped in several cases (and later re-adopted) when circumstances emerged which urged the adoption of a bilateral system of social classification. These circumstances can only be guessed at, but Dyen and Aberle favour an explanation in which the physical environment figures as the crucial player. Eastern Athabaskans, for example, never developed a sedentary lifestyle based on a fishing economy as did some of the western matrilineal groups. Bilaterality among easterners, say Dyen and Aberle, is indicative of greater flexibility in social organization.[14] The recent borrowing of matrilineality by some of the eastern groups is a third phase which correlates with the movement of these groups into areas previously dominated by matrilineal peoples.[15] Dyen and Aberle more or less accept the trade hypothesis at face value since it is not a crucial proposition for their purposes. Some modern evidence supports their arguments, they say. Dendogram scores of language distance suggest that Sekani is closely affiliated with Kechika River Kaska, although Sekani and Sarcee share sufficient specific innovations to posit extensive contact at some point.[16] A location just south of the Sarcee around 1650 would account for the present linguistic distribution.[17] In essence Dyen and Aberle are proposing a three-tiered evolutionary scheme. A reign of matrilineality on the plains was followed by a period of bilaterality. After moving to the Trench the Sekani (and the Kechika River Kaska, it is implied) fell under the influence of coastal groups and adopted matrilineality once again.

I have examined Dyen and Aberle's arguments in some detail because they clarify all the essential points in the important debate on bilaterality and matrilineality. The weight of the evidence and arguments, whatever their source, points to the recent adoption of matrilineal phratries by the Sekani. There is no doubt that the Pacific Coast people influenced the interior by means of trade in prehistoric times. Two hypotheses emerge: either phratries were adopted by the people of the interior in order to regulate trade (the diffusion hypothesis), or they were adopted in order better to regulate access to resources located within the homeland (the territorial hypothesis). The latter case could obviously be accounted for by diffusion as well, but the focus here is on the internal social-structural arrangements to which phratries are attuned. Hence, I do not label it 'the innovation hypothesis', although it could, strictly speaking, bear that name. Given that the Sekani were recent arrivals in the Trench and met with a frosty welcome, the territorial hypothesis seems to be the more reasonable of the two. As we shall see, there are other problems with the trade hypothesis.

Phratries and Clans: Innovation or Diffusion

Evidential support for the diffusion hypothesis rests by and large on the importance of the iron trade between the Sekani and the people of the Coast. The hypothesis, however, is not supported by weight of evidence. Many of the arguments in its favour have been either general or deductive and have not benefited from a close examination of the trade record. In 1870 Fort Grahame changed the focus of trade from the Coast to the interior, and it is precisely at that point that phratries were adopted. The post was founded because the northern Sekani would no longer trade at Bear Lake in Gitksan country. No good reason suggests itself to explain why these Sekani would adopt (or be forced to adopt) phratries in order to regulate trade when the trade for coastal iron was all but ended. On the other hand, it remains problematical that similarities exist between the phratric systems of the McLeod Lake Sekani and the Stuart Lake Carrier. This points to a common origin. Yet even here the evidence which others have used to support the diffusion hypothesis is far from unequivocal. First, there is no strict correspondence between the phratric systems, despite general similarities. If diffusion did occur, the subsequent changes in the phratric systems of the McLeod Lake Sekani, the Stuart Lake Carrier and the T'lotona Sekani must still be accounted for. If trade was to be regulated by means of phratries, then their specificity of function would encourage accurate and complete borrowing. I see no reason why differences would emerge unless phratries had an internal role as well. Yet table 8.1 clearly shows that differences do indeed exist between the various systems. While similar, they are far from congruent. Even Jenness, whose arguments place him in the diffusionist camp, provided sufficient evidence to discount the diffusionist viewpoint:

> [The McLeod Lake Sekani] say that the Carrier of Stuart Lake had five phratries. The Sekani of McLeod Lake tried to arrange themselves into similar phratries under Chiefs, and they even held one or two potlatches to establish the system; but they quickly abandoned the attempt when they discovered that it did not help them under the new conditions of life, and merely provoked the scorn of the Europeans. Yet if a McLeod Lake native today visits Stuart Lake to take part in any ceremony, the Stuart Lake Carrier consider him to belong to the Tsayu phratry, and would forbid his marriage to a woman of that phratry.[18]

The conclusion seems obvious: a McLeod Laker's own phratry had little bearing on the identity conferred upon him by the Stuart Lake Carrier. They were all placed in the same Carrier phratry when in Carrier country.[19] This makes sense if phratries were used to regulate trade from the Carrier point of view –

trade with outsiders simply follows the already existing lines of political and economic alliances – but obviously weakens the case for simple borrowing by the Sekani.

To discount diffusion does not automatically lead to an understanding of how the phratric system worked for the Sekani and why they tailored the foreign categories to their own needs. A small insight into the internal role of phratries can be gleaned from the Hudson's Bay Company journals. I have already mentioned that burial arrangements were contracted ("arranged", says Jenness) to members of associated phratries. Only one case of such an arrangement is recorded in the trading post journals. An old man named Pierre was refused credit at the store when he specifically tried to obtain food for a burial feast. This "old custom" should be "cut out until better times," said the trader.[20] The feast was held none the less and an invitation extended to the trader (no doubt this is why the story figures in the post journal). The trader called it "their feast for the dead".[21] We know that the Sekani held no such feasts before the full development of the fur trade economy.[22] The dead were usually abandoned in the last shelter occupied or placed on a scaffold. Neither of these practices rule out the possibility of a later commemorative feast, but a list of the foods served at Pierre's feast points to a relatively late adoption of the custom; it does not appear likely that the large quantities of redistributed food could have been accumulated before people were in some ways settled in a semi-sedentary lifestyle. This piece of evidence about the internal role of phratries does not negate the diffusionist hypothesis but does render it almost inconsequential.

Additional evidence from the system of relationship terms, examined in Chapter 4, also hints at the role of phratries in Sekani social organization. The merging of terms for brother/ brother's daughter and sister/sister's daughter for female speakers in contrast to the separate categories used by male speakers hints that the Sekani may have possessed a classic Crow-type matrilineal system of kinship terms. The identity between the McLeod Lake and Fort Grahame terms in this respect points to an indigenous provenance of a matrilineal principle, since the terms resemble each other but the phratric categories do not. It does not prove or even hint that phratries are indigenous (just the opposite, in fact) but does show that the Sekani were predisposed towards matrilineality before matrilineal phratries were adopted around 1870. It is unclear why the Sekani had 'weak' and recently adopted phratries but clear evidence of relationship terms typical of a matrilineal system. This suggests that phratries were attuned to local needs rather than to atavistic social structural requirements.

Land and Marriage: Division

One theme recurs throughout these considerations: there is an intimate link between territorial expansion, lineality and relations with foreigners, especially as these are linked to claims of land ownership. Descriptions of land ownership in band societies is at best ambiguous. For example, 'proprietary interest' could refer to the vested claim which the Sekani maintained through more or less continuous occupation. Yet whether this is 'ownership' in the same manner in which we use the word is problematic, since the absence of sovereignty in band societies implies that there is no conception of legal ownership among its members (I think that it is more accurate to say that there is either no means or desire to enforce claims based on sovereignty). 'Possession' is a weak term which ignores some of the very concrete rights claimed by the local groups. These rights are at their strongest when the local band (or hunting band) is occupying land for a season or two. 'Occupation' implies the use of physical force, in fact or in theory, to ward off rival claims which may or may not be legitimate. While 'usufruct' implies definite rights to use land on a temporary basis – which best describes the movements of the local bands or hunting groups – it ignores the important question, whose property is being occupied? As Gluckman points out, usufruct specifically implies the right of one person to use the property of another.[23] Hence, the term cannot be applied to local bands without some important qualifications. A hunting band can be said to be exercising rights of usufruct, but only in terms of the entire regional band of which it is a necessary constituent. The Sekani have a proprietary interest in their entire domain while simultaneously recognizing that various levels of usufruct rights devolve upon the various smaller groups and networks of which the whole is constituted. This obviously begs the question of where these rights come from and how they are claimed.

As VanStone noted, the Sekani were more aggressive than other Athabaskan groups in making claims of ownership; they were willing to fight to keep outsiders out.[24] Yet they themselves were outsiders to the Trench and sometimes fought to claim land from others. Hence it is not surprising that Sekani territorial claims were expressed more concretely than by mere occupation and

were not dependent on some sort of jural expression of ownership before ownership would be defended. On the other hand,
their small numbers and the dispersal of the hunting groups
rules out the constant use of force as a means of establishing
their claims. It could be expected that a more sophisticated ideological stance would emerge under these conditions. Yet it must
have been clear to the Sekani that merely developing statements
of greater subtlety or ideological complexity would hardly facilitate recognition of their claims by rivals. Sekani statements
about the ideology of land ownership reflect this ambivalence,
as do their actions. More than once we have seen evidence of
battles and accommodation, Carriers and Shuswaps killed and
northerners peacefully trading at Fort Grahame. In a word, they
can hardly have been expected successfully to resolve the question once and for all and still maintain the flexibility which an
organization based on small and mobile hunting groups gave
them. The Sekani solution is a compromise – discontinuous occupation accompanied by the occasional use of force on the one
hand, and a definite basis for the emergence of ideologies of
ownership and unity on the other. This compromise lies somewhere between occupation and sovereignty, between the purely
concrete and the purely legal. The Sekani, as far as hunters and
gatherers are concerned, appear unusual in this respect.

One reflection of these separate tendencies is the manner in
which hunting groups circulate throughout the band range.
Turner and Wertman's examination of Cree social structure
suggests that two aspects emerge as a consequence of the propensity for constant movement over the band range: a certain
size and a particular political structure.[25] They argue that political autonomy of the band is best maintained by establishing a
sufficiently large range and correspondingly small population
such that self-reliance is possible. 'Small enough' and 'large range'
depend on the number of people who could survive in times of
severe scarcity of resources. Hence, people are rarely forced to
move into ranges claimed by outsiders or into areas of which
they have little knowledge. The sensibility of the hunter is informed not so much by immediate success or failure in the hunt
but by the imminence of diminishing returns in an area. A relatively low population density fuels a tendency for groups often
to change location. This is accompanied through the agency of a
chief or council whose duties include urging people to move
into areas which are ought to be occupied for the sake of demonstrating ownership. The difficulty lies in reconciling what
might be good for the entire band with what might best serve

the short-term interests of people in the hunting group. It is no accident that most, if not all, Indian band societies place a premium on communal ownership of land while generally disdaining attachments to particular areas of land.[26] In brief, the separate existence of the small hunting groups is maintained by mobility. These groups are what constitute the band as a self-defined entity.

Land and Marriage: Unity

It is obvious that this is only a partial insight into the dynamics of political self-definition and claims of ownership. If the Sekani, like other band societies, place a premium on autonomy and the movement which guarantees it, they also demand a certain cohesion beyond a mere adherence to a belief in common ownership. Once divided, the hunting groups must unite. Marriage plays a crucial role in creating this unity. In the Sekani case, however, contact and conflict with outsiders made this somewhat more difficult in practice than in theory. Each writer who has examined the phratric question agrees that intense and problematic contact brought about the diffusion of the phratric ideal. I have suggested that the emphasis on diffusion avoids the issue of the origin of phratries and their internal role. Yet contact between the Sekani and their neighbours has, time and time again, played such an important part in their history that it would be surprising if this were not a fruitful line of enquiry.

Given their small numbers and a history of troublesome contacts with neighbours with conflicting claims to slices of the Trench, it is not surprising that the Sekani have continually shown concern with regulating access to areas whose occupation is discontinuous. Such marginal areas, more often than not at the periphery of Sekani territory, have naturally invited occupation by foreigners. In band societies there are always problems of demonstrating ownership by means of intermittent occupation. Despite their newly emergent tribal identity, the Sekani were little more than dispersed interlopers in the Trench during the first half of the last century. This made their claims of ownership precarious indeed. No doubt a defensive and proprietary attitude was heightened by their failure to move beyond the confines of the Trench (I am referring to the Shuswap war) and by continued hostility on the Gitksan and Beaver frontiers. The tendency towards fragmentation and isolation of the many small groups to which we hesitatingly apply the term 'Sekani' in the last century was aggravated by the mountainous terrain of the Trench. Each hunting group, then as now, encountered widely different ecological and climatic conditions. Hence, what constituted the 'periphery' for any particular hunting group no doubt acquired an air of mystery and even danger. Paul Haworth, an American traveller exploring the upper reaches of the Peace River in 1915, noted that:

> [The Provincial Government Surveyor] got only as far as the "Fishing Lakes" [source of the Finlay, west-northwest of Fort Ware], where he found many moose. He attributes the number of animals in that locality to the fact that the [Sekani] have a superstitious dread of the country; those who accompanied him could hardly be prevailed upon to enter its precincts. At Fort Grahame one of the Indians drew in the sand for [the surveyor's] edification a sketch of a footprint he declared he had seen, and it was fully three feet long. Later one of the Indians deserted rather than face the reputed monsters.[27]

This territory is adjacent to Gitksan holdings and was not heavily used by the Sekani at the time. If the Sekani had a tendency to aggregate where game and furs were plentiful, then the converse is also obviously true; they sometimes abandoned less favoured areas as a result of the relatively dramatically diverse micro-environments typical of mountainous regions. The effect was not only psychological. The people of Fort Ware repeatedly told me and continually demonstrated that information on local conditions was and is the prime currency in interaction.[28] An atmosphere of uncertainty about the future no doubt contributed to feelings of isolationism. While there is no hard evidence of continual warfare, the written and oral evidence suggests that altercations with neighbouring peoples were frequent, especially at the periphery. In sum, isolation and fragmentation paved the way for the later acceptance of a new definition of unity.

If land is a question, then marriage is, and was, viewed as one possible answer. The Sekani see alliances as a means of legitimating links between themselves and foreigners, although the evidence on the extent to which people follow this dictum is not without gaps.[29] Not surprisingly, marriages of this sort created some problems in the past which contributed to the acceptance of the phratric ideal. In the short run, however, strategic marriages appeared as a viable response to a threatening situation. The record of one such marriage from this era reveals as much by what was forgotten as by what was remembered. Chief Davey of the Long Grass Band, north–northwest of the Fort Grahame people in the Kechika–Fox River basins, chose husbands for his four daughters with the same "great care" as he himself chose a wife.[30] Davey had split from the Tseloni Sekani to the south–southeast in "a spirit of antagonism" yet this did not prevent him from marrying a Tseloni woman in order to secure hunting rights to Tseloni land.[31] Not surprisingly, the evidence in Jenness suggests that the marriage took place after, not before, the split.[32] Such strategic marriages exacerbated one of the problems which are inherent and always emerging in Sekani social organization: the extent of the autonomy of the hunting or local band. In other words, Davey got greedy. But so did the Tseloni, as Davey's marriage tells us.

Davey's northern location places him squarely in the path of a southwards and increasingly intense migration of moose. I have already commented on the absence of moose in the period after 1890 and on their 1913 arrival from the north in McLeod Lake. If moose were indeed following a southwards path along the relatively nerve Trench valley, then Davey was ideally situated to reap a rich harvest. Whether through simple luck or by aggressive threats (for which there is not a shred of evidence), Davey became an important man. From the viewpoint of a less fortunate individual, what better way to gain access to a rich area than by becoming Davey's son-in-law. From Davey's viewpoint, what better way to guarantee his continued hold over the territory than by 'ceding' temporary access to other Sekani. Davey's sons-in-law were from widely scattered areas: one was a Kaska from the Upper Liard River, another a Sasutchan[33] from around Fort Grahame, one was a "half-breed Kaska", while the identity of the last is unknown.[34] The important point here is that Davey's strategic location was respected by other Sekani; autonomy and individualism apparently run deep in Sekani tradition. Still, the tension must have been sufficiently convincing of the need to create some ties with potential rivals. As advantageous as the marriages were in the short run, no permanent ties emerged from them, nor would we expect such ties to surface given that conditions change continually. Only one of his daughters is remembered in Fort Ware and his grandchildren (interestingly, only the women are noted) all married people from outside the region.

This account is consistent with an important belief of the people of Fort Ware and McLeod Lake. Men state that while they occasionally married women from outside "here", i.e. their regional bands (today, read: 'community') "their" (so they state) women never married men from other bands. What happened to the 'surplus' women? Of course, there were none. Just as Davey's strategic marriages were carried out through the agency of women of whom no detailed memories survive, Sekani men acknowledge alliances they make when outsiders are brought in but deny those alliances when insiders leave. This characteristic ambivalence towards such marriages points to a weakness in this strategy, the same weakness which Davey discovered (or was willing to risk): dissolution of the boundaries of the group. 'Foreign' marriages led to the dissolution of Davey's band, the Long Grass People, as an identifiable group. Jenness was aware of its impending fate, although he is silent of the role of demographic or natural causes in its disintegration.[35] His Fort Grahame informants had no doubt been vague on Davey's status as head of a separate band; boundaries are broken as potential enemies become actual (in the sense of 'present') members of the group. Conversely, Davey was incorporated into the northern Finlay River people. The weakening of boundaries between regional bands is one of the contributing factors which led to the development of phratries in the north.

There are two very practical problems associated with strategic marriages which phratries alleviate. First, if people marry outsiders then they are obviously not renewing their ties to other hunting groups in the regional band. Second, the period of initial matrilocal bride service associated with such marriages is normally one year, according to the literature and to the people of Fort Ware. Phratries permit continued association despite a lessened frequency of contact and of intermarriage. Phratries bypass the criteria of location and interaction as a means of creating links. While it is true that a re-affirmation of a weakened sense of band unity need not be remedied by phratries, it was unlikely that the Sekani would choose to strengthen the importance of the regional band by stressing the contribution of the hunting groups which composed it. Their small numbers, isolation and mountainous location all urged the Sekani to adopt a new principle of unity. Although 'unity' per se is a catch-all phrase referring mostly, at this point, to the means whereby ownership is demonstrated, at least two circumstances arose such that phratries appeared as a germane response to problems of ownership. These circumstances, like the weakness in the strategy of marrying people outside the band, were the final and sufficient conditions which made phratries an appealing and apposite proposition.

Politics and Phratries

After the failed attempt at southern expansion into Shuswap territory, the northern Sekani had reversed direction and were moving northwards. This in turn was temporarily halted by the aggregation of people around Fort Grahame in 1870. This was the turning point, coming on the heels of the problems engendered by strategic marriages which encouraged the Sekani to adopt phratries. The period immediately after the 1870 founding of Fort Grahame, which drew Sekani and outsiders into its immediate area, was a temporary interlude in the process of northwards movement which probably began around 1850, when tensions in the western sector at Bear Lake trading post were on the increase.

The evidence which bears on this point is admittedly scant. We know, for example, that the Sekani had unfavourable relations in the south, east and west. They were relatively friendly with the Kaska to the north, however,[36] very likely because the Kaska were not middlemen in trade with the Sekani after the 1870s.[37] We also know that migrating moose were more likely to arrive from the north following the valley formed by the Trench than to cross the continental divide in the south. At some point moose also encouraged a northern orientation among the northern Sekani, who tended to walk north in their hunts and raft south with their kill. Fourth, we also know that at some point after the 1850s and definitely before 1870 White trappers and prospectors started moving into the area from the south. Some were interested, towards the end of the last century, in using the Trench as a corridor of transport to the Klondike gold fields. Well before this time, however, others were interested in exploring for gold in the area, especially in the Omineca mountain range, where it was discovered in 1868.[38] Many of these prospectors were to settle in the area after their initial hopes were not met. Many trapped in order to support themselves and hence came into direct competition with the Sekani. They almost never traded with the Hudson's Bay Company for supplies but prefered to go south to Prince George.[39] By 1850 the southern routes were well developed, as opposed to the more difficult routes through the mountains via older posts on the eastern side such as Fort Saint John.[40]

The influence of these White trappers cannot be underestimated. Although rarely mentioned in the Hudson's Bay Company records (not surprising, since they rarely traded with the Company), local tradition in Fort Ware is especially clear on this point. Disputes with the Sekani were common and apparently continued well into this century. Government officials in Prince George cite competition between the Sekani and Whites as a reason why registered traplines were introduced in 1926. And some men in Fort Ware will candidly admit that more than a few of "their" women married White trappers (although the details are not remembered or are deliberately forgotten), thus exacerbating an already tense situation in the typically ambivalent Sekani fashion. In brief, the Sekani were developing a northern vision, partly of their own volition and partly pushed in that direction by newly arrived rivals from the south.

This alone did not lead the Sekani to adopt phratries. It is, however, the retrenchment of this northern orientation which was the touchstone for the change. In 1870 an economic problem with political overtones arose which precipitated the adoption of phratries. Between 1870 and 1885 the Fort Grahame Sekani increasingly restricted the range within which they hunted and trapped. I have already mentioned the consequences and hinted at the causes of this in the previous chapter. It remains compelling that phratries were adopted at the same time and reached their strongest expression in Fort Grahame rather than in McLeod Lake, since Fort Grahame was the newest post and the tradition of sedentarism was recent. Without movement over the entire band range there is little alternative to which the Sekani could turn in order to demonstrate the claims of the regional band over its territory. Hunting group exogamy is the strongest expression of regional band unity and is the social counterpart of spatial displacement of the hunting groups. When the absence of movement into one area results in a weakened claim, marriage to other hunting bands who are more closely linked to such areas will succeed, at least temporarily. Yet in 1870 the Fort Grahame Sekani were diminishing their range of movement and increasing the frequency of marriages to outsiders because, as I have shown in the previous chapter, outsiders were now arriving in increasing numbers in the Fort Grahame region. As the boundary around the hunting group became less significant in terms of exogamy and of membership in the regional band, the Sekani defined a new context for exogamy. The newly emergent categories of phratric descent bypass those problematic criteria, location and proximity.[41] The already strengthened autonomy of the hunting groups made reinforcement of that particular boundary a redundant proposition. The major consideration here is the influence of the fur trade, which, as Jenness argued and as the Hudson's Bay

Company records show, emphasized the independence of the hunting group.[42] Jenness was unequivocal on this point: family hunting territories "have come only in recent times".[43] Before this time the solidarity of the family as such did not even exist, a point which agrees with observations from the fur traders.[44] There is not much doubt, whatever the source of evidence, that the bureaucratic structure of the fur trade led to pressures on individuals and eroded traditional ties in much the same way as Leacock described social change among the Montagnais/Naskapi.[45] These pressures undoubtedly were exacerbated by the type of hunting opportunities offered to the Sekani by the Trench environment: definite yet unpredictable cycles and geographic and ecological diversity. The subsequent development of a patrilineal bias in the inheritance of land use rights by the hunting band must have been, at that particular conjunction of events, especially distasteful to the Sekani since it would have entailed even greater restrictions on movements and flexibility. In sum, the weight of circumstances all urged the Sekani to rethink the exogamic rule by which the boundary around the hunting groups was inexorably reinforced. Phratries bypassed these problems; or so it seemed at first. Phratries, like hunting groups, divide people without, however, creating smaller corporate units. They do not constitute people in networks which are automatically imbued with the attributes of corporateness.

I am suggesting that phratries were introduced in part to counter the weakened sense of band solidarity that resulted from a combination of forces which were impinging on the political autonomy of the Sekani. It is a perhaps unusual argument, largely because our commonsensical instincts tell us that when people aggregate more, not less, solidarity should emerge. But in the Sekani case, and I suspect in similar band societies, the exact opposite outcome is engaged whenever people come together beyond a particular threshold. When exogamy is defined in terms of a hunting band, and a hunting band implies a common and unique history of occupation, and when it is no longer feasible to imbue the hunting band with a unique status, then everything that is implied by the hunting band is also threatened. In this case, circumstances created a crisis which the Sekani met by redefining exogamy so as to re-create wide networks while bypassing the criteria which are at the root of the problem. In fact, not only were these bypassed, they were, in a sense, inverted. The tangibly limiting criteria of location and proximity became the abstract and, in theory, universally applicable criterion of phratric brotherhood. I am not so sure, however, that the Sekani would see this as an inversion. For them these are two possibilities which are quite distinct but not mutually exclusive.

It is obvious that I am speaking in dramatic and simple terms only to clarify my position. There was no general meeting of Sekani in which a new political consensus was formed, no (recorded) sounding of alarms that foreigners were arriving, no concern that there were too many moose in too limited an area (an almost ridiculous thought to the Sekani in any case). There was, probably, a sense of unease about their identity as Sekani when some of the core traits – local economic and political independence reinforced through marriages with people in other local bands – which defined that identity were undermined. Phratries were known since the days when the Sekani had depended on Coastal peoples for iron and were probably taken out of the closet in a desultory fashion. The actual process of breathing new life into the phratries did not entail rearrangements of alliances, just a switch in masks, so to speak, which identified marriage in new terms. All the elements for the emergence of a new political philosophy were already in place. It should also be clear from this brief discussion that while phratries might very well appear to be an answer to particular problems, they were a palliative at best. Simply redefining networks does not impress outsiders with one's willingness to enforce one's claim of ownership to land. And it is not surprising that the Sekani resumed moving over a wider area around 1890. The process by which the Sekani abandoned phratries is noteworthy and instructive of the limitations of brotherhood in its own right. Phratries imply clans, and the evidence in table 8.1 suggests that the Sekani indeed adopted the phratric sub-units like a hand in a glove. The Fort Grahame Sekani had a total of nine clans and, in 1894, a population of ninety-nine people. Hence, each clan was composed on average of about eleven people, a number suspiciously close to the size of the hunting bands. Hence the Sekani, inadvertently or not, resurrected and reaffirmed one of the elements which had led to the crisis of 1870, the over-developed autonomy of the hunting band. Moreover, the three Fort Grahame phratries developed a territorial base, along with a political organization which also bore a strong resemblance to the regional band. Three chiefs were acknowledged by the Hudson's Bay Company in the 1890s. They were: Woolthley, the Portage chief (whom we have already met playing off independent traders against the Hudson's Bay Company);

Natchay, the Long Chief; and Cahtah, the Bear's Lake Chief.[46] All three are associated with areas which are not only widely separated but located along the most troublesome areas along the perimeter of Sekani territory: Bear Lake was the Gitksan-Sekani frontier in the west, the Portage Chief 'guarded' the Peace River Portage east of Fort Grahame and the area closest to the traditional enemy of the Sekani, while the Long Chief was associated with the area around McLeod Lake in the south.[47] It is noteworthy that no Chief (or phratry) was 'assigned' to the relatively peaceful northern frontier. It is only speculation, but perhaps it is this 'grounding effect' which, by 1924, turned the vestigial memories of the three northern phratries into three northern regional bands. It is noteworthy that in 1924 Jenness was told of an old quadripartite scheme which was said to have been in force at the turn of the last century. It is certainly possible that the 'grounding effect' acted as a screen through which only four of the six groups identified in Chapter 5 were allowed to pass: the three phratric-derived regional bands in the north and the southern regional band centred around McLeod Lake. This quadripartite scheme has to this day formed the basis for enquiries into fur trade era Sekani social organization,[48] despite the fact that no one has questioned the dynamics by which four distinct groups could emerge during the turbulent years of the early fur trade and on the heels of the forced arrival of the Sekani into the Trench. In sum, the Sekani essentially merged the new ego-centric category of phratry and the older socio-centric category of regional band. It is no wonder that they merely fore-stalled but did not alleviate the pressures which had led to their political crisis. I have already examined the evidence which bears on the resumption of Sekani movement in 1890. Let me merely re-emphasize that in the fur trade era the Sekani rarely moved away from a trading post when there was a shortage of food. The record of the food shortage of 1829 mentioned in the previous chapter makes no mention of the Sekani going farther afield. Quite the opposite is implied; people were reluctant to leave unless the trader gave them some stores. In 1890 there was a shortage of moose, judging from the available figures, but there was no shortage of outsiders in the Trench. The only significant difference between the two eras is the presence of outsiders in the later period. If anything, the Sekani should have demonstrated a greater reluctance to leave a better sup-plied trading post in 1890 than in 1829, but there is no mention of this in the records. It is the political undercurrent to a rela-tively mundane (but no less pressing) problem which ended the

phratric era and saw the hunting and regional band system re-
gain its former pre-eminence.

Conclusion

Between the constant circulation of small and relatively discrete
hunting groups in the past and the somewhat truncated hunting
practised by individuals today arose a form of organization that
stood intermediate between mere occupation and the heavily
ideological pose of pan-Indianism. This is the Sekani concept of
brotherhood. It was invoked in order to solve a particular problem of ownership of land, but its origin in the Sekani notion of
unity implies important repercussions for other social arrangements. Many current traits, including the boundaries imposed
on pan-Indian political unity, the tension between men and
women and the more or less 'traditional' reliance on patronymics as a basis for bonding, cannot be understood without
taking into account the particularly dynamic and variable quirks
with which the Sekani imbue their notion of unity. Phratries
were the strongest antecedent expression of brotherhood, yet
they divide as much as they unite. Hence, it is not surprising
that they fail to mediate the tension between the unity of the
regional band and the autonomy of the hunting group and
individual.

Phratries are linked to the emergence of a triad of problems
facing the Sekani in the last century. First, they helped regulate
trade and hence were used as a means of gaining access to iron
before the Sekani had their own supply. Second, phratries provided a counterpoint of unity to the increasingly divided Sekani,
who accentuated the process of fragmentation while attempting to minimize conflict by marrying rivals from the outside.
Finally, phratries allowed a new definition of unity to emerge
against the background of a crisis of self-definition which had
been precipitated by the arrival of foreigners into the Trench
during a period of relative security and wealth. 'Unity', as I have
warned, is just a word; a newly defined rule of exogamy was the
actual mechanism by which people reaffirmed their ties to one
another despite divisive economic and political forces. Larger
networks were created, and, more important, these networks
could leave in place the other mechanisms by which mundane
social arrangements were developed.

I have not speculated on why the phratries were matrilineal.
I have left it implicit that this is a feature that was adopted from

the Pacific Coast. However, I think that matrilineality emerged precisely because the 'other' criteria of unity, proximity and location, were expressive of a patrilineal, patrilocal and patriarchal tendency.[49] If these criteria were involved in the mechanisms which created a crisis of political autonomy, then it is credible that the Sekani preferred to stress the alternative when attempting to prevent what today would be called the Balkanization of their homeland.

Notes

1. D. Jenness, *The Sekani Indians of British Columbia*, Ottawa: National Museum of Canada, Bulletin No. 84, 1937, p. 49.
2. When Jenness is speaking of dates it is not clear whether he is referring to his visit in 1924 or the date of publication of his report (1937).
3. Jenness, *The Sekani Indians*, p. 50.
4. Jenness did not refer to an earlier discussion of this problem which had been in print for nearly thirty years at the time of his work. Father Morice, writing in *The Western Denes*, concluded that despite the clear rules of matrilineal clan membership among the Carrier: "it is unknown among the Sekanais [sic] and Eastern Nah'anes [Kaska] who owing to the geographical position of their territory, have adhered to their primitive usages and kept aloof from foreign practices. As a result father-right is the only law which regulates succession among them." Jenness also ignores another writer. Swanton believed that clan organization moved from the Pacific Coast to the interior, but that the trend had not been embraced by the Sekani. Perhaps Jenness deliberately ignored Swanton, since he was apparently no authority on the Sekani: in one map Swanton placed the westernmost frontier of Sekani territory almost on the shore of the Pacific Ocean. See A.G. Morice, *The Western Denes, their Manners and Customs*, The Canadian Institute, Proceedings for 1888–1882, vol. 7, 1890, p. 121; J.R. Swanton, 'The Development of the Clan System and Secret Societies among the Northwestern Tribes', *American Anthropologist* 6(3); 477–87, 1904.
5. I. Goldman, 'The Alkatchoo Carrier of British Columbia', in Ralph Linton, ed., *Acculturation in Seven American Indian Tribes*, New York: Appleton-Century, 1940, p. 342.
6. F. de Laguna, 'Matrilineal Kin Groups in Northwestern North America', in *Proceedings, Northern Athapaskan Conference, 1971*, ed. A. McFadyen Clark, Vol. 1, pp. 17–145, 1975, p. 58. Sib refers to a lineally defined clan. Sept refers to a clan whose membership is negotiable and is based on bilaterally-extended linkages. Phratry refers to an assemblage of clans. I use the term 'sib' to refer to matrilineally defined clans.
7. Ibid., p. 56.
8. V.H. Kobrinsky, 'The Tsimshianization of the Carrier Indians', in

J.W. Helmer, S. VanDyke and F.J. Kense, eds., *Prehistory of the North American Sub-Arctic: The Athapaskan Question*, Calgary: Archaeological Association of the University of Calgary, 1977.

9. Ibid., pp. 201, 202.

10. Ibid., p. 207.

11. De Laguna, 'Matrilineal Kin Groups', p. 136.

12. I. Dyen and D.F. Aberle, *Lexical Reconstruction: The Case of the Proto-Athapaskan Kinship System*, London: Cambridge University Press, 1974, p. 291.

13. Ibid., p. 363.

14. Ibid., p. 402.

15. Ibid.

16. Ibid., p. 248.

17. Ibid., p. 251.

18. Jenness, *The Sekani Indians*, p. 47.

19. Jenness and Morice disagree about the number of phratries. See ibid., footnote.

20. HBC Arch. B249/1/9, p. 301.

21. HBC Arch. B249/1/9, p. 303.

22. J. White, ed., *Handbook of Indians of Canada*, Ottawa: Appendix to the Tenth Report of the Geographic Board of Canada, 1913. Reprinted Toronto: Coles, 1971, p. 413. A.G. Morice, 'The Fur Trader in Anthropology', *American Anthropologist* 30(1): 60–84, 1928, pp. 576, 577.

23. M. Gluckman, *Politics and Law in Tribal Society*, Oxford: Basil Blackwell, 1971, p. 36.

24. J. VanStone, *Athapaskan Adaptations: Hunters and Fishermen of the SubArctic Forests*, Chicago: Aldine, 1974, p. 50.

25. D.H. Turner and P. Wertman, *Shamattawa: The Structure of Social Relations in a Northern Algonkian Band*, Ottawa: National Museum of Canada, Canadian Ethnology Service Paper No. 36, 1977.

26. D.H. Turner, *Dialectics and Tradition: Myth and Social Structure in Two Hunter-Gatherer Societies*, London: Occasional Paper No. 36 of the Royal Anthropological Institute of Great Britain and Ireland, 1978.

27. P. Haworth, *On the Headwaters*, p. 240.

28. This is reflected in the normal manner in which greetings are offered in Fort Ware, for example. People often volunteer information about their activities immediately preceding the encounter. The description includes a detailed description of the speaker's movements that brought him to his present location.

29. Yet Harmon's journal and Morice both mention marriages by the Carrier as an attempt to gain access to Sekani land and as an attempt by the Sekani to obtain better trade terms for iron. See Morice, 'The Fur Trader in Anthropology', p. 81. D.W. Harmon, *Sixteen Years in the Indian Country: The Journal of Daniel Williams Harmon 1800–1815*, ed. W.K. Lamb, Toronto: MacMillan, 1957, p. 256.

30. D. Jenness, 'The Sekani Indians of British Columbia', *Transactions of the Royal Society of Canada* 25(2): 21–34, 1931, p. 29.

31. Ibid., p. 30.

32. Ibid., p. 29.

33. Saschut'qenne, in Morice's classification, A.G. Morice, *Notes on the Western Dene*, Toronto: Transactions of the Canadian Institute, 1892/3, p. 29.

34. Jenness, 'The Sekani Indians of British Columbia', p. 29.

35. Idem, *The Sekani Indians*, p. 50.

36. Ibid., p. 19.

37. E. Allard, 'Notes on the Kaska and Upper Liard Indians', *Primitive Man* 11 (1, 2): 24–36, 1929, pp. 24, 25.

38. R.M. Patterson, *Finlay's River*, Toronto: Macmillan, 1968, p. 68.

39. The history of these White trappers has yet to be written. Local tradition at McLeod Lake is rich, and the various accounts tend to confirm one another. These trappers are rarely mentioned in the Hudson's Bay Company journals.

40. The southern transport route along the Crooked River from the southern height of land to McLeod Lake was so well used that to this day there are still traces of the old dams which were used to increase temporarily the depth of the shallow channel of the Crooked River for the heavily laden boats. As the water rose these dams were breached. The flood carried the boat along to the next dam, where the process was repeated. These dams are crude and are little more than boulders rolled quickly into position.

41. It might be easier to suggest that hunting group exogamy follows automatically from the genealogical closeness of its members. This, however, begs the question. First, there is no exact knowledge of the genealogical composition of these hunting groups. They were almost certainly based around one or two families but almost equally certainly included others. Second, an explicit statement about exogamy formulated in reference to a social group rather than a network of kin indicates a concern with the jural aspects of group solidarity. Third, the composition of the hunting groups appears to have changed with sufficient frequency so as to obviate any concern the Sekani may have had for the negative genetic results of continued endogamy.

42. Jenness, *The Sekani Indians*, p. 44.

43. Ibid.

44. Ibid.

45. E.B. Leacock, *The Montagnais 'Hunting Territory' and the Fur Trade*, American Anthropological Association Memoir No. 78, 1954.

46. HBC Arch. B249/d/3, fo. 16d., 17; HBC Arch. B249/d/9, p. 71.

47. HBC Arch. B249/d/3.

48. G. Denniston, 'Sekani', in *Handbook of North American Indians, vol. 6: The Subarctic*, ed. J. Helm, Washington: The Smithsonian Institution, 1981, pp. 433–45.

49. I have argued much along the same lines when examining Tsimshian matrilineality in M. Korovkin and G. Lanoue, 'On the Substantiality of Form: Interpreting Symbolic Expression in the Paradigm of Social Organization', *Comparative Studies in Society and History* 3(3): 13–68, 1988.

Chapter 9

Conclusions

Much by way of specific conclusions about Sekani political structure and the modern situation has already been alluded to in the previous chapter. Here I will confine myself to some general summarizing comments and observations.

Clearly, what I have written about is not exactly nor even necessarily representative of what I saw every day during my nineteen months with the Sekani. What I saw in McLeod Lake was despair and violence but also people still trying to carry on with whatever routine activities they deemed necessary to their normal lives against a background of uncertainty about the future and, even worse, grave doubts about the value of holding on to the past in the modern world. The people of McLeod Lake were caught in a spasm of non-confidence in their culture which they countered with a renewed emphasis on what they believe comprises its core. I hinted at the conditions in McLeod Lake in the second chapter, and most people and certainly all anthropologists can read enough between the lines to appreciate some of the difficulties involved in describing or analysing such a situation. Since I could not write about everything I saw, I set about to make sense of what I instinctively felt was a nonsensical situation. I went to Fort Ware and saw people who, although worried about what had happened to their southern cousins, were more traditional in their orientation. There, I was able to get a more complete view of Sekani life.

'Traditional' as a value in itself means very little to the Sekani, of course, but it means a lot to me. Anthropologist or not, I am no more or less a product of my society and training than the Sekani are of theirs. Apart from the obvious theoretical reservations that all anthropologists have or should have about indiscriminately using terms like 'alienation', 'tradition' 'relations of production' and the like, at some point emotions and biases take over and it is no longer possible to use a deterministic model where all the pieces fit together neatly. After all, I was there and so I must have been part of the puzzle insofar as people's reactions were concerned. I am not addressing the high-school debating club issue of cultural relativism and the possibility of undertaking bias-free science. I am trying to write about what it means to be human, the Sekani and I in the same stew with all of us trying to work out what the other meant to one's sense of self. It is an important question and not only theoretically; it so happens I am White and not Indian, and the Sekani never let me forget the fact. They did so without malice or political cynicism, but there it was: two societies, two people, two backgrounds and one wall behind which one could discern grey outlines without at the same time ever being sure that one wasn't just looking at a steamy mirror.

In the long run, these ruminations help put theoretical propositions into their proper perspective. They help us remember that anthropology deals with people in a much more tangible way than models generally allow. In short, there is no question in my mind that any person who wants to call him- or herself an anthropologist must realize that there is no one model that makes sense of what we see and that we cannot even be certain of what we are looking at. While at McLeod Lake and Fort Ware it would have been easy to slip into a more classical stance and speak of alienation and its effects rather than try to imagine what could possibly be a meaningful reason to the Sekani for the outward manifestations of what I thought I was seeing. And, after all, the Sekani dress more or less as I dress, watch hockey games on television on Saturday night while drinking beer and go to supermarkets to buy food (in McLeod Lake, at least). Yet everything I saw, even these mundane activities, reflected an interplay between Sekani traditions and the modern world. The point is simple: if an anthropologist sees someone watching a hockey game and cheering wildly when a team 3,000 miles away puts a piece of rubber into a net, it is relatively straightforward to claim that these people are fans who like hockey. But then, while musing on the symbolism of hockey, the ideas of controlled competition, the dynamic tension of the individual versus the collective, vicarious thrills for impotent and semi-alienated people and the like will creep in because of the word 'fan' and what it means in White North America. But what if the Sekani cheer just as wildly when the other team scores a goal? What if they don't even know where the teams' home towns are? There is something going on here that is not easily amenable to instant analysis.

What impressed me most was the tenacity with which the Sekani hold on to certain ways of interacting despite the nearly overwhelming economic and political pressures which urge them to adopt expedient and pragmatic values. Pragmatism is present but, given the distressing circumstances in which the Sekani find themselves, the continued use of a particular way of forming relationships is not only surprising, it is bewildering. All sorts of 'traditional' patterns were easily discernible, but I was continually amazed at the unexpected dimensions that these patterns took. What I hope I have been able to suggest is the way in which a continual dynamic interaction is maintained between the past and present; how individuals make sense of their history in terms of the present, in other words.

The theoretical point I am trying to make is that there must be some way in which Durkheimian mechanical solidarity develops into organic solidarity by the agency of choice. Durkheim ultimately agreed with Marx in that the basis of organic solidarity lay in the pragmatic and overlapping networks we call the division of labour. Durkheim believed that the more differentiated basis of solidarity had implications for the creation of a self-defined and self-sustaining polity (*Suicide, The Division of Labour in Society*), even if he was unclear about the origins or political implications of mechanical solidarity (for example, his discussion of totemism in *Elementary Forms of the Religious Life*). If civil society is self-sustaining, then it certainly has an impact on the pragmatic arrangements into which people enter. Not so unlike Marx, after all. Like Durkheim, I have tried to explore these implications of how self-definition emerges. Unlike Durkheim I suggest that the basis for the way in which the solidarity of the polity (i.e. for people who live in civil society characterized by organic solidarity) may be expressed lies ultimately in the implicit beliefs which people hold about how being human is defined. In the case of the Sekani I make no claim to understanding the complexity of their thoughts on this matter. I have merely tried to show how these thoughts have had some impact in their political and social choices.

In the introductory chapter I had hypothesized that a particular type of tension existed in Athabaskan societies and that this was the result of the kinds of bonds into which people entered. The particular problem I had set out to study was not so much to discern the presence of this tension but the particular comprises which made the tension manageable. The 'resolution' held important consequences for the manner in which people formed associations. What I saw in McLeod Lake and Fort Ware was an important category, the patronymic, acting as a boundary around which most daily tensions were focussed. Furthermore, the presence of pan-Indian sentiments in McLeod Lake implied a similar type of boundary and tension: between Indians and Whites, between McLeod Lake and other Sekani groups and between the individual and the group. The common thread in all these categories was the way in which they were defined, by invoking an abstract definition of what constitutes the community, the base for hunting partnerships and, ultimately, the individual as seen in the world, White or Indian. I sought to understand the historical basis for this view of the world and discovered that in the phratric regime matrilineal phratries and patriarchal organization of labour had created an ideological focal point for the emergence of the group. I emphasize the word 'resolution' because I hope that I have made clear that the tension is maintained by the 'resolution' as much as it is eliminated. It is the interplay of tension and its 'solutions' which defines Sekani social organization. The particular compromise the Sekani engaged was as well-suited to the need to reproduce these tensions as to hide them. In brief, what they emphasized in the domain of social activity they de-emphasized in their ideological descriptions about their social organization. That is, no matter how 'ideological', 'abstract' and arbitrarily postulated the rule of group formation may be, it is no less 'true' and 'real' for all that. Of course, all people live in terms of their culture, but the twist in this case is that in Sekani society the constant switching of commitment between the 'real' and the 'ideal' is their culture.

For example, descriptions of social structure in band societies which stress egalitarianism are no less (or more) correct than models which stress hierarchy. An undifferentiated and basically egalitarian band could easily co-exist with pragmatic and hierarchical categories in the form of various degrees of partnerships which link domestic groups with one another. This is not surprising, after all. What I realized, however, was that hierarchy is not a concession exacted from everyday life, nor is egalitarianism some sort of mechanism of social control which keeps the peace so that people can get along in the harsh northern environment. Instead, each of these tendencies could be described, in our terms, as a particular political philosophy. I say 'could' because in the Sekani case neither hierarchy nor egalitarianism as such are the specific forms of discourse that inform the choices people make in mundane activities. Hierarchy and egalitarianism are, however, structural principles that allow an easy jump to the mundane level: pan-Indianism is an explicitly egalitarian form of discourse, and community and individual self-definition operate in a hierarchical context. In sum, I discovered that the Sekani valorize their ideology of pan-Indianism so that it is an effective blanket, but I also found that valorized ideology is as much the engine which drives social action and guides social change as is the need for hunting partnerships.

Sekani socio-political development reflects the application of their notion of unity expressed as limited brotherhood, especially as these limits are interpreted by the Sekani in terms of spatial location and frequency of interaction. We know that something like local bands and hunting groups probably existed at the time of early contact. We are not sure how these groups were integrated into the larger category of regional band, but the weight of the evidence suggests that marriage was most likely the strongest expression (i.e. with the most far-reaching consequences) of the political interdependence and autonomy of the hunting groups. The resulting political self-consciousness of the band was further enhanced as much by confrontations with its neighbours as by common work interests and ownership. Hence, the template for phratric association is certainly implicit in the notion of 'band'.

The evidence dealing with the political development of tribe and phratry is more complicated and elusive, however. The Sekani attempted to deal with intrusion (theirs and others') in two ways. First, they moved constantly, as much to demonstrate their continued interest in land as to avoid confrontation. Indeed, the Sekani do not appear, on balance, to be the most timid of Athabaskan groups in this regard. Second, and this is anthropologically unique in its historical documentation, they developed phratric organization; they became tribalized, in other words. Phratries expressed links among people who may have effectively ceased intermarrying. People apparently diminished the frequency of marriages among hunting groups in order to marry people outside the boundaries of the regional band. As viable as the strategy of marrying foreigners may have appeared in the short run, it contributed to the weakening of solidarity among the hunting groups. The boundary of the hunting group ceased to hold any meaning as far as the self-definition of the group was concerned. Phratries inadvertently undermined the importance of the regional band as the ownership groups since they were now the exogamic categories. Sekani phratries even came to be imbued with a sense of regional identity as their members asserted their claims of ownership over peripheral territories.

The demise of phratries tells us much about their role, perhaps as much as their inception reveals. As greater importance came to be placed on occupation-as-ownership when people renewed their visits to peripheral territories around 1885, phratries evolved (or perhaps, devolved) into little more than local bands. Each phratry had a chief and, more importantly, a specific tract of land associated with it. In brief, phratries changed from categories in which membership was unrelated to a person's location and to the nature of his personal relationships to networks with definite social and spatial expression. They became redundant as a means of inculcating solidarity as long as strategic alliances 'solved' the question of access to peripheral land. In their original conception, in other words, Sekani phratries initially appear to have been akin to small tribes rather than large local bands but after several years once again began to resemble local bands and all that this implies. In my opinion, the new spatial and regionally discrete dimension of phratric identity was caused by the all too successful Sekani policy of marry-your-enemy. In-laws now acquired 'rights' over areas of land whose use may have been previously disputed but whose ownership was apparently never called into question. The paucity of the evidence, I have constantly cautioned, does not permit unassailable conclusions, but I think that no other interpretation fits the evidence so well.

In the Sekani case their ideology of unity, which in many Athabaskan societies remains rather implicit (and hence not as much 'ideological' or 'political' as it is 'religious' or 'cultural' in the broad sense), was rendered explicit at a particular conjuncture of events. The phratry emerged as the specific expression of the bonds of brotherhood. I have also argued that the Sekani notion of unity has more than one dimension. On the one hand, the Sekani are not altogether new to the idea of revitalization based on universalizing the categories they use in everyday life. On the other hand, the attempt to unite otherwise autonomous (I cannot say 'alienated', since it is as theoretically inapplicable as it is descriptively correct) people within the same category has been expressed by the notion of tribe, not to mention the patronymic category, which is suspiciously evocative of the concept of local or hunting band. Hence, it is not surprising that an ideologically expressed definition of unity, with its inevitable politicization of relationships, has once again emerged in this latest of crises, nor is it surprising that pan-Indianism is now interpreted as limited brotherhood. The close of the last century saw the idea of brotherhood applied on a different scale, however. The new category of phratry was intermediate between the largest network, the tribe, and the smallest pragmatic group, the hunting band. The phratry was used as a means of redefining the ties that linked people to one another so that their existence as a group could be clarified and strengthened. The crisis which precipitated this drastic change was something akin to what political scientists would, in the modern context, call a threat to sovereignty. Over the years the circumstances of that crisis have changed, such that phratries have become little more than patronymic networks which act as significant categories in linking people to one another. After being limited to this lower level, however, the idea of brotherhood has once again re-emerged in a larger and more abstract form as pan-Indianism. Once again, foreigners appear as a threat to the survival of the Sekani as a self-defined people. Once again, this 'invasion' is countered by an attempt to increase the strength of the solidarity of the group. Once again, this emergent unity is largely based on the exclusiveness of a category which is defined in highly abstract and all-encompassing terms. Unlike the political crisis of the phratric era, however, the scale of the problem has increased dramatically, just as the social organizational traits which characterized the contemporary Sekani are different than those of the past. Fragmentation in the modern context is much more pronounced compared to the past. Hence, it is not surprising to find that the idea of unifying people by means of membership in an abstract category has also increased in scale and strength. The phratric principle of bounded unity – defining inclusion by means of exclusion – is now used, ironically, to unite "all" Indian people.

There is another major difference between phratric brotherhood and pan-Indian brotherhood. Each allows different consequences to emerge. Although phratries seemingly bypassed the criterion of location by creating descent-based networks, they were exclusive in theory only. The northern regional band was divided into three phratries and each one tended to anchor itself to an identifiable location. Hence, in the end, phratric brotherhood came to resemble something akin to the regional band. Phratries, in other words, are a division of a larger category as much as they are a union of smaller units. Pan-Indian brotherhood, on the other hand, suggests no such limitation, neither through the notion of membership it embodies ("all Indians") nor through geographical boundaries. Boundaries are necessarily allowed to emerge on a pragmatic basis, something which does nothing for the elimination of the factionalism which pan-Indianism 'resolves' in the first place.

In sum, two planes of Sekani social and political life intersect to produce four distinct levels of social integration, but each plane remains structurally distinct in the process which gives birth to it. On the one hand, membership in one of two categories – the phratry or the 'tribe' (the modern designation) – is given by birth regardless of location or a person's parent's work histories. On the other hand, membership in the hunting band or regional band depends very much at any point on a person's pragmatic links within well-defined spatial boundaries. It is tempting to think of these four levels as representing different degrees of socio-political integration. This, however, ignores the very real traits with which the Sekani imbue each level. Throughout this work I have tried to deduce these traits, in the same way that a political scientist might deduce what 'nation' means to a group of people by looking at what they do as much as by listening to what they say. The result of this analytical procedure quickly puts to the lie the widespread but inappropriate assumption that each level represents greater inclusiveness. Phratries, for example, are larger (in the sense of having more members) than the local band but they are exogamous, while local bands tend towards endogamy. Tribes are more or less endogamous compared to the phratry, yet phratries emerge precisely at the point in which a practice of tribal endogamy was redefined as exogamy. There is a great deal of overlap between all of these categories because some of the traits which characterize one often emerge in another. These traits are, after all, merely different ways of uniting people; it is not surprising that the Sekani appear to have somewhat contradictory and redundant principles of social organization. It is not unexpected that as groups grow in size they tend towards a more abstract definition of inclusion, since more people implies a greater diversity of interests; the hunting group is defined in a much more concrete manner than the regional band, for example. As some abstract categories shrink in their inclusiveness they tend to become groups, just like, for example, the phratries. On the other hand, phratries (and now patronymics) are ways of dividing people who are otherwise all members of the same regional band (now, the government-defined Band or community). Limits to unity, therefore, are incorporated in the Sekani notion of brotherhood no matter what category happens to be dominant at the time. Today, these limits surface as tension and violence along the patronymic frontier. The theoretically significant point of this study is that social and political categories emerge from a dynamic process which is unrelated to simple growth or a change in technology.

The tension and violence I have described in the second and fifth chapters and explored in the rest of the work could have many origins. Many people will argue with the interpretation I offer by pointing out, quite correctly, that tensions between men and women, husbands and wives, are never absent in any society and that spousal violence has increased in many contemporary Indian societies that are under stress. I am not arguing that the Sekani case is not part of a general phenomenon, nor am I arguing that the Sekani are emblematic of whatever is happening elsewhere. Rather, I am suggesting that, whatever its ultimate source, tension in Sekani society emerges precisely at the seams of structural integration and that such manifest tension (Sahlins's 'structure in history') informs much of social and political discourse. There is a corollary conclusion with implications for anthropological methodology. If the phenomenon of tension and violence is so complex in one society, perhaps our facile understanding of general trends ought not to be invoked quite so readily. And what is, after all, our understanding of the general picture except, literally, generalizations forged from the study of many small and discrete societies? To those who would argue that general phenomena such 'the fur trade', 'socio-cultural clash with the White world', 'alcoholism', 'competition for scarce resources', 'the disruptive influence of missionary teachings', etc. all had a part to play in what can too easily be called the disintegration of Sekani society, I answer that the onus of proof is on them to show that these notions, which evolved in our cultural context, make any sense when applied elsewhere. I have tried to anticipate such viewpoints by examining such classic domains of enquiry as demographic pressure, demand for scarce trade goods, distribution of money and land use. Everywhere the data have suggested the same interpretation: complex Sekani notions that do not correspond to our understanding of sociocultural processes were and are at work in organizing even these mundane aspects of daily life. These are not easily described by terms that we often use to describe social and cultural processes. Violence, especially spousal violence, is usually interpreted in only one way in the received wisdom of Western social science, as an index of disintegration. Yet Sekani society is not disintegrating.

In general, I am arguing that violence is positively correlated with the increasing emphasis on pan-Indianism. Pan-Indianism by itself does not cause violence. It merely allows violence to emerge at particular points in the social organization. Pan-Indianism contributes to violence only in the sense that its universalism contains no practical guidelines for the formation of boundaries and distinctions. Hence, the crisis in social relations, particularly in McLeod Lake, allows the traditional dichotomy in the Sekani conception of brotherhood to emerge in a more potent form.

Although it is a common belief that violence arises out of situations of despair – and there is no doubt that the situation in McLeod Lake and to a lesser extent in Fort Ware is very serious – I am suggesting that it is possible that violence falls into the pattern which embodies the categories people use. Conditions outside Sekani society have created a sense of uncertainty and even desperation among many people. The results are predictable enough: stress, violence and disorganization. The guarantee of survival which the Sekani have managed to inculcate despite everything demands that violent interaction be imbued with the significance of cultural reaffirmation. Violence is about individual despair, but it is transformed into a social and historical gesture by the context of brotherhood.

Appendix I

Population figures for Fort Ware, Fort Grahame and McLeod Lake

	1839[1]	1858	1894	1895	1896	1897	1898	1899	1900	1901	1902	1903	1904	1905	1906	1907	1908	1909	1910	1911	1912	1914
Fort Grahame Nomads[2]	202	151																			32	32
McLeod Lake			95	93	93	94	93	91	91	93	95	96	99	99	99	99	99	98	85	91	90	76
Fort Grahame			99	97	99	99	97	95	95	93	96	93	91	91	89	89	89	88	88	94	92	59
Finlay River Band[3]																						
Fort Ware[4]																						

	1915	1916[5]	1921[6]	1924	1929	1934	1939	1944	1954[7]	1956	1958	1959	1960	1961	1962	1963	1965	1966	1968	1969	1970
Fort Grahame Nomads	32	35	50[8]	41	40																
McLeod Lake	76	72	56	61	82	81	85	93	118	127	136	140	147	144	142	142	152	156	165	168	174
Fort Grahame	56	56	96	99	129	133	135	145	83	83	84										
Finlay River Band												182	198	207	218	222	233	249	264	275	281
Fort Ware										85	83										

1 From *The Beaver*, Autumn 1965, p. 27.
2 Refers to a northern group of Sekani who occasionally traded at Fort Grahame but did not reside there.
3 Finlay River Band refers to Fort Grahame and Fort Ware (sometimes called Whitewater).
4 1978 and 1979 population figures are given in the text.
5 Note attached to 1916 census: "There are some 2,500 Nomadic Indians in British Columbia who cannot be correctly classified."
6 'Indian Affairs Files: 1921 Census', Ottawa: Public Archives of Canada, RG ID vol. 3161, File 365.009–2A
7 McLeod Lake figures are undoubtedly too high since 1953, since that is the year of the opening of the highway between Prince George and Dawson Creek.
8 The figure is not identified as belonging to the Fort Grahame Nomads in this census. The classifications used are as follows: Bear Lake 39, Manson [Creek] 3, Blackwater [Creek] 8, "Bear Lake" could be referring to the Caribou Hide People (more closely affiliated with Tahltan speakers than with Sekani) rather than the Sekani *per se*.

Source: B. Steventon, unpublished research project, n.d. except where noted.

Appendix II

Fur harvest, McLeod Lake

	1824	1826	1827	1828	1829	1830	1831	1832	1846	1847[1]	1848
Black bear	2		8	11	13	6	29				
Brown bear										} 15	
Grizzly bear											16
Large beaver	377	930	1070	1297	1340	1345	1224	67		} 491	
Small beaver	130	496	705	687	598	699	427	38			
Silver fox										1	
Cross fox										1	
Red fox											7
Fisher		1									
Ermine											
Lynx	15	2		4	8	32	15	2		15	33
Marten	1	321	129	301	168	454	20	52		745	734
Muskrat		9	4	5	10	8	2			6	4
Otter	3	29	24	28	36	43	26	6		18	16
Wolverine		3	1	1	2	12	1	1		6	
Wolf											
Squirrel											
Coyote											
Moosehides											24
Caribou hides	1										
Mink	1	9	4	5	10	8	2			6	4

1846: Not listed by species for this year. Total returns: 12 packs @ 80 lbs. per pack.

Source: Hudson's Bay Company Archives, except for [1], Glenbow Foundation Archives, BB12.M165, p. 20.

Fur harvest, Fort Grahame

	1892	1893	1894	1896	1897	1908	1915	1920
Black bear	41	40		74	59	9		3
Brown bear	2	3		11	2			1
Grizzly bear	9	15		19	17			2
Large beaver	} 536	} 439		} 695	} 614	} 153		
Small beaver								
Silver fox				2	2			
Cross fox	1	4		3	4			
Red fox	1	1		8	1	1		1
Fisher	1	12		20	12	8	4	3
Ermine								
Lynx	72	191		269	86	61	2	
Marten	608	664		867	536	1	59	16
Muksrat	39	30		34	5			
Otter	4	6		15	3			
Wolverine	14	15		21	27		1	1
Wolf		2		2	5			
Squirrel								
Coyote								
Moosehides		129.5	151	225	123.5			
Caribou hides		15	3		5			
Mink	11	14		11	3	2		1

Source: Hudson's Bay Company Archives.

Fur harvest, Fort Ware

	1976[1]	1977[2]	1978[3]
Black bear			2
Brown bear			
Grizzly bear		1	
Large beaver	} 56	} 59	} 177
Small beaver			
Silver fox			
Cross fox			
Red fox		1	
Fisher			1
Ermine	44	30	14
Lynx	2	8	3
Marten	142	333	311
Muskrat	16	28	35
Otter	2		6
Wolverine	6	3	2
Wolf		2	
Squirrel	424	384	814
Coyote		2	1
Moosehides			
Caribou hides			
Mink	16	10	30

[1] Based on November and December returns only.
[2] Based on four months' returns.
[3] Complete; based on six months' returns.
Source: Van Somer's Store; Ft. Ware; BC Fish and Wildlife Branch, Mackenzie.

Appendix III

Debt at McLeod Lake trading post, 1902 in MB

Women	Debt	Payment	Balance due
Mrs Achee	28.5	22	6.5
Mrs Alexie	22	22	
Mrs Chayah	11.5+28.5		40
Mrs S. Chingee	26	13	13
Mrs Cook	8+16.5	34.5	10 (credit)
Mrs Dan	25	20	5
Celina	15		15
Mrs Henry	23	23	
Mrs High Yallie	22.5		22.5
Mrs Solonas	20	11	9
Maritine	12		12
Mrs Two Dick	26.5	24	2.5 (cancelled)
Dan Ma	22	22	
Francis Ma	15		15

Men	Debt[1]	Payment[2]	Balance due[3]
Chayah	126.5		
S. Chingee	87.5	49	38.5
Inyallie	121		121
Isadore	59.5	31	28.5
Francis	60		60
Dan	90	41	49
Nancie	74+50.5	91	17
Pierre	43	42	1
Solonas	75+49		124
E. Solonas	15+23.5	13.5	10 (15 cancelled)
S. Solonas	41.5	33	18
Two Dick	132	56	76
Yatse	51	51	0[4]
Theodore	20		20
Duncan	15.5+6.5	7	15
Achee	43+22.5+9	28	46.5 (cancelled)
Mat	22.5	7	15.5
Challus	56	56	
Alexie	51.5+65	21	95.5
Bill	18.5	18.5	
Bazil	32	19	13

[1] Represents June and July debt, plus 1901 debt carried forward, expressed in Made Beaver.
[2] Payments made in October 1902.
[3] Balance owing; cancellations at time of trade listed as such in original.
[4] Actual amount paid equalled 49 MB; 2 MB cancelled but not entered.

Bibliography

PUBLISHED SOURCES

Aberle, D.F. 'The Prophet Dance and Reactions to White Contact', *Southwestern Journal of Anthropology* 15: 74–83, 1959.

Allard, E., 'Notes on the Kaska and Upper Liard Indians', *Primitive Man* 11(1, 2): 24–36, 1929.

Asch, M., 'The Impact of Changing Fur Trade Practices on the Economy of the Slavey Indians: Some Preliminary Conclusions Regarding the Period 1870–1900', Winnipeg: paper delivered at the Canadian Ethnology Society symposium on early mercantile enterprises, 1976.

——, 'The Dene Economy', in M. Watkins, ed., *Dene Nation: The Colony Within*, Toronto: University of Toronto Press, 1977.

——, 'The Economics of Dene Self-Determination', in G.A. Smith and D.H. Turner, eds, *Challenging Anthropology*, Toronto: McGraw Hill-Ryerson, 1979.

——, 'Steps Toward the Analysis of Athapaskan Social Organization', *Arctic Anthropology* 17(2): 46–51, 1980.

——, *Home and Native Land: Aboriginal Rights and the Canadian Constitution*, Toronto: Methuen, 1984.

Babcock, B., ed., *The Reversible World: Symbolic Inversion in Art and Society*, Ithaca: Cornell University Press, 1979.

Bailey, A.G., *The Conflict of European and Algonkian Cultures 1504–1700*, New Brunswick Museum Series No. 12, 1937.

Balikci, A., 'Perspectives on the Atomistic Type Society: Bad Friends', *Human Organization* 27(3): 191–9, 1968.

Bancroft, H.H., *History of the Northwest Coast; vol. II: 1800–1846*, San Francisco: The History Company, 1886.

Barbeau, M., *Indian Days in the Canadian Rockies*, Toronto: Macmillan and Co., 1923.

Bergson, H., *Le Rire: essai sur la signification du comique*, 399th edn, Paris: Quadrige/PUF, 1981.

Black S., *Black's Rocky Mountain Journal, 1824*, E.E. Rich, ed., London: Hudson's Bay Record Society, 1955.

Brown, J.S.H., *Strangers in Blood: Fur Trade Company Families in Indian Country*, Vancouver: University of British Columbia Press, 1980.

Burridge, K.O.L., *New Heaven, New Earth: A Study of Millenarian Activities*, Oxford: Basil Blackwell, 1969.

de Laguna, F., 'Matrilineal Kin Groups in Northwestern North America', in *Proceedings, Northern Athapaskan Conference, 1971*, ed. A. McFadyen Clark, Vol. 1, pp. 17–145, 1975.

Denniston, G., 'Sekani', in *Handbook of North American Indians, vol. 6: The Subarctic*, ed. J. Helm, Washington: The Smithsonian Institution, 1981.

Douglas, M., *Purity and Danger*, London: Routledge and Kegan Paul, 1966.

Dunning, R.W., *Social and Economic Change among the Northern Ojibwa*, Toronto: University of Toronto Press, 1959.

Dyen, I., and D.F. Aberle, *Lexical Reconstruction: The Case of the Proto-Athapaskan Kinship system*, London: Cambridge University Press, 1974.

Fraser, S., *Simon Fraser, Letters and Journals 1806–1808*, ed. W.K. Lamb, Toronto: Macmillan, 1960.

Fumoleau, R., *As Long As This Land Shall Last*, Toronto: McClelland and Stewart, 1974.

Geertz, C., 'Deep Play: Notes on the Balinese Cockfight', *Daedalus* 101, 1972: 1–37.

Glenbow Foundation, 'McLeod's Lake Journal 1845–1848', Calgary, Alberta, n.d.

Gluckman, M., *Politics and Law in Tribal Society*, Oxford: Basil Blackwell, 1971.

Goldman, I., 'The Alkatchoo Carrier of British Columbia', in R. Linton, ed., *Acculturation in Seven American Indian Tribes*, New York: Appleton-Century, 1940.

Goldschmidt, W., 'Social Organization in Native California and the Origins of Clans', *American Anthropologist* 50: 444–56, 1948.

Harmon, D.W., *Sixteen Years in the Indian Country: The Journal of Daniel Williams Harmon 1800–1816*, ed. W.K. Lamb, Toronto: Macmillan, 1957.

Harris, M., *Cannibals and Kings*, New York: Random House, 1977.

——, *Culture, People, Nature*, New York: Harper and Row, 1980.

Haworth, P., *On the Headwaters of the Peace River*, New York: Scribners, 1917.

Helm, J., 'Kin Terms of the Arctic Drainage Dene: Hare, Slavey, Chipewyan', *American Anthropologist* 62: 279–385, 1960.

——,'Bilaterality in the Socio-Territorial Organization of the Arctic Drainage Dene', *Ethnology* 4: 361–85, 1965.

Helm-MacNeish, J., 'Leadership Among the Northeastern Athapaskans', *Anthropologica* 2: 131–63, 1956.

Helm, J., and E.B. Leacock, 'The Hunting Tribes of Subarctic Canada', in E.B. Leacock and N.O. Lurie, eds, *North American Indians in Historical Perspective*, New York: Random House, 1971.

Hertzberg, H.W., *Search for American Identity Modern Pan-Indian Movements*, Syracuse: Syracuse University Press, 1971.

Honigmann, J.J., *Culture and Ethos of Kaska Society*, Yale University Publications in Anthropology No. 40, New Haven: Yale University Press, 1949.

——, *The Kaska Indians: An Ethnographic Reconstruction*, Yale University Publications in Anthropology No. 51, New Haven: Yale University Press, 1954.

——, 'Interpersonal Relations in Atomistic Communities', *Human Organization* 27(3): 220–9, 1968.

Ingram, G.C., and D.A. Harris, 'New Caledonia and the Fur Trade', *Western Canadian Journal of Anthropology* 3(1): 179–94, 1972.

Jackson, B., 'Deviance as Success', in B. Babcock, ed., *The Reversible World: Symbolic Inversion in Art and Society*, Ithaca: Cornell University Press, 1979.

Janes, R., 'The Athapaskan and the Fur Trade: Observations from Archaeology and Ethnohistory', *Western Canadian Journal of Anthropology* 4(3,4): 159, 1975.

——, 'Culture Contact in the 19th Century Mackenzie Basin, Canada', *Current Anthropology* 17(2): 344–5, 1976.

Jarvenpa, R., *The Trappers of Patuanak: Towards a Spatial Ecology of Modern Hunters*, Ottawa: National Museum of Canada, Canadian Ethnology Service Paper No. 67, 1980.

Jenness, D., 'The Sekani Indians of British Columbia', *Transactions of the Royal Society of Canada* 25(2): 21–34, 1931.

——, *The Indians of Canada*, Ottawa: National Museum of Canada, Bulletin No. 65, 1932.

——, *The Sekani Indians of British Columbia*, Ottawa: National Museum of Canada, Bulletin No. 84, 1937.

Jobson, K., G. Ferguson, M. Fus, B. Ferstman and K. Kaiser, 'Report on Northern Justice', unpublished paper, Victoria: University of Victoria, 1978.

Karamanski, T.J., *Fur Trade and Exploration*, Vancouver: University of British Columbia Press, 1983.

Knight, R., 'A Re-examination of Hunting, Trapping and Territoriality Among the Northeastern Algonkian Indians', in A. Vayda and E. Leeds, eds, *The Role of Animals in Human Ecological Adjustments*, Washington: The American Association for the Advancement of Sciences, 1965.

Kobrinsky, V.H., 'The Tsimshianization of the Carrier Indians', in J.W. Helmer, S. VanDyke and F.J. Kense, eds, *Prehistory of the North American Sub-Arctic: The Athapaskan Question*, Calgary: Archaeological Association of the University of Calgary, 1977.

Koolage, W.W., 'Conceptual Negativism in Chipewyan Ethnology', *Anthropologica* N.S. 17(1): 45–60, 1975.

Korovkin, M.A., and G. Lanoue, 'On the Substantiality of Form: Interpreting Symbolic Expression in the Paradigm of Social Organization', *Comparative Studies in Society and History* 30(3): 613–48, 1988.

Krause, A., *The Tlingit Indians: Results of a Trip to the Northwest Coast of North America and the Bering Straits*, Vancouver: Douglas and McIntyre, 1979. Originally published 1885 and translated 1956 by Erna Gunther, University of Washington Press Monograph 26, American Ethnological Society.

Krech, S., 'Disease, Starvation and Northern Athapaskan Social Organization', *The American Ethnologist* 5(4): 710–26, 1978.

———, 'The Influence of Disease and the Fur Trade on Arctic Drainage Lowlands Dene, 1800–1850', *Journal of Anthropological Research* 39(2): 123–46, 1983.

LaBarre, W., 'Materials for a History of the Studies of Crisis Cults: A Bibliographic Essay', *Current Anthropology* 12(1): 3–44, 1971.

Lanoue, G., 'Flexibility in Hare Social Organization', *The Canadian Journal of Native Studies* 1(2): 259–76, 1981.

———, 'Continuity and Change: The Development of Political Self-Definition Among the Sekani of Northern British Columbia', Ph.D. dissertation, Department of Anthropology, University of Toronto, 1984.

———, *Images in Stone: A Theory on Interpreting Rock Art*, Rome: Art Center, 1989.

———, 'Beyond Values and Ideology: Tales from Six North American Indian Peoples', *Quaderni di Igitur*, 3: 1–137, Rome: Nuova Arnica Editrice, 1990.

———, 'La Désunion Fait La Force: Survie et tensions chez les Sekani de la Colombie-Britannique', *Anthropologie et Sociétés* 14(2): 117–41, 1990.

———, 'Breakdown and Ethnographic Consciousness: The Sekani Case', *The European Journal of Native Studies* 4(2): 45–52, 1990.

———, 'Language Loss, Language Gain: Cultural Camouflage and Social Change Among the Sekani of Northern British Columbia', *Language in Society* 20(1): 87–115, 1991.

———, 'Orpheus in the Netherworld in the Plateau of Western North America: The Voyage of Peni', *Proceedings, Orpheus Seminar Series*, ed. G. Masaracchia, Rome: Dipartimento di Studi Classici, Universita' di Roma "La Sapienza", 1991 (in press).

Leacock, E.B., *The Montagnais 'Hunting Territory' and the Fur Trade*, American Anthropological Association Memoir No. 78, 1954.

Lee, R.B., and I. Devore, eds, *Man the Hunter*, New York: Aldine, 1968.

Lejacq, Fr, 'District de N.-D. de Bonne Esperance; Lettre du R.P. Lejacq a Mgr. Herbourg', *Missions de la Congrégation des Missionaires Oblats de Marie-Immaculé* xii: 346, 1874.

Lévi-Strauss, C., *The Savage Mind*, London: Weidenfield and Nicolson, 1966.

Levy, M., Jr, *Modernization and the Structure of Societies: A Setting for International Affairs*, Princeton, NJ: Princeton University Press, 1966.

Lurie, N.O., 'The Contemporary American Scene', in N.O. Lurie and E.B. Leacock, eds, *North American Indians in Historical Perspective*, New York: Random House, 1971.

McDonald, A., *Peace River: A Canoe Voyage from Hudson's Bay to the Pacific*, Ottawa: J. Durie and Sons, 1872.

McDonnel, R.F., 'Kasini Society: Some Aspects of the Social Organization of Athapaskan Culture between 1900–1950', Ph.D. dissertation, Department of Anthropology, University of British Columbia, 1975.

———, 'Symbolic Orientations and Systematic Turmoil: Centering on the

Kaska Symbol of Dene', *Canadian Journal of Anthropology* 4(1): 39–56, 1984.

McGhee, R., 'An Archaeological Survey in the Area of the Portage mountain Dam Reservoir', Victoria: Archaeological Sites Advisory Board, 1963.

McKennan, R.A., *The Chandelar Kutchin*, Arctic Institute of North America, Technical Paper No. 17, 1965.

——, 'Athapaskan Groupings and Social Organization in Central Alaska', in David Damas, ed., *Contributions to Anthropology: Band Societies*, Ottawa: National Museum of Canada, Bulletin No. 228, 1969.

MacKenzie, A. *The Journals and Letters of Sir Alexander MacKenzie*, ed. W.K. Lamb, Toronto: Macmillan, 1970.

McLean, J., *Notes on Twenty-Five Years Service in the Hudson's Bay Company*, London: Richard Bentley, 1849.

McNickle, D., *Native America Tribalism: Indian Survivals and Renewals*, New York: Oxford University Press for the Institute for Race Relations, 1973.

Michae, J., 'Les Chitra-Gottineke: essai de monographie d'un groupe Athapascan des Montagnes Rocheuses.' Ottawa: *National Museum Bulletin* 190: 49–93, 1963.

Miller, C., *Prophetic Worlds: Indians and Whites on the Columbia Plateau*, New Brunswick: Rutgers University Press, 1985.

Mills, A.C., 'The Beaver Indian Prophet Dance and Related Movements Among North American Indians", Ph.D. dissertation, Harvard University, 1981.

Mooney, J., *The Ghost Dance Religion and the Sioux Outbreak of 1890*, Chicago: University of Chicago Press, 1965.

Morantz, T., 'The Impact of the Fur Trade on 18th and 19th Century Algonquian Social Organization: An Ethnographic, Ethnohistoric Study of the Eastern James Bay Cree from 1700–1850', Ph.D. dissertation, Department of Anthropology, University of Toronto, 1980.

Morgan, L.H., *Systems of Consanguinity and Affinity of the Human Family*, Smithsonian Contributions to Knowledge 17: 1–590, Washington: Smithsonian Institute, 1871.

Morice, A.G., *The Great Dene Race*, St Gabriel-Modling, Austria: Administration of *Anthropos*, n.d.

——, *The Western Denes, their Manners and Customs*, The Canadian Institute, Proceedings for 1888–1889, vol. 7, 1890.

——, *Notes on the Western Dene*, Toronto: Transactions of the Canadian Institute. 1892/3.

——, *Au Pays de l"Ours Noir: Chez les sauvages de la Columbie Britanique*, Paris: Delhomme et Briguet, 1897.

——, 'La femme chez les Dénés', *Proceedings, International Congress of Americanists*, 15th session, vol. 1: 361–84, 1906.

——, *The History of the Interior of British Columbia (formerly New Caledonia) from 1660–1880*, London: John Lane, 1906.

——, 'About Cremation', *American Anthropologist* 27: 576–7, 1927.

——, 'The Fur Trader in Anthropology', *American Anthropologist* 30(1): 60–84, 1928.

Murdock, G.P. *Social Structure*, New York: Macmillan, 1949.

Murphy, R.F., and J.H. Steward, 'Tappers and Trappers: Parallel Process in Acculturation', *Economic Development and Culture Change* 4. Reprinted in R.A. Manners and D. Kaplan, *Theory in Anthropology*, New York: Aldine, 1956.

Nelson, R.K., *Hunters of the Northern Forest*, Chicago: University of Chicago Press, 1973.

Norbeck, E., 'Rites of Reversal of North American Indians as Forms of Play', in E. Norbeck and C.R. Farrar, eds, *Forms of Play of Native North Americans*, Proceedings of the American Ethnological Society, 1979.

Osgood, C., *The Distribution of the Northern Athapaskan Indians*, Yale University Publications in Anthropology 7: 1–23, New Haven: Yale University Press, 1936.

Parsons, T., *The Social System*, Glencoe, Ill.: The Free Press, 1951.

——, 'The Professions and Social Structure', in *Essays in Sociological Theory*, New York: The Free Press, 1954.

——, 'Democracy and Social Structure in Pre-Nazi Germany', in *Essays in Sociological Theory*, New York: The Free Press, 1954.

——, *Structure and Process in Modern Society*, Glencoe, Ill.: The Free Press, 1960.

Patterson, F.G., *The Canadian Indian: A History Since 1500*, Don Mills, Ont.: Collier-Macmillan Canada, 1972.

Patterson, R.M., *Finlay's River*, Toronto: Macmillan, 1968.

Perry, R.J., 'Variations on the Female Referent in Athabaskan Cultures', *Journal of Anthropological Research* 33(1): 99, 1977.

Petitot, E., *Dictionaire de la langue Déné-Dindjie*, Paris: Leroux, 1876.

——, *The Amerindians of the Canadian Northwest in the 19th Century, as seen by Emile Petitot: vol. II, The Loucheux Indians*, Ottawa: Northern Science Research Group, 1970.

Price, J., 'U.S. and Canadian Indian Periodicals', *Canadian Review of Sociology and Anthropology* 9: 150–62, 1972.

Quimby, G.I., *Indian Life in the Upper Great Lakes 11,000 B.C.–1,000 A.D.*, Chicago: University of Chicago Press, 1960.

Radcliffe-Brown, A.R., *Structure and Function in Primitive Society*, London: Cohen and West, 1952.

Ray, A.J., 'History and Archaeology of the Fur Trade', *American Antiquity* 43(1): 26–34, 1978.

Ray, A.J. and Freeman, D., *'Give Us Good Measure': An Economic Analysis of Relations Between the Indians and the Hudson's Bay Company before 1763*, Toronto: University of Toronto Press, 1978.

Riches, D., *Northern Nomadic Hunter-Gatherers*, London: Academic Press, 1982.

Ridington, R., 'Kin Categories versus Kin Groups: A Two Section System Without Sections', *Ethnology* 8(4): 460–7, 1969.

——, *Swan People: A Study of the Dunne-Za Prophet Dance*, Ottawa: National Museum of Man, Mercury Series No. 38, 1978.

Sahlins, M., *Stone Age Economics*, Chicago: Aldine, 1974.

Savishinsky, J.S., 'Kinship and the Expression of Values in an Athabascan Bush Community', *Western Canadian Journal of Anthropology* 2: 31–59, 1970.

——, 'Stress and Mobility in an Arctic Community: The Hare Indians of Colville Lake', Ph.D. dissertation, Department of Anthropology, Cornell University, 1970.

——, 'Mobility as an Aspect of Stress in an Arctic Community', *American Anthropologist* 73: 604–18, 1971.

Service, E., *Primitive Social Organization: An Evolutionary Perspective*, New York; Random House, 1962.

Sharp, H.S., 'The Caribou-Eater Chipewyan: Bilaterality, Strategies of Caribou Hunting and the Fur Trade', *Arctic Anthropology* 14(2): 35–40, 1977.

——, 'Shared Experience and Magical Death: Chipewyan Explanations of a Prophet's Decline', Ethnology 25(4): 257–70, 1987.

——, *Chipewyan Marriage*, Ottawa: National Museum of Man, Mercury Series, Canadian Ethnology Service Paper No. 58, 1979.

Sherwood, A., 'Some Remarks About the Athapaskan Indians', *Anthropologica* 6–8: 51–6, 1958/9.

Shkilnyk, A., *A Poison Stronger Than Love: The Destruction of an Ojibwa Community*, New Haven: Yale University Press, 1985.

Slobodin, R., *Band Organization of the Peel River Kutchin*, Ottawa: National Museum of Canada Bulletin No. 179, 1962.

Spier, L., 'The Distribution of Kinship Systems in North America', *University of Washington Publications in Anthropology* 1: 69–88, 1925.

——, *The Prophet Dance of the Northwest and its Derivatives: The Source of the Ghost Dance*, Menasha, Wisc.: George Banta Publishing Company, 1935.

Spier, L., W. Suttles and M. Herskovits, 'Comments on Aberle's Thesis of Deprivation', *Southwestern Journal of Anthropology* 15: 84–8, 1959.

Steward, J., 'The Economic and Social Basis of Primitive Bands', in J. Steward, ed., *Essays in Anthropology Presented to A.L. Kroeber*, Berkeley: University California Press, 1936.

——, *Basin-Plateau Aboriginal Socio-Political Groups*, Washington: Smithsonian Institution, Bureau of American Ethnology, Bulletin No. 120, 1938.

Swanton, J.R., 'The Development of the Clan System and Secret Societies among the Northwestern Tribes', *American Anthropologist* 6(3): 477–87, 1904.

——, *Haida Texts and Myths, Skidegate Dialect*, Washington: Smithsonian Institution, Bureau of American Ethnology, Bulletin 29, 1905.

——, 'The Social Organization of American Tribes', *American Anthropologist* 7: 663–73, 1905.

Tanner, A., *Bringing Home Animals: Religous Ideology and Mode of Production of the Mistassini Cree Hunters*, London: Hurst, 1979.

Teit, J., *The Shuswap*, Memoirs of the American Museum of Natural History 4(7): 443–813: New York. Reprinted as volume 2(7) of the Jesup Expedition, New York: AMS, 1909.

Turner, D.H., *Dialectics and Tradition: Myth and Social Structure in Two Hunter-Gatherer Societies*, London: Occasional Paper No. 36 of the Royal Anthropological Institute of Great Britain and Ireland, 1978.

Turner, D.H. and P. Wertman, *Shamattawa: The Structure of Social Relations in a Northern Algonkian Band*, Ottawa: National Museum of Canada, Canadian Ethnology Service Paper No. 36, 1977.

VanStone, J., *The Changing Culture of the Snowdrift Chipewyan*, Ottawa: National Museum of Canada, Bulletin No. 209, Anthropological Series No. 74, 1965.

——, *Athapaskan Adaptations: Hunters and Fishermen of the SubArctic Forests*, Chicago: Aldine, 1974.

Walker, D.F., 'New Light on the Prophet Dance Controversy', *Ethnohistory* 16: 245–55, 1969.

Weaver, S.M., *Making Canadian Indian Policy: The Hidden Agenda 1968–70*, Toronto: University of Toronto Press, 1981.

Westermarck, E., *The History of Human Marriage*, London: Macmillan and Co., 1894.

White, J., ed., *Handbook of Indians of Canada*, Ottawa: Appendix to the Tenth Report of the Geographic Board of Canada 1913. Reprinted Toronto: Coles, 1971.

Williams, B.J., *A Model of Band Society*, Memoirs for the Society for American Archaeology No. 29, 1974.

Worsley, P. *The Trumpet Shall Sound*, London: Paladin, 1970.

Wright, J.V., 'A Regional Examination of Ojibwa Culture History', *Anthropologica* 7: 189–277, 1965.

Yerbury, J.C., 'The Social Organization of Subarctic Athapaskan Indians: An Ethno-Historical Reconstruction', Ph.D. dissertation, Simon Fraser University, 1980.

Unpublished Sources

Anonymous, 'Correspondence, Western New Caledonia District', Winnipeg: Hudson's Bay Company Archives, B119/b/1, 1823–4.

——, 'Journals, Eastern New Caledonia District', Winnipeg: Hudson's Bay Company Archives, B119/a/1, B119/a/3, 1823–4.

——, 'Report, McLeod Lake Post', Winnipeg: Hudson's Bay Company Archives, B119/a/3, 1823–4.

——, 'Post Journal, McLeod Lake', Calgary: Glenbow Foundation Archives, BB12.M165, 1823–48.

——, 'Report, McLeod Lake Post', Winnipeg: Hudson's Bay Company Archives, B119/e/1, 1824.

——, 'Journal, McLeod Lake Post', Winnipeg: Hudson's Bay Company Archives, B119/a/4, 1824.

——, 'Journal, Dunvegan Post', Winnipeg: Hudson's Bay Company Archives, B56/a/2, 1824–5.

——, 'Report, Western New Caledonia District', Winnipeg: Hudson's Bay Company Archives, B188/a/5, 1826.

——, 'Journals, Western New Caledonia District', Winnipeg: Hudson's Bay Company Archives, B188/a/8, B118/a/10, 1827.

——, 'Journals, Western New Caledonia District', Winnipeg: Hudson's Bay Company Archives, B188/a/12, B188/a/13, 1828–9.

——, 'Journal, Western New Caledonia District', Winnipeg: Hudson's Bay Company Archives, B188/a/14, 1829–30.

——, 'Correspondence, Stuart Lake Post', Winnipeg: Hudson's Bay Company Archives, B188/b/8, 1829–30.

——, 'Journal, Western New Caledonia District', Winnipeg: Hudson's Bay Company Archives, B188/a/17, 1831–2.

——, 'Journal, Fort Dunvegan Post', Winnipeg: Hudson's Bay Company Archives, B56/a/3, 1834–5.

——, 'Ledger, McLeod Lake Post', Winnipeg: Hudson's Bay Company Archives, B119/d/1, 1887–8.

——, 'Ledger, McLeod Lake Post', Winnipeg: Hudson's Bay Company Archives,, B119/d/2, 1887–9.

——, 'Ledger, McLeod Lake Post', Winnipeg: Hudson's Bay Company Archives, B119/d/3, 1889–90.

——, 'Ledger, McLeod Lake Post', Winnipeg: Hudson's Bay Company Archives, B119/d/8, 1889–1900.

——, 'Report, McLeod Lake Post', Winnipeg: Hudson's Bay Company Archives, B119/a/2, 1891.

——, 'Journal, McLeod Lake Post', Winnipeg: Hudson's Bay Company Archives, B119/a/5, 1891.

——, 'Account Books, Fort Grahame Post', Winnipeg: Hudson's Bay Company Archives, B/249/d/1, 1891–3.

——, 'Journal, Fort Grahame Post', Winnipeg: Hudson's Bay Company Archives, B/249/a/1, 1891–3.

——, 'Account Books, Fort Grahame Post', Winnipeg: Hudson's Bay Company Archives, B/249/d/4, 1891–5.

——, 'Account Books, Fort Grahame Post', Winnipeg: Hudson's Bay Company Archives, B249/d/8, 1891–7.

——, 'Ledger, McLeod Lake Post', Winnipeg: Hudson's Bay Company Archives, B/119/d/6, 1892–3.

——, 'Account Books, Fort Grahame Post', Winnipeg: Hudson's Bay Company Archives, B249/d/2, B249/d/5, 1893.

——, 'Journal, Fort Grahame Post', Winnipeg: Hudson's Bay Company Archives, B249/a/2, 1893.

——, 'Account books, Fort Grahame Post', Winnipeg: Hudson's Bay Company Archives, B249/d/3, 1893–4.

——, 'Journal, Fort Grahame Post', Winnipeg: Hudson's Bay Company Archives, B249/a/2, 1893–4.

——, 'Report, McLeod Lake Post', Winnipeg: Hudson's Bay Company Archives, B/119/a/6, 1893–5.

——, 'Ledger, Fort Grahame Post', Winnipeg: Hudson's Bay Company Archives, B249/d/6, 1893–6.

——, 'Account Books, Fort Grahame Post', Winnipeg: Hudson's Bay Company Archives, B249/d/10, 1893–1901.

——, 'Journal, Fort Grahame Post', Winnipeg: Hudson's Bay Company Archives, B249/a/3, 1895–6.

——, 'Journal, McLeod Lake Post', Winnipeg: Hudson's Bay Company Archives, B119/a/7, 1895–6.

——, 'Ledger, McLeod Lake Post', Winnipeg: Hudson's Bay Company Archives, B119/d/7, 1895–7.

——, 'Account Books, Fort Grahame Post', Winnipeg: Hudson's Bay Company Archives, B249/d/9, 1895–8.

——, 'Report, Fort Grahame Post', Winnipeg: Hudson's Bay Company Archives, B249/e/1, 1896.

——, 'Journal, Fort Grahame Post,' Winnipeg: Hudson's Bay Company Archives, B249/a/4, 1896–9.

——, 'Ledger, McLeod Lake Post', Winnipeg: Hudson's Bay Company Archives, B119/d/9, 1896–1902.

——, 'Ledger, Fort Grahame Post', Winnipeg: Hudson's Bay Company Archives, B249/d/7, 1897.

——, 'Journal, Fort Grahame Post', Winnipeg: Hudson's Bay Company Archives, B249/a/5, 1899.

——, 'Journal, Fort Grahame Post', Winnipeg: Hudson's Bay Company Archives, B249/a/6, 1899–1902.

——, 'Report, Fort Grahame Post', Winnipeg: Hudson's Bay Company Archives, B249/e/2, 1900.

——, 'Report, McLeod Lake Post', Winnipeg: Hudson's Bay Company Archives, B119/e/4, 1900.

——, 'Journal, McLeod Lake Post', Winnipeg: Hudson's Bay Company Archives, B119/a/10, 1901–2.

——, 'Journal, Fort Grahame Post', Winnipeg: Hudson's Bay Company Archives, B249/a/7, 1902–5.

——, 'Journal, MacLeod Lake Post', Winnipeg: Hudson's Bay Company Archives, B119/a/11, 1902–5.

——, 'Journal, Liard Post', Winnipeg: Hudson's Bay Company Archives, B299/a/1, 1904–5.

——, 'Journal, McLeod Lake Post', Winnipeg: Hudson's Bay Company Archives, B119/a/12, 1905–11.

——, 'Journal, Fort Grahame Post', Winnipeg: Hudson's Bay Company Archives, B249/a/8, 1906–8.

——, 'Journal, Liard Post', Winnipeg: Hudson's Bay Company Archives, B299/a/2, 1906–11.

——, 'Journal, Fort Grahame Post', Winnipeg: Hudson's Bay Company Archives, B249/a/10, 1917–22.

Government of Canada, 'Letter from S. Carmichael and J.P. Shaw to N.W. White, Chairman of the Royal Commission on Indian Affairs for the Province of British Columbia', Ottawa: Department of Indian Affairs and Northern Development, file no. 482191, 1915.

———, 'Indian Affairs Files: 1916 Census', Ottawa: Public Archives of Canada, RG 10 vol. 4003, File 215.037–2, 1916.

———, 'Indian Affairs Files: 1921 Census', Ottawa: Public Archieves of Canada, RG 10 vol. 3161 File 365.009–2A, 1921.

———, 'Indian Affairs Files: Memorandum of Proposed Treaty with Northern Indians', Ottawa: Public Archives of Canada, RG 10 vol. 3848 File 75.236–1, n.d.

———, Unclassified DIAND files in Prince George office, various dates.

Canada Department of Indian Affairs and Northern Development, Indian Affairs Branch, Ottawa and Prince George files, n.d.

Cassidy, S. *et al.*, 'Preliminary Report on the Archaeological Potential of Those Areas Affected by the McGregor Diversion Project', Victoria: Archaeological Sites Advisory Board, 1976.

Kelly, J.P., 'A Historical Review of the Interest and Management of Fur Trapping in North Central British Columbia', Victoria: British Columbia Fish and Wildlife Branch, Department of Recreation and Conservation, 1975.

LeBaron, B., 'Fort Ware Resource Uses', unpublished paper prepared for the Fort Ware Indian Band, Fort Ware, BC, 1979.

Steventon, B., 'Population Study of the Northern Athabaskans', unpublished manuscript, n.d.

Woodward, J., 'Report to the Legal Services Commission on the McLeod Lake Indian Band', unpublished paper, 1978.

Index